T0310475

The Poor and the Plutocrats

The Poor and the Plutocrats

*From the Poorest of the Poor
to the Richest of the Rich*

FRANCIS TEAL

OXFORD
UNIVERSITY PRESS

OXFORD
UNIVERSITY PRESS

Great Clarendon Street, Oxford, OX2 6DP,
United Kingdom

Oxford University Press is a department of the University of Oxford.
It furthers the University's objective of excellence in research, scholarship,
and education by publishing worldwide. Oxford is a registered trade mark of
Oxford University Press in the UK and in certain other countries

Published in the United States of America by Oxford University Press
198 Madison Avenue, New York, NY 10016, United States of America

British Library Cataloguing in Publication Data

Data available

Library of Congress Control Number: 2020941872

ISBN 978-0-19-887014-2

Printed and bound in the UK by
TJ Books Limited

In memory of Caroline Dinwiddy

Preface

Incomes in the world range from less than £1,000 a year to the hundreds of millions—the poor and the plutocrats of the title of this book. How has a world come about that has this extraordinary level of inequality? In this book I seek an answer to that question. The answer proposed in the book is that the fate of the poor depends on how the price of relatively unskilled labour is changing. Its dramatic rise in most now-rich countries, which occurred in the first three quarters of the twentieth century, is the key to understanding the decline in both poverty and inequality that occurred in that period within those countries. The poor own their labour and sometimes low-quality land. Plutocrats own a lot more, partly more skilled labour, partly more capital and partly more high-quality land. Just as the fortunes of the poor depend on how the price of its most important asset—its labour—changes, so the emergence of the plutocrats depends on how the prices of their assets are changing. We document in detail those changing fortunes for both the US and the UK.

While the level of current plutocratic incomes is a phenomenon which dates from the late twentieth century, poverty is not. Being poor has been the fate of almost everyone in human history, until the last 300 years. It is not poverty we need to explain, it is why some countries have exited it, by such large amounts, and some have not exited it at all. The poorest of the poor almost always live in countries which are poor. So, the path we wish to understand, from the poorest to the richest, crosses country boundaries first, and then focuses within rich countries on the fate of the relatively poor and rich there. In the world's richest economy, the US, the price of relatively unskilled labour stopped rising in the 1980s, in the UK it fell substantially after the financial crash of 2007–08. In both countries that reversal of fortunes for the relatively poor in those countries was the background to a political revolution in the shape of the Trump presidency and the decision by the UK to leave the EU. Both represent radical breaks with the past political processes in those countries.

Political rhetoric in both countries speaks of the resulting inequality as a 'rigged system', the abuse by the 1 per cent of political processes to distort economies to benefit the few, not the many—to paraphrase two currently used political slogans. In the chapters that follow I look in detail for the US and the UK at how the relatively poor and rich have fared under the different parties since the advent of the premiership of Margaret Thatcher and the presidency of Ronald Reagan; what is often described as the coming of neoliberal economics. I show that the popular picture of their periods in office, as ones where the rich gained far more than the poor, is wholly accurate. However, while in the US, in the main, that pattern continued, in the UK it was decisively reversed by New Labour whose period in office saw faster rises in income for the bottom 20 per cent than the top 20 per cent. Further, under that administration the incomes of the bottom 10 per cent rose to exceed the bottom 10 per cent in the US. New Labour's success in these respects is one of the best-kept secrets of the current leadership of the Labour Party.

In the latter chapters of the book I explore how current plutocratic levels of income have arisen, how at the top of the distribution, in both the US and the UK, those at the very top have raced way from the rest of the rich. It is not simply that these plutocrats have seen their incomes grow relatively to the poor, it is that they have grown very rich relatively to most of the rich. These super-rich individuals are hard to find in the data as they are so scarce but in Chapter 8 I provide estimates. While in the UK the average incomes of the top 0.1 per cent in 2014 was $1.5 million, some 100 individuals had incomes that exceeded $30 million. These numbers are dwarfed by those for the US where, in 2014, the average income of the top 0.1 per cent was $3.6 million. Within that top 0.1 per cent, some 100 individuals had incomes that exceeded $100 million.

It is the super-rich, within the rich, who have been so visible. They are not short of critics and the source of their incomes has been contentious. Is it, as their critics argue, that they are the beneficiaries of markets distorted by the free flow of capital and the decline of worker power, summarized as globalization? Alternatively, can some at least of their income be seen as reflecting a combination of talent with the new digital age technology. The pay of the top Premier League football players exceeds £200,000 a week, enough comfortably to make the top 0.01 per cent in either the UK or the US. I try and evaluate how much of the incomes of the super-rich can be seen as reflecting these alternative sources in Chapter 10.

My objective has been to understand the sources of both those high and those vastly lower incomes. To provide you with a map that enables you to see the path from the poorest of the poor to the richest of the rich. It is a path whose length has been steadily increasing for many years.

Francis Teal

London
March 2020

Acknowledgements

Providing this map has required a large number of data sources and my principal debt is to those researchers who have made comparative data available so that what would have, in the past, required months of painstaking work now requires a click of a mouse. On inequality the data provided by the late Tony Atkinson and his collaborators has transformed our knowledge of both inequality and the incomes of the very rich. Two vital web-based data sources are *The Chartbook of Economic Inequality* and the *World Wealth and Income Database (WID)*. Researchers at the Institute for New Economic Thinking (INET) at the John Martin School in Oxford have brought together a large number of data sources and provided a comparative perspective. The World Bank has organized the collection of data on poor countries which has given us an unparalleled insight into the comparative incomes of the poor, presented at *PovcalNet*. Economic historians, looking to provide a measure of how incomes have changed over the long term, have ensured that we can now see the long-run changes of income in a comparative historical context across both poor and rich countries. Much of this work has been consolidated by the *Maddison Project* which is extending and updating the work of Angus Maddison. The Maddison data is combined with the GDP data from the *PENN World Tables 9.0*. In this version of the Tables it is possible to use different GDP series depending on whether it is the time series or cross-country dimension which is the focus of analysis. Longer time series of GDP and earnings have been compiled on the *Measuringworth* website for the UK and the US, of which I have made extensive use, and *The Billionaire Characteristics Database* provided vital information on the world of the richest. Needless to say, all this data is contentious, with disagreement as to the accuracy of measurement and of interpretation. However, without such data we would be arguing about the sources of inequality and poverty without the basic tools to make progress, namely data. In the chapters that follow I acknowledge those sources more fully. It is the authors of these sites who have made this book possible.

Three anonymous reviewers for Oxford University Press made very valuable suggestions for improvements and pointed out errors as well as directing me to data sources of which I was unaware. Only I am responsible for the uses made of the data and any misinterpretations and errors are entirely my responsibility.

Table of Contents

List of Figures and Tables

Figures

Tables

1

From Hundreds to Billions of Dollars of Income

The Poor and the Plutocrats

In August 2018 Apple became the first company with a market capitalization of US$1 trillion—a trillion is a million million. In recent years its net income has been running at an annual rate of about US$50 billion—a billion is a thousand million. In 2014, the most recent year for which readily comparable data is available, the size of the world economy was US$100 trillion (approximately, what's the odd trillion between friends). So, the net income of Apple is some 0.05 per cent of the income of the whole world. Some 100 countries in the world had total incomes in 2014 less than the revenues of this one company. The population of these countries was just under 750 million and in those countries per capita incomes for some 50 per cent of the people there were US$4,000 a year or less (that's less than US$350 per month).[1]

As trillions are a bit hard to imagine let us come down from the stratosphere of mega US tech companies to the humble UK taxpayer and ask what, in 2014, income you would need to get into the top 0.05 per cent of taxpayers. The answer is about £2 million or in current US$ about US$2.6 million. To get into the top 1 per cent you would 'only' need £150,000 as your annual income. Indeed 95 per cent of UK taxpayers in 2014 had incomes below £70,000 and that income would be unimaginable wealth for those at the bottom of the UK income scale.[2]

This book is about what can explain these extraordinary numbers. In particular we want to explain the co-existence of people with incomes in the hundreds with those whose incomes is in the hundreds of millions, even

---

[1] The basis for these figures is comparative data for national incomes provided by PENN World Tables 9.0. This data is described in Feenstra, R.C, R. Inklaar, and M.P. Timmer (2015). Details of this data can be found at: https://www.rug.nl/ggdc/productivity/pwt/.
[2] The source is the data from HMRC *Survey of Personal Incomes* for 2014–15.

billions—the poor and the plutocrats. We are not short of explanations. The principal villain (or hero, possibly depending on whether or not you are an Apple shareholder) is globalization which is seen as having benefited the elites of the top 1 per cent at the expense of the bottom 99 per cent. There are other candidates for the gross inequalities these numbers suggest—they include openness to trade, the threat posed by migrants to domestic workers and the demise in much of the rich world of the role of trade unions. The attempts to prevent workers organizing, which has a history as long as labour movements have existed, by governments controlled by the mega rich seems to many an obscene abuse of the relatively powerless. A mirror image of the view that trade unions are a conspiracy against those who need jobs as their activities price them out of employment.

The figures on inequality which are widely cited, and which form the basis for the impact of Thomas Piketty's book *Capital in the Twenty-First Century*, add fuel to the fires of resentment. That the share of the top 1 per cent in incomes in the US is argued to have increased from some 8 to nearly 20 per cent from the 1980s until the early part of the twenty-first century and the share in the UK from 5 to 15 per cent, over a similar period, while wages for the relatively unskilled in the US have stagnated seems the basis for revolution.[3] While those advocating less inequality would be horrified by its methods, a revolution is just what is currently taking place in the US. The UK is not far behind with immigration being the toxic issue which has rendered advocacy of membership of the EU politically impossible for both the major UK parties.

In this book I seek to address these issues from a longer-term historical perspective. The quality and extent of information that is currently available on both incomes and inequality, through the efforts of many researchers making their data readily available, is without parallel. My objective is to use this information, and put it into a narrative, as to what has determined the fall, and rise, of inequality over the last 300 years.

Incomes across the World: Absolute and Relative Poverty

How has a world emerged when incomes can range from a few hundred dollars to ones in the billions; in other words, how can so many be so poor

---

[3] This data is from *The Chartbook of Economic Inequality* which can be found at: https://www.chartbookofeconomicinequality.com/ (accessed 7 August 2020).

and so few plutocrats be so very rich? Posing the question in that way, as is often done, suggests a world of tiny islands of the super-rich surrounded by a rising tide of massed, and increasing, poverty. In fact, exactly the opposite is true. For the first time in human history we live at a time when the numbers of people who are absolutely poor—living on less than US\$2 per day—is falling.[4] The picture often painted of rising inequality at the country level is simply false. It is true that the 100 countries with annual incomes less than Apple's net income are mired in acute poverty. However, in contrast stands China and, to a much lesser extent India, whose combined populations is 2014 were some 2.7 billion and whose incomes, since their reforms of the late 1970s, have been rising rapidly. Once we allow for differences in population across countries we will see that, at the country level, there has been a more or less continuous decline in inequality since the 1980s.

Within countries it is a different story and for measures of poverty to be interesting a relative approach is essential. Pointing out to the average worker in the richer world that their incomes of US\$20–30,000 are unimaginable wealth for those in the poorest countries is not a winning political strategy. Relative poverty is determined by the extent of inequality in a country and, in many rich countries since the 1970s, inequality has been rising. For some in those countries their wages have not risen for decades, for some this has meant their incomes have fallen. Changes in inequality within a country arise because incomes grow at different rates. If, as was the case from the early part of the twentieth century until the 1970s, the relatively poor saw faster rates of growth of their incomes than the relatively rich then inequality will fall. If this process reverses as has happened in *some* countries for *some* periods since the 1970s then inequality will rise. There is a measure—the Gini coefficient—which offers us a way of summarizing the shares that the relatively poor obtain of total income and we will use it to show how inequality is related to levels of income in Chapter 5.

Once a longer term and comparative perspective is taken on incomes and inequality we see that our problem is not to explain a rising tide of poverty— there isn't one—nor is it to explain how capitalism generates ever-increasing inequality—it hasn't. Our problem is much more complicated. What can explain such large *changes* in both incomes and in inequality as have occurred since the start of sustained global growth in the early part of the nineteenth century? We need to reformulate our question so that it is not

---

[4] Data justifying this assertion is presented below in Chapter 6.

about the levels of income and inequality but about what determines their changes. We start with incomes.

Do You Want to Get Richer Faster than Others?

If you do you need to be aware that rates of growth have differed greatly across countries and over time as we show in Chapter 4. These differential growth rates are by far the most important factor in explaining where the poor have lived and where they live now. So, if you want to be rich the first step is to make sure you are born into a rich country. The second step is to make sure you own an asset whose price is increasing relative to that of other assets. In this context labour is an asset and for many it is their only asset. If that is your asset you need to make sure you live during a period when the price of labour is rising rapidly. So, best to avoid the twenty-first century, and opt for the middle part of the twentieth century—and, of course, make sure it's a relatively rich country. In his book *A Farewell to Alms* Gregory Clark documents the scale of the success in raising the price of labour initially in the US and the UK and then spreading out from there, albeit to only a small part of the world until very recently.

It may seem a little odd, in an age dominated by the visible incomes of super-rich people, to be talking about the poor seeing faster growth in their incomes than the rich. Indeed, a little self-contradictory, as wouldn't the poor soon cease to be the poor? Odd yes, but that is exactly what happened for most countries that were rich relative to others at the start of the twentieth century. For the next seventy years the income of relatively unskilled labour rose very rapidly and their share of incomes rose too. Now, given the size of the gap between the rich and the poor at the start of the twentieth century, the rich were still ahead, even after seventy years of a closing gap, but they were very much less ahead.

It is the reversal of that process from the 1980s onward in now-rich countries that dominates current political discourse and on which we too wish to focus. However, the longer-term perspective is important. If inequality fell due to the rise in the price of the unskilled labour then logic dictates that it may well rise once that rise ceases as, at different times, and to varying extents it has, in most rich countries.

The big exception, currently, to the general rule that the poor only own their labour, and that labour is unskilled, which is why an increase in its price is essential for them to exit poverty, is sub-Saharan Africa where the poor, in many of those countries, own their land as well as their labour. Poverty here flows, as it did in all countries before the nineteenth century, from the low productivity of that land. More generally the rise in the price of any asset depends on increases in its productivity. It is the link from ownership of assets (whether it be labour, land or capital) to their productivity that explains, in part, why some get so much richer than others. The other part of the explanation is when individuals capture for themselves the productivity of assets they steal. Kleptocratic rulers not being a new phenomenon, although the productivity of the assets they can steal is.

Productivity and Skills

While productivity is widely discussed it is less widely understood; both in the sense that its meaning is not understood, and in the sense that the reasons for its change are not well understood. When we talk of the productivity of an asset we mean how much output it produces per unit of input. Thus, you could measure the productivity of an acre of land by how much output was produced on that land. You could also measure the productivity of labour on that land by knowing how much was harvested per year by a labourer. So that would give you a measure of land and labour productivity respectively. However, rather obviously, you need both land and labour to produce the farm's output. So how do we measure the productivity of a farm? To do that you need a way of combining the inputs to jointly produce the output. That economists can do so with a joint measure of inputs, then we can ask how much output those inputs combined will produce. Robert Gordon's (2016) *The Rise and Fall of American Growth* provides a comprehensive account as to how this can be done. We can do this not only for farms, we can do it for factories where we need labour and capital and a new asset—skills. It is not that farms don't need skills, it is assumed they need less (economists tend not to farm).

Now let's move from a farm, or firm, to an economy, which is the basis for Robert Gordon's study. We have already said that the growth of the output of economies has varied enormously. Why is that? Well you might have thought that the rather obvious answer to that is that input growth has varied enormously too. It is true it has, but one of the major puzzles in economics is that when we measure inputs and outputs we find that much of the increase in outputs is not explained by those inputs. When physicists discovered that the universe was expanding, and they did not know why, they invented the term 'dark energy' to explain the expansion. Now economists are just as good as physicists in thinking up names for things they don't understand, so they term this mysterious factor increasing output 'total factor productivity' (TFP). As with dark energy, while we don't know what it is, we do know that whatever it is, it is very important. If TFP acts to increase the demand for labour—and it appears to have done so for long periods of time—then that is very good news for the owners of labour whose productivity, and price, will go up. But, of course, it may not help labour, it may help capital, or it may all be tied up in the brain of Steve Jobs inventing Apple. In which case the price of labour, particularly of the unskilled kind, will not rise.

As with poverty only a relative definition of skills is useful for understanding the evolution of incomes in an economy. Since the late nineteenth century there has been a steady expansion of education levels so that jobs which required simply secondary education now require university degrees. It is those at the bottom of the education ladder, however long that ladder is, that constitute the unskilled in that society. In poor countries low skills means those with no education, in rich countries they have ten years but leave with no formal qualifications.

You may well think that the obvious factor we have not mentioned so far that will be driving TFP is 'skills' broadly defined so it can include the ability of Steve Jobs to invent Apple. However, if by skills we mean the more prosaic kind, such as years of education, then the news is not good. Such measures explain relatively little of TFP—the mysterious X factor continues to dominate the factors that drive output.

Inequality in Markets and Inequality across Households

But we are in search of the plutocrats. So, given that people are seeing different changes in their incomes, is that all we need to know for what drives the inequality that gives us the plutocrats? The answer is clearly no as these prices drive market outcomes, not personal and household incomes. There has, since the Napoleonic Wars, been some form of tax on incomes although not continuously—it was formally repealed in 1816, a year after the Battle of Waterloo, but it was reintroduced in 1842 by Sir Robert Peel to deal with a massive public deficit (some things never change)—so there is a gap between what workers earn and what they can spend. Nowadays there is much more than income taxes to consider. Further there is more to the incomes of labour than the wage rate. We have, so far, not mentioned the self-employed who are in many poor countries most earners and are increasingly important in rich countries.

In Chapter 7 we will use data for both the UK and the US for the current range of benefits and taxes which drive the gap between what the market pays labour and what the household with that income can afford to spend. In the case of the UK the distinction made by the Office of National Statistics (ONS) is between 'Original Income' which is what we have been considering so far, the direct cash benefits that a family may receive, and 'Final Income' which allows for all the direct and indirect taxes and transfers and implicit benefits that households receive. For the US we will make a similar distinction, although the data is organized differently from that of the UK ONS. There is indeed a large gap between original and final incomes.

When analysing inequality we need to be clear not only which income we are considering but whether we are considering the distribution of an individual's income or that of the household. In the chapters that follow we will look at both individual incomes and that of households. As we want to compare rich and poor countries, we begin our comparison with households as that allows us, for the moment, to sidestep the problems of societies where incomes are hard to measure as many do not work for wages. The income measure in Figure 1.1 below is based on household per capita incomes.[5]

The measure of inequality on which we will mainly focus is the Gini and the Gini has a ready graphical representation. We show two examples in Figure 1.1 of plots which will give rise to different values of the Gini. The curve in the chart shows how much income any percentage of the population captures, it is the Lorenz curve, named after its inventor. In the top panel we show a Lorenz curve for data we will be using in Chapter 8 for incomes in Ghana in 2012/13. Ghana is a relatively poor country compared to countries in Europe and America but certainly not among the poorest countries in the world. In the bottom panel we show a Lorenz curve for the population of the world in 2008.

On the horizontal axis we show the percentage of people, on the vertical axis the percentage of the total income they have. So, the graph shows that for Ghana the bottom 20 per cent of people get less than 5 per cent of total

---

[5] In fact, Figure 1.1 uses both household income and household consumption to measure 'income'. This distinction will prove very important later when, in Chapter 6, we distinguish between rich and poor countries.

income while the top 20 per cent get more than 50 per cent and the top 10 per cent 35 per cent of income. A rather unequal distribution of income you may well think. The Gini coefficient is one means of summarizing this fact. The Gini coefficient is the area A in the figure divided by (A+B). In words, it is the proportion of the area under the 45-degree line which is above the Lorenz curve. The word proportion in that last sentence is important. The Gini coefficient is telling us about the proportional distribution of income. It is not telling us how big is the gap between incomes. In the figure the Gini coefficient for Ghana is 45.0 which tells you that the Lorenz curve divides the area under the 45-degree line roughly into half. Now it is clear from the figure that the more unequal is income the further to the right will be the

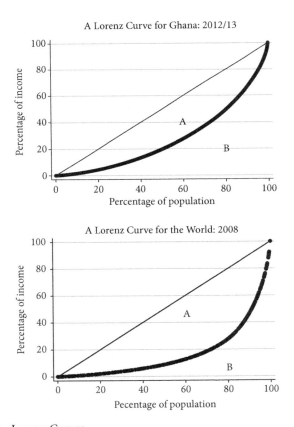

Figure 1.1. Lorenz Curves

Sources: Ghana GLSS survey and author's calculations using unweighted data. World Lorenz curve data from Lakner and Milanovic (2013) World Panel Income Distribution (LM-WPID) database.

Lorenz curve so if we look at the bottom panel, we see that here the area A is much bigger and in fact the Gini for the world in 2008 is 66.5. You can read off the graph that the top 20 per cent of people in the world get some 85 per cent of its income. Even more unequal, and there are reasons to believe this number may *understate* the true extent of inequality which we will discuss in Chapters 5 and 6.

Now we are interested in more than simply proportions. We are also interested in how big is the gap in incomes between the rich and the poor. To measure that gap we need to measure incomes and doing so is difficult and much of our concern in the chapters that follow will be to compare incomes both within and across countries. To anticipate some of that discussion we need to note two problems when it comes to comparing incomes. The first is that a dollar in a poor country buys far more than a dollar in a rich country. One implication is that the numbers we used above, comparing the incomes of very poor countries with the net revenue of Apple, will be misleading. The second is that inflation changes the purchasing power of any currency. Currently Venezuela holds the prize for the fastest rate of inflation ever.

Now economists have sought to make allowances for the first problem by using not actual exchange rates to convert Ghanaian Cedis (the national currency) into US dollars but what are termed 'purchasing power parity' (PPP) exchange rates. These rates allow for the fact that the purchasing power of a dollar differ and if we want to compare incomes across countries we need to use PPP exchange rates. The second problem, namely that inflation both reduces purchasing power at different rates over time and over countries, is allowed for by standardizing all prices, say to 2011 US$ dollars. Both of these adjustments are not without their problems. However, they are our best methods so far devised of enabling us to compare incomes across very different economies.

Our first use of these will be to look at incomes in Ghana in 2012/13. The bottom 25 per cent of Ghanaians in 2012/13 had annual incomes of less than US$700 (PPP 2011) while the top 5 per cent had incomes above US$ (PPP 2011) 5,200, a gap of nearly 7 times in proportional terms and an absolute gap of US$ (PPP 2011) of US$4,500. The data we have used for our World Lorenz Curve has also been converted into PPP (2011) US$ and there the bottom 25 per cent in 2008 had incomes of US$1,000 (PPP 2011) while the top 5 per cent had incomes of US$(PPP 2011) 26,000, a gap of 26 times. Again, we will show in Chapter 7 that this does not at all reflect the true extent of the gaps between the richest and the poorest.

It is important to recognize that these gaps in income can increase even if the Gini does not change. If all the incomes in Ghana were to double the Gini would not change, proportions are exactly the same but the gap between the bottom 25 per cent and the top 5 per cent would double to US$9,000. People within Ghana might well think inequality had increased as the gap between the poor and the rich had doubled but that would not be reflected in the Gini. That, of course, is not to criticize the Gini; it is simply to note that if we want to understand the spread of incomes from those of hundreds of dollars to the billions, which we do, we need to understand how much of that is due, not to any change in the distribution of income within a country, but to changes in their average incomes. As we will show this widening gap as average incomes rise is an important part of the creation of the plutocrats in rich societies.

Armed with a value of the Gin, a clear definition of what we mean by incomes—is it incomes before or after benefits and taxes—and a means of measuring incomes across countries we can ask how has the spread of incomes changed over time and across and within countries. That we will investigate in Chapters 5 and 6.

Top Income Shares: Looking for the Plutocrats

As well as the Gini as a summary measure of inequality there has been much interest in the share of the top 1 per cent, data for which is presented in Table 1.1. The income in the Table is gross income, that is income before any taxes. As it is drawn from tax records it is sometimes of individuals and sometimes of tax units, which may be household based, depending on the country and the time period. It is necessary to use tax data to find the super-rich as they are too few to turn up in other data sources. In Chapter 7 we will compare incomes across the whole distribution for both the US and UK using comparable definitions and allowing for taxes and transfers.

Two countries with relatively high shares of the top 1 per cent are the US and the UK. The focus of much recent political rhetoric has been on the fact that for the US this share is believed to have risen from some 8 per cent in the mid-1970s to over 18 per cent in the period after 2006. In Table 1.1 we report data from *The Chartbook of Economic Inequality* which shows it peaked at 18.9 per cent in 2012 and saw no decline at the time of the financial crisis of 2008–09. In the UK the low point for the share was also in the mid-1970s when the share stood at 6 per cent, it then rose

Table 1.1. Share of the Top 1 Per Cent

	Average 1900 to 1930	Average in the 1970s	Average from 2000
Australia	11.4	5.1	7.6
Canada	13.9	8.1	14.1
Finland	17.4	9.0	8.5
France	20.6	8.4	8.5
Germany	17.1	10.5	11.9
Japan	18.2	7.4	9.3
Netherlands	20.4	6.9	6.6
New Zealand	11.0	6.7	8.3
Norway	15.9	5.5	9.3
South Africa	20.7	11.7	18.3
Sweden	21.0	5.2	6.5
United Kingdom	19.4	6.4	13.7
United States	17.1	7.9	17.2

Source: *The Chartbook of Economic Inequality*—https://www.char tbookofeconomicinequality.com/ (accessed July 2017).

to 15.4 per cent in 2009 and then has fallen back since the financial crisis to 12.7 per cent in 2012. That 1 per cent of earners can obtain between 12 and 18 per cent of total incomes might seem rather extraordinary. In fact, it is not. Such shares were the norm at the start of the twentieth century as we show in Table 1.1. The countries shown in the table are those for which a comparison can be made over this long period.

The current concern, of course, is not with the early twentieth century, but with what has been happening over the last one or two decades. Two of the countries with the fastest rate of growth of the share of the top 1 per cent are the United Kingdom (UK) and the United States (US). So how rich do you need to be to get to be very rich in these countries? The answer is in Figure 1.2 which shows from 1990 the average incomes of those not only in the top 1 per cent, but those in the top 0.05 and top 0.01 per cent.

The top chart in Figure 1.2 shows incomes for the UK, in 1913 GB£, for the rich and the very rich, the chart on the right shows incomes, for the US, in 2014 US$. To get the UK numbers into 2014 US$ you need to increase them by about 30 per cent. There is a rather striking similarity across the two countries and an equally striking difference.

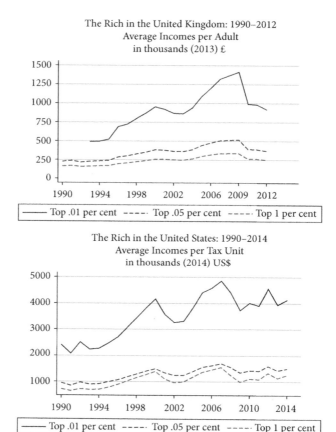

Figure 1.2. The Rich in the UK and the US from 1990

Note: This is tax-based data so its gross earnings of individuals.

Source: Facundo Alvaredo, Anthony B. Atkinson, Thomas Piketty, Emmanuel Saez, and Gabriel Zucman, The World Wealth and Income Database, http://www.wid.world (accessed 7 August 2020).

The striking similarity is the large, and increasing, gap between the top 0.01 per cent and the top 0.05 or 1 per cent. The striking difference is how much richer the rich are in the US than in the UK. Looking at the very rich, within the rich, top incomes peaked at US$5 million in the US, the top 0.01 per cent in the UK had to get by on a mere £1.5 million. You may well feel that either incomes are more than adequate. However, these are averages.

Within this average some earnt very much more. Indeed, we will argue in Chapter 8 that it is possible some have *incomes* in the billions.

There is sometimes a confusion in discussions of inequality between incomes, what you earn each year, and wealth which is the value of the assets you own. Wealth is more unequally distributed than income and can change for very different reasons from why inequality in incomes is changing. Our focus will be almost exclusively on incomes. Where the incomes of the very wealthiest can only be inferred from their wealth we will focus on that wealth. It is certain that the wealth of the richest people in the world runs into billions and Forbes reports that a billionaire is being created in China every two weeks. While incomes in the billions may be confined to a very small number it is clear that among the richest people in the world many of these billionaires have incomes in the hundreds of millions of US$. That some people have *incomes* far in excess of the *wealth* of almost everyone is another indicator of the extent of the inequality we observe in the world.

Absolute and Relative Poverty in the UK

In the opening section of this chapter we reviewed the incomes that you need to be among the richest of UK taxpayers. How many are there at the other end of the scale who can be regarded as poor, or very poor, currently in the UK and how has this number changed over the last two decades? Just as we need a data source which captures the very rich, namely the tax data, to ask questions about the rich so we need a very different source to ask questions about the incomes of the poor. Since the mid-1990s such data is available from the Family Resources Survey results from which are presented in the Reports of Households Below Average Incomes (HBAI). This is the source for the Joseph Rowntree Foundation's analysis of poverty trends in the UK.

We stressed above the need to make a distinction between absolute and relative poverty. Just such a distinction is possible using the HBAI data. The absolute definition of poverty is those with incomes less than 60 per cent of 2010/11 median household income *held constant in real terms*. The relative measure uses 60 per of contemporary median income. In 2016/17 median household incomes were some £425 per week so in 2016 to be relatively poor household income would be below £255 per week or £13,260 a year.

To be absolutely poor they would have to have an income below £240 per week or £12,480 (all in 2016 prices and after allowing for housing costs).

In the top chart of Figure 1.3 we show that from 1994 to 2016 the rate of absolute poverty halved in the UK, while the rate of relative poverty changed very little. The reason for these two results is simple. Median incomes rose rapidly over part of this period and, contrary to what is widely believed, inequality changed very little. The bottom panel translates these

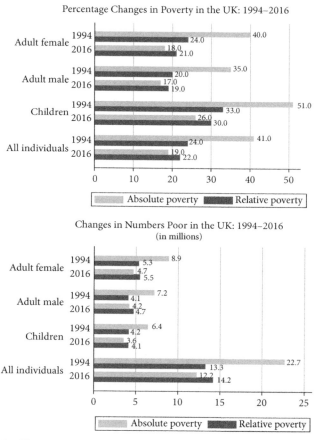

Figure 1.3. Changes in Poverty in the UK 1994–2016

The income concept used in this data is equivalized disposable income.

Source: ONS HBIA Surveys. The relative poverty line is less than 60 per cent of median household income. The absolute poverty line refers to 2010/11 median household income held constant in real terms. Both relative and absolute poverty are after allowing for housing costs.

percentage rates of poverty into the actual number of the poor, for both definitions of poverty, in the UK in these two years.

How much poverty there is in the UK depends on whether we are using a relative or absolute measure of poverty. The Joseph Rowntree Foundation Report confines its attention to the relative measure.[6] With a relative one we will find poverty wherever these is not complete equality—that is, everywhere. We have introduced the Gini coefficient in Figure 1.1 where the larger its value the higher the level of inequality and, whatever cut-off we assume in the distribution, it will generally be true that the higher is the Gini the more poverty we will have.

In contrast, with an absolute measure of poverty, once we have defined a poverty line we can, providing we can measure incomes when incomes are very low, talk about rises and falls of poverty quite separately from inequality. Indeed, poverty in this sense can be falling while inequality is rising. It just depends on how fast the incomes of the poor are changing relative to the median. The bottom chart in Figure 1.3 shows the importance of the distinction. The numbers of the relatively poor increased by 7 per cent from 13.3 to 14.2 million between 1994 and 2016 while the absolutely poor (using median incomes in 2011/12 as the basis) nearly halved from 22.7 to 12.2 million.

This halving of both the rate and the numbers of the absolutely poor between 1994 and 2016 was roughly similar across adults and children. However, these totals hide very significant differences within the adult population. As Figure 1.4 show among pensioners, whether single or living as a couple, the falls in poverty were much greater than the averages shown in Figure 1.3.

The implication is, of course, that poverty fell much less than the average for younger adults. Clearly for the vast majority of these pensioners their falls in poverty are the result of transfers enacted through the tax system. The income measure used Figures 1.3 and 1.4 is disposable household income with an adjustment for household size and composition which we will discuss more fully in Chapter 5. The income measure includes

[6] The Joseph Rowntree Foundation produces an annual report on poverty trends in the UK where in the 2018 report 'the poverty indicator used throughout this report is when a family has an income of less than 60% of median income for their family type, after housing costs (AHC)' (UK Poverty, 2018, p. 11).

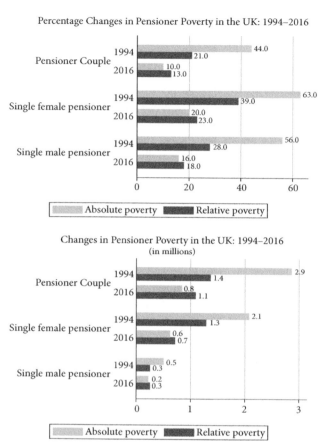

Figure 1.4. Pensioner Poverty in the UK 1994–2016
Source: as for Figure 1.3.

contributions from earnings, state support, pensions, and investment income among others, and is net of tax. An allowance has been made for changes in prices and the measure given in the Figures are after housing costs which can be a major expense for poorer households.

Over the last twenty years in the UK the problem for young people has not been the increase in inequality but the income implications of the outcomes from the financial crisis of 2008–09 which we show in Chapter 9 led to substantial falls in wages, particularly for young workers, combined with a tax system increasingly designed to benefit the old.

The Question to Which We Seek an Answer

The basic question we which we seek an answer is framed by the data presented in this chapter. We began with the mega earnings, and valuation, of a large tech company, Apple, formed in the mid-1970s. We then showed that annual incomes of the super-rich in the UK in 2014 exceeded a million pounds. Those defined as poor within the UK in 2014 had incomes less than £15,000. In the next chapter we are going to show that those in the bottom 5 per cent have incomes of £6,300 while those in the bottom 1 per cent have incomes below £3,500.

In summary within the UK we need to explain incomes ranging from a few thousand to more than a million. As has been hinted at by the numbers for Ghana—we have not yet got the numbers of a comparable basis but will in Chapter 8—poverty is much greater there than in the UK. Indeed, that is implied by the Lorenz curve for the world, and as will be elaborated in the chapters that follow, differences will be shown to be an order of magnitude greater across rich and poor countries than within the UK.

2

The Poor and the Rich in the UK in the Twenty-First Century

Imagine

Imagine you have an income of £500 per year in the second decade of the twenty-first century. You would certainly feel very poor. Indeed, you would be unsure if you could survive at all in twenty-first-century Europe or North America. Now imagine an income of £25,000 per year. As a single person not only would you feel sure you could survive but you would be aware that many had lower incomes. However, you would not consider yourself rich or even moderately well off. Now up your imagined income to £70,000 which, as we saw in the last chapter, would put you in the top 5 per cent of UK taxpayers. More than comfortable you would, I think, feel. But still not rich? Now up your income to £150,000 into the top 1 per cent. Very well off, more than just about managing? Even with those school fees and foreign holidays? Now up your income to £1.9 million, the average income of the top 0.05 per cent. Surely everyone is going to agree you are now very rich indeed? Well maybe—or maybe not. Within the top 0.05 per cent some incomes are substantially higher than that.

Hunting the Very Rich in the Data

One of the reasons seeking the very rich is difficult is that their incomes will not appear in most data sources simply because they are so scarce. However, the data source we have just used is based on UK tax revenues which does report the incomes of the top 0.05 per cent who constitute (again we are talking about 2014) some 15,000 taxpayers out a total population of taxpayers of about 30.5 million—you can see why they are hard to find in the

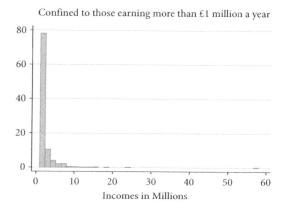

Confined to those earning more than £1 million a year

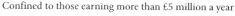

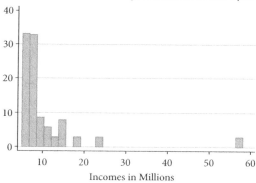

Figure 2.1. The Distribution (in percentages) of UK Annual Income for Tax Purposes for the Rich

Source: HMRC Tax Data for 2014–15.

data. Now we can see how those whose income is 'only' £1 million will feel so hard done by.

In Figure 2.1 above, we plot in the top panel the distribution of incomes for those whose incomes are over £1 million and in the bottom panel we plot those whose incomes were over £5 million. Rather remarkably, some incomes exceed £20 million with the highest incomes grouped at £50 million. Even when we confine the data to those with incomes above £5 million there remains a large spread among those incomes.

Incomes of the Rest

The individuals whose income we have been observing are millionaires in the sense that they earn a million each year. Such incomes are unimaginably large for most workers in the UK in the second decade of the twenty-first century and feed the perception that 'the rich' do live in another world. As a first step to seeing what most people earn in the UK we will exclude the highest earners who are such a small percentage of the total. Now while this data excludes our annual millionaires, all of whom are comfortably in the top 1 per cent, it does not include the poorest members of society who are too poor to pay any tax. To find those we need other data sources which we will come to below. With that reservation in mind what did 'normal' people earn in the UK in 2014?

In the top panel of Figure 2.2 we show the range of incomes from £10,000 to £150,000 so that only excludes the top 1 per cent. In the bottom panel we show the range from £10,000 to £70,000 which excludes those in the top 5 per cent. Remember the poorest are excluded from this data as they pay no tax.

We see that the shape of the distribution we have shown is always the same whatever the range of incomes we present. The shape is a slope with a long right tail. This shape has important implications for how we try and summarize the range of incomes we observe. We want a number which tells us what 'most' people earn. One number which is often quoted is average income. Now we get the average by adding up all the incomes and dividing by the number of people. That sounds like a good idea as to how to summarize what a typical person earns. However, there is a problem when the income distribution looks like it does in our charts—'most' people earn much less than the average. One rather obvious definition of 'most' is the income that divides the population in half, with half getting more than that number and half getting less. That number is called the median and the implication of our charts is that the median is less than the mean, possibly very much less. In the case of our tax data if we take the whole population earning more than £10,000 a year then average incomes are £31,000 while the median income is £22,000, nearly one third less.

The reason for this difference can be seen in the charts. As there are far more people with low incomes than with high ones, averaging will include those high earners—our £50 million earner is equivalent to 5,000 workers on £10,000 a year. It is indeed the shape of this distribution which people are implicitly quoting when they present data showing how much of total income is obtained by a relatively small number of individuals. As we will see the distribution always has this form. If we wish to understand the inequality of incomes, we need to understand why the income distribution takes the form we see in our figures.

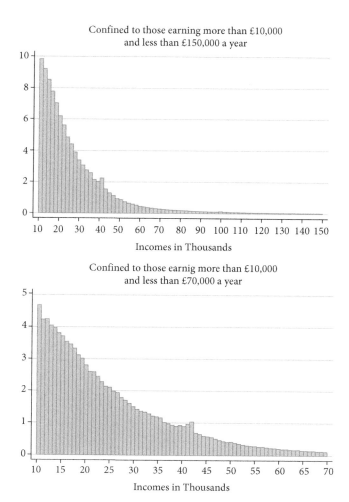

Figure 2.2. The Distribution (in percentages) of UK Annual Income for Tax Purposes Excluding the Richest

Source: As for Figure 2.1.

However, before doing that we need to find data that enables us to view workers who earn too little to be taxed. So next we turn to consider those earning below the minimum wage when it was first introduced in 1998.

Earnings and the Minimum Wage in the UK: 1997–2016

In Figure 2.3 below we show the distribution of earnings for most workers for both 1997 and 2016. A key policy for Labour in the 1997 general election, and a key piece of legislation in 1998, was the introduction of the national

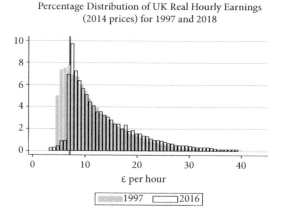

Percentage Distribution of UK Real Hourly Earnings (2014 prices) for 1997 and 2018

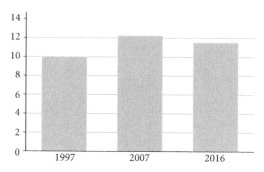

Median UK Real Earnings (£ per hour) (2014 prices) for 1997, 2007 and 2016

Figure 2.3. UK Real Hourly Earnings from 1997 to 2016

Note: The vertical black line shows the National Living Wage for 2016 (in 2014 prices) of £7.10 per hour.

Source: ONS Data from Annual Survey of Hours and Earnings (ASHE) (October 2016).

minimum wage which came into force on 1 April 1999 at £3.60 per hour for adult workers over the age of 22 and £3.00 for those aged 18–22. The national living wage, a new name of the minimum wage, came into effect on 1 April 2016 for workers aged more than 25 at £7.20 per hour. Now to ensure comparability of these numbers with those for our annual million-aires above we have converted all incomes to 2014 prices, so in 2014 prices the minimum wage in 1997 was £5.15 per hour and the national living wage in 2016 was £7.10 per hour.

The grey area in the top panel shows how incomes were distributed in 1997 while the black boxes show what the distribution looked like in 2016. It is clear from the figure that the numbers earning less than the national living wage have fallen dramatically. In 1997 25 per cent of workers earned less than £7.10 per hour while by 2016 that percentage had fallen to less than 5 per cent. You will also notice from the figure that there are actually fewer of the largest incomes in 2016 than there were in 1997 (remember all these numbers are converted to 2014 prices). It looks from the figure as though the inequality of incomes of those included in this data has gone down. What is also striking is that the highest incomes recorded in this data are about £40 per hour. If we convert that to a full-time 35 hour per week, 52 weeks a year, job we get an annual income of just over £70,000 into the top 5 per cent of taxpayers but way below our annual millionaires.

Poverty in the UK in 2014

While our Figures 2.1 and 2.2 show people at the top end and Figure 2.3 those much lower down the income scale, neither captures the very richest or the very poorest even in the UK. The reason we cannot observe the very richest is that they are so scarce the tax data is coded so they cannot be seen as if they were in the publicly released data, it would compromise the anonymity of the data. The reason neither of the data sources we have used so far captures the poorest is that they don't have jobs so we cannot observe their incomes from data on wages.

To see the bottom end of the distribution in Figure 2.4 below we use data that enables us to measure non-labour as well as labour income. Now once we try and capture incomes from, for example, pensions, child credit, and unemployment pay, it makes sense to measure 'incomes'—now meaning all sources of income—on a household basis. Further to ensure that households are as comparable as possible rather than taking the total household income and dividing it by the number of adults we make an allowance for the fact that children 'cost' less than adults. This leads to what is described as an equivalized scale which means we take total household income and divide it by the number of 'equivalent' adults. Doing that enables us to compare households across that part of the distribution where the poorest will be located. While we can see the poorest households, we cannot see the richest as the data we are using is 'top-coded' which means that any income above a certain level, in his case just over £100,000, are coded as that. The result can be seen in Figure 2.4 where the number of higher incomes declines steadily as the incomes rise until we reach just over £100,000 when the number of

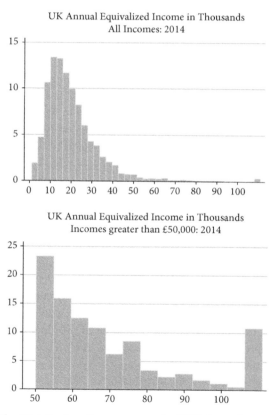

Figure 2.4. The Distribution (in percentages) of UK Annual Equivalized Incomes in 2014

Note: All prices are current 2014 prices.

Source: ONS Living Costs and Food Survey 2014 using unweighted data.

households increases. This can be seen most clearly in the bottom panel of the figure where incomes are confined to over £50,000 per equivalent adult and there is a very clear jump up in the number of households with incomes per equivalent adult of just over £100,000. This is not because the numbers do increase but because all incomes above that level are classed as having that income.

How poor are the poorest people we observe in this sample? Those in the bottom 5 per cent have incomes of £6,300 while those in the bottom 1 per cent have incomes below £3,500. While the numbers are not directly comparable these numbers can be seen in the context of a minimum wage earner on £7.10 (2014 prices) per hour earning, if the job is full time, of £13,000 a year. Clearly minimum wage earners are not by any means the poorest members of society.

Household Expenditures

Now it is possible incomes will be a misleading measure of how well off is a family. Incomes may fluctuate, especially for the poorest whose sources of incomes may vary a lot from year to year. Fluctuations in income may also be important for the self-employed who will be included both among the poorest—the delivery driver—and the richest—the corporate lawyer. To allow for this we can look at household expenditures rather than incomes as those are likely to be far more stable than income. Doing so has other advantages. We will want to compare these UK households with households in much poorer countries than the UK and in these countries most households do not have wage incomes so measuring expenditures is a much better guide to living standard than hard-to-measure income sources. We will take advantage of that when seeking to compare levels of income across rich and very poor countries.

In Figure 2.5 below we present the data for household expenditure per adult equivalent. As can be seen it appears the shape of the distribution is very similar although the top end has not been top coded as the highest expenditures reported are more than double the highest income at over £200,000. With that exception, which is purely an artefact of how the data has been made available, expenditures are lower than incomes. This is consistent with the view that expenditures are a better guide to the long-run income available to households than their actual incomes as households seek to smooth their consumption and not change it when income, for some

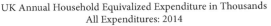

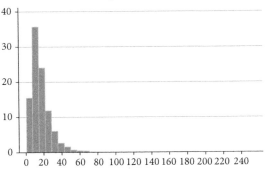

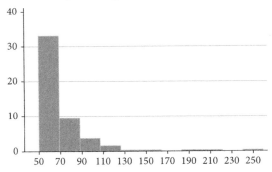

Figure 2.5. The Distribution (in percentages) of UK Annual Equivalized Expenditure in 2014

Note: All prices are current 2014 prices.

Source: As for Figure 2.4.

random short-term reason, changes. If we accept that view then Figure 2.5 is our first view of the range of what we can think of as 'permanent' incomes for most, but crucially, not all households in the UK in 2014. The poorest families have permanent incomes of less than £2,000, the richest ones of more than £200,000—a 150-fold difference.

That though almost certainly understates the range. The data used as the basis for Figures 2.4 and 2.5 is from survey data and excludes the very richest for reasons we have already given—there are so few of them that a relatively small survey is not going to capture them. That indeed is why we began with tax data. It is rather likely, although not certain, that those with incomes of over £1 million a year will have a higher expenditure per adult equivalent than £200,000. The reason we cannot be sure is that we began with data for wages, while Figures 2.4 and 2.5 are on a household basis. While incomes are determined by the market opportunities open to individuals, households form as a result of individual decisions and the link from incomes of individuals to household expenditures is a complex one.

However, while much household income accrues from non-market sources, household-based data is our best basis for measuring differences in incomes across societies as incomes gets translated into expenditures and it is our ability to consume which ultimately determines how well-off we are. Thus, we will use the data in Figure 2.5 as our first step in understanding the range of incomes we need to explain. As we are going to show in the chapters that follow, the UK is a relatively rich country and the poor in the UK are very rich from the point of view of the poor in a poor country.

Combining the data sources we have presented we are faced with seeking an explanation for incomes and expenditures ranging from a few thousands to ones in the tens of millions. Is such inequality a recent phenomenon, as much popular discussion suggests, or has that level of inequality a long history? And, if it has, what generates it and can it be altered? These are the questions to which we seek answers.

The Shape of the Distribution

Why does the distribution take the shape it does? The shape is a common one across all the data we have looked at for tax incomes, incomes around the minimum wage, and household incomes, which ensures that most earn relatively little—the data is bunched to the left—and the long right-hand tail means that the larger the incomes the fewer the people who get them. It will prove instructive to compare the distributions we have observed with the normal distribution which is familiar as the bell curve shown below in Figure 2.6.

For the standard normal distribution, 68 per cent of the observations lie within 1 standard deviation of the mean; 95 per cent lie within two standard deviation of the mean; and 99.9 per cent lie within 3 standard deviations of the mean. Further the distribution is completely described by its mean and its standard deviation which is the measure of how spread out is the distribution. Finally, the mean and median coincide. In summary if the distribution is normal it is very easy to characterize its shape, that is not

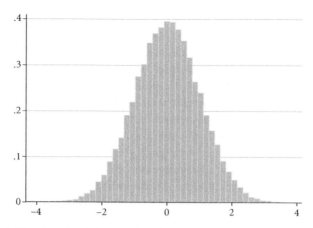

Figure 2.6. The Standard Normal Distribution

the case in the distributions we have been finding for incomes and expenditure, they are conspicuously *not* normal.

However, let's see why it matters that our distributions are so far from normality by considering how different the world would look if incomes were normal. Rather than observing a few very rich people and large numbers of very poor we would observe similar numbers of both the rich and the poor. Further most people would earn the average income and the median and average would coincide. As we have already pointed out, the average can be far higher than the median with the distributions we do observe. Now the normal distribution is very commonly observed, the most generic example being heights and, a rather more contentious one, being intelligence. Now the reason we observe such distributions is well known. It is an implication of a theorem in statistics called the central limit theorem (see the Appendix for a formal statement of the theorem).

So, what does this theorem suggest might be determining height? If the height of an individual is the result of lots of different factors, which are independent of each other, then if we average those factors the distribution of that average will have a normal distribution. So, if we look at the distribution of heights what we are looking at is the average of those factors in each individual.

Now our question is this: why does that *not* describe the process driving income? Think about the factors that may be affecting income, say a shock to the economy that reduces the demand for workers. Now the theorem we have just summarized talks about summing the variables affecting height but if we are dealing with income that does not really make sense. A £100 shock to someone on £1,000 a year is a very different shock to someone on £10,000. So how could we make the shocks comparable? Well, rather than talking about the level of a variable we could talk about the percentage change. So, we don't talk about a shock of £100 but one of say 10 per cent. Now the numbers are much more comparable. For the person on £1,000 a year £100 is 10 per cent while for the person on £10,000 a year 10 per cent is £1,000.

So, can we find a measure where the difference in the measure is a percentage change. The answer turns out to be yes if the percentage change is small. We need to rescale our variables and this rescaling creates what are termed logarithms. There is a note at the end of this chapter explaining how this new scale works in algebraic terms but, if you don't like algebra, all you need to know is that logarithms, logs for short, give us a better way of looking at the charts by rescaling the data. Table 2.1 shows the rescaling we are going to use to rescale the data shown in Figure 2.4.

We begin with a small change of 4 per cent from £2,980 to £3,100 which in our new log scale goes from 8 to 8.04 so the difference in logs, as shown in the Table, is the percentage change in the level variables. Now as you can see from the other calculations in the table this does not work for bigger percentage changes. For that we need another rule which is explained in the Appendix. But we don't need that for now so we just note that changes in our new log scale work well as growth rates if we are looking at growth rates of less than 10 per cent which, on an annual basis, is almost always the case. The large numbers in the table come from measuring changes over long periods of time. But notice what our new scale has done for the expenditure data we want to graph. Instead of the scale going from just over 3,000 to just

Table 2.1. From Levels to Logs

Level of household equivalized incomes	Log scale	Percentage change in level of incomes	Difference in the log scale × 100
2,980	8.0	3,100/2,980 =	
3,100	8.04	1.04 = 4%	4%
8,103	9.0	8,130/3,100 =	
		2.62 = 161%	0.96 = 96%
22,026	10.0	22,026/8,103 =	
		2.72 = 172%	1.0 = 100%
59,874	11.0	59,874/22,026 =	
		2.72 = 172%	1.0 = 100%

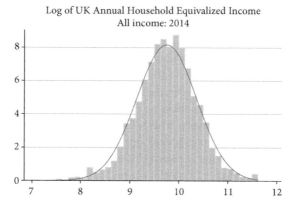

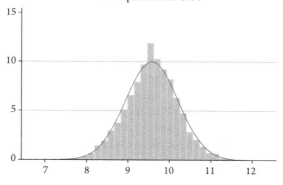

Figure 2.7a. The Distribution (in percentages) of the Log of UK Annualized Incomes and Expenditures (showing log scale)
Source: As for Figure 2.4.

under 60,000 it goes from 8 to 11. With this new scale we are going to be able to see details that would be invisible if we used the levels data.

In Figure 2.7a we use this new scale to represent our data for household incomes and consumption.

In Figure 2.7b we represent this same figure but replacing the measure in logs on the horizontal axis with the actual level of incomes.

Whereas our data in Figure 2.4 was clearly not normal, once we use the log of the variable the distribution is strikingly close to normality. In Figure 2.4 the area under the curve told us the probability of observing a household between two levels of income. In the top charts in

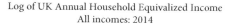

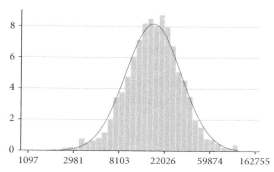

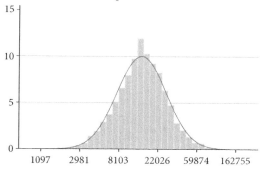

Figure 2.7b. The Distribution (in percentages) of the Log of UK Annualized Incomes and Expenditures (showing levels scale)

Notes: The sample is confined to whose reporting incomes of more than £500 a year. The horizontal axis has been converted to actual incomes and expenditures but distribution is of the logs of those variables. All prices are current 2014 prices.

Source: As for Figure 2.4.

Figure 2.7a and b the area under the curve is telling us the probability of observing the log of that income. The symmetry of the log distribution implies that the probability of observing a household with an income between 2,981 and 8,103 is, close to, the probability of observing one with an income between 22,028 and 59,874. While the gap between the two ranges is very large in level terms, in percentage terms they are the same change—a 2.7-fold increase in income. Look back at Figure 2.4 and you see its shape ensures there are far more households on low incomes than high ones so to get the same number of households we need a much larger range of income to ensure the number in poorer and richer parts of the distribution are the same. The change in scale though does far more than represent the data. Just as normality in levels results from a lot of independent variables impacting on the level, so normality in logs results from a lot of such variables impacting on growth rates. That is the key to understanding why gaps in incomes can grow while the proportions of incomes earned by households do not.

Before considering the possible implications of this let us see how our other data fares when we use a log scale. In Figure 2.8 we represent the data

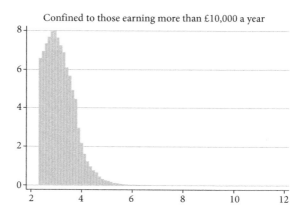

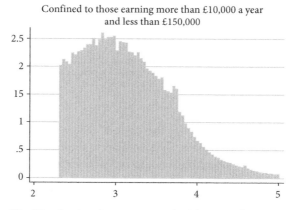

Figure 2.8. The Distribution (in percentages) of the Log of UK Annual Incomes for Tax Purposes in 2014–15

Note: All prices are current 2014 prices.

Source: As for Figure 2.1.

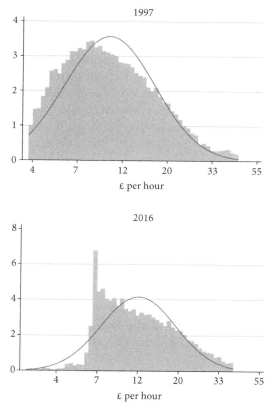

Figure 2.9. The Distribution (in percentages) of UK Real Hourly Earnings (2014 prices) for 1997 and 2016

Note: The horizontal axis has been converted to actual hourly earnings but the distribution is of the logs of those earnings. All prices are current 2014 prices.

Source: As for Figure 2.3.

of Figure 2.1. Given that the data is truncated by the fact that no one earning under £10,000 is in the data we see in Figure 2.8 a shape now much closer to the right-hand side of a normal curve.

With a log scale we can now put everyone on the same chart. Measuring income in thousands on a log scale £60 million converts to 11. It is clear that the tail is far too long for the log normality assumption to hold. For reasons we need to investigate there are far too many very rich people, albeit very few. Put another way—and it's crucial for our ability to understand why we have the super-rich—it looks as though the tiny number of super-rich have escaped the mechanism driving the incomes of everyone else.

We can see this more clearly if we confine our sample to the bottom 99 per cent. If we did not know about the long right tail we would think log normality worked quite well in describing what we see.

While a gap between 3 on the log scale (which is £20,000) and 5 (which is £150,000) is large it is clearly nowhere near as large as the gap from £150,000 to £50 million. What of the wage data presented in Figure 2.3 which we present using our log scale in Figure 2.9? While the distribution for 1997 could be described as very roughly log normal—very roughly as clearly any formal test for log normality would reject that—the change to 2016 is such that log normality is clearly a non-starter for describing what is going on. Indeed, we know what is going on in that the government by introducing a minimum wage law—and it appears ensuring it was enforced—has radically changed the distribution of income at the lower end. In other words, it is *not* the result of a lot of independent variables impacting on the growth rate. It is the result of the government's intervention in the market.

The Log Scale and the Long-Run Change in the Price of Labour

Some, but by no means all, of our data has shown that the distribution of incomes and expenditures is close to log normality. We have argued that a process by which a lot of independent shocks impact on the growth of incomes will result in a log normal pattern. However, we have said nothing about what that growth of incomes has been and what factors may be driving its underlying level. As we are now going to show the incomes that we have shown for 2014 are many times the level of incomes of 20 or 200 years ago.

Poverty is due to low incomes. For most of the poor their only asset is their labour and their income then depends on the 'price' of that labour and the employment opportunities open to them. While being unemployed may be a source of poverty it is certainly possible to be poor and employed if the 'price' the labourer can command is sufficiently low, as indeed it has been for the vast majority of human history. It is natural in the context of now-rich countries to think of the 'price' of labour as its wage or earnings, the difference being bonuses and benefits. However, again in the long run of history, wage employment has been the exception rather than the rule.

The earnings of labour have been from farming, from own production in the household, from self-employment as a trader or artisan. In fact, the rise in wage labour has been inextricably linked to the decline in poverty as being employed for wages is a key aspect of raising the 'price' of labour. The other key aspect of reducing poverty is not only that the wages of labour should rise but so should employment expand with the growth of population. Combing high, and rising, wages with full employment is indeed the mix that when it works dramatically reduces poverty but, unfortunately, it often does not work and indeed has stopped working in many now-rich countries as we will see in later chapters. Here we want to see how, in the long term in the UK, this 'price' of labour has changed.

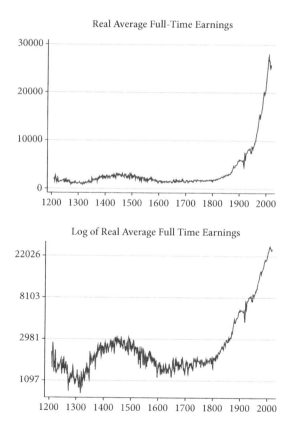

Figure 2.10. UK Earnings (in 2014 prices) 1200–2015

Note: In the bottom figure on the vertical axis the logs have been converted to actual incomes.

Sources: Earnings data from Gregory Clark, What Were the British Earnings and Prices Then? (New Series), MeasuringWorth, 2016, URL: http://www.measuringworth.com (accessed 7 August 2020). Updated from ONS data.

Definition: Earnings represent an estimate of the total monetary value of the compensation an average worker in full-time employment would get each year. Earnings thus includes wages, non-cash (in-kind) payments, bonuses, commissions, remuneration per output accomplished ('piece-rate payments'), and overtime supplements. From 1870–1962 earnings are estimated from weekly wages, and are just those wages multiplied by an assumed 52 weeks of payment per year. 1209–1869 earnings are estimated from daily wages, assuming each worker worked for 312 days per year (6 days a week, for 52 weeks). For the modern period, 1963 to the present, the earnings data covers all full-time workers. For the earlier years average earnings are projected backwards looking just at the movement of earnings in a sample of occupations. Before 1869 these occupations are just those of men in farming (which employed typically 60 per cent of the population before 1750), coal mining, and skilled and unskilled building workers—carpenters, bricklayers, painters, masons, plumbers, glaziers, plasterers, thatchers, and labourers. Average wages are inferred on the assumption that the relative wages of women relative to men did not change 1209–1869, and that the share of women employed also did not change in these years.

Thanks to the work of economic historians we can observe this 'price' over very long periods of time and we present that data in Figure 2.10. In the top panel we use the level scale, in the bottom panel we use our log scale. As we would expect the pattern of changes is clearer in our log scale as it allows us to much better compare very small and very large numbers. However, the use of a log scale has another advantage. As we have shown a change in the log can be interpreted as a growth rate. So, the slope of the line in our bottom log chart shows us the growth rate of wages. If it is a straight line—which visually appears to be a good approximation after 1820—then that is telling us that the growth rate has been constant.

Now what Figure 2.10 shows is full-time average earnings from 1200 to 2015. This is based, as explained in the Appendix, on various sources for hourly or weekly earnings. These numbers have been summed to full-time earnings by assuming the worker is fully employed. So, the data in Figure 2.10 combine the two elements which are the key to understanding poverty—the 'price' of labour and the number of hours the labourer can work—thus creating a measure of incomes that can be compared over this long historical period. It needs to be stressed that this is only income if you are fully employed.

The patterns shown in the data are both clear and dramatic. From 1200 to 1800 the incomes of labour fluctuated but with no long-run trend. Over these six centuries average incomes never rose above £5,000 a year in 2014 prices. Then shortly after 1800 they took off and rose it appears, with some blips, continuously until the present.

Indeed, the increase we show in the figure is a substantial underestimate of how well people did as it makes no allowance for the decrease in weekly hours worked since the start of the nineteenth century. As the definition of earnings under Figure 2.10 explains, no allowance has been made for changes in hours worked. The author of the data, Gregory Clark, writes that 'since 1820 hours of work, even for full-time workers, are now much less than the typical 3,000 hours per year of pre-industrial England'.

In Figure 2.11 we compare hourly earnings with the average earnings from Figure 2.10—we have scaled up the hourly earnings numbers to an annual basis so it fits on the same scale in the figure. It might appear from the chart that the growth rates of the two series are similar. In one sense they are in that hourly earnings increased at a trend rate of 1.6 per cent per annum while average earnings increased by 1.3 per cent per annum. However, over a period as long as from 1820 to 2015, what appears a small difference in growth rates results in for the average earnings data a 13-fold increase, while for hourly earnings there was a 23-fold increase.

But are appearances deceptive? In Figure 2.10 we have a very long period of time so the details of decades can be hidden and people worry about their incomes over years, not over decades or centuries. To get a clearer picture of what has been happening in the last decades the top panel in Figure 2.11 shows the data from 1997, the advent of the New Labour government. From 1997 to 2008, the eve of the financial crisis, real hourly earnings increased by 3.2 per cent per annum, nearly double the long-term trend shown in the bottom panel of Figure 2.11. The clear break in the series is apparent, since the financial crisis earning have fallen back to where they were a decade earlier. You have to go back to before the First World War to find a similar decade of no growth in real hourly earnings.

We want to know why this has happened and whether, and how, the previous trend can be restored. One of the features of both Figure 2.10 and 2.11 is that the series for earnings looks very smooth, going up very regularly over the long term. That is why the period since the financial crisis has been such a shock. However, that smoothness hides great diversity. If we look at the growth rate of earnings, as we do in Figure 2.12, we get a very different picture.

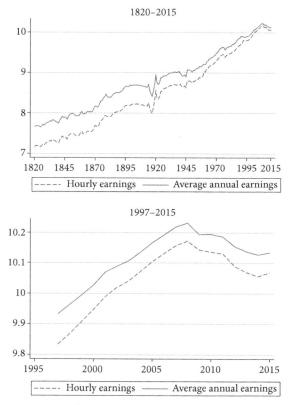

Figure 2.11. Earnings in the United Kingdom: 1820–2015 Log of Real Hourly Earnings and Log of Real Average Annual Earnings (2014 prices)

Note: Real hourly earnings are presented on an annual basis to ensure comparability.

Source: As for Figure 2.10.

Indeed, rather than being impressed by how smooth is the series it now looks like a radio wave with large year-to-year fluctuations in the growth rate. In fact, the series has a name, it is called a random walk for reasons which are apparent from the figure. It appears you cannot predict, once you look at growth rates, what is likely to happen next. From this perspective what has happened since the financial crisis looks much less unusual as we see much larger changes in growth rates in the past than what has happened since 2008. However, if we abstract from the period of the two World Wars in the twentieth century, it does look as though the sustained negative

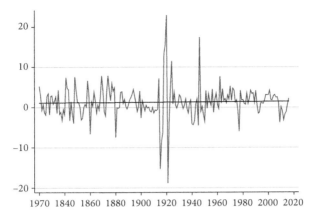

Figure 2.12. Annual Growth Rate of Real Average Earnings in the UK (%pa) 1820–2015

Source: As for Figure 2.10.

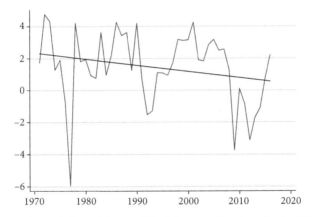

Figure 2.13. Annual Growth Rate of Real Average Earnings in the UK (%pa) 1970–2015

Source: As for Figure 2.10.

growth rates since 2008 may be unusual. Let us look in more detail for the period since the 1970s—Figure 2.13.

Here we see something much more worrying than a break in the upward trend, we appear to see a downward trend in the growth rate of earnings and this downward trend can be traced back to the advent of the premiership of

Margaret Thatcher. In the Thatcher period growth of average earnings was some 3 per cent per annum, the figure after the financial crisis was about -2 per cent per annum—a change in the growth rate of about 5 percentage points, more than sufficient to explain the unhappiness of British workers in the recent past. However, you might well wish to object that the line has a very shallow slope and may well be hiding not a long-run decline in growth rates but a shift by which, with the financial crisis, growth rates shifted down substantially from their pre-crash high. Something happened at the time of the financial crisis in the UK. We need to understand not simply the results of the financial crisis, but whether something is driving down the ability of the economy to produce higher earnings.

Inequality, Poverty, and Growth in the UK in the Twenty-First Century

We began this chapter with tax data showing the range of incomes in the UK for 2014 for those who pay tax. That range was very wide from the minimum amount you need to earn to pay tax at £10,000 to incomes in the tens of millions. We placed these current earnings in a historical context showing that since 1820 there had been a 13-fold increase in average earnings and a 23-fold increase in hourly earnings. Over this period workers have been able to work much shorter hours for much higher rates of pay. The obvious question is how they have managed that. As we are going to show in the chapters that follow most countries have not succeeded in doing so. We will introduce measures of poverty where to be poor is defined, roughly, as having a daily income of less than £2. If we look back in time for the UK we can see that average daily earnings, for a full-time worker, were more than twice this in 1800. Now while we have no data on the distribution of incomes in 1800 similar to that used earlier in this chapter, we can be fairly certain it was very unequal so many would have incomes well below £4 per day. We have also shown that average earnings have shown a pattern of sustained growth over the very long term from 1820 with clear evidence of a slowdown in this growth rate in recent decades. Looking at expenditures per adult equivalent for the UK in 2014 we found that from the richest to the poorest the range in logs was nearly 4 which translates into differences of 55 times.

Our objective is to understand the factors that explain what appears to be extraordinary inequality. However, before doing so we need to look wider than the UK. As we will now see, such inequality as we have observed in the UK is as nothing to the scale of inequality when we look at a world-wide scale. We tackle that issue in two steps. In the next chapter we will look at incomes across five countries: the UK, the US, Brazil, China, and India. In Chapter 4 we move to include the rest of the world. The UK will then be seen as a middle-income rich country with a middle-income level of inequality with, by global standards, almost no absolutely poor people.

Appendix: The Central Limit Theorem

The central limit theorem (CLT), which is one of the most powerful results in statistics, suggests why we may often observe normal distributions. The CLT states that if we have N random variables $\{Y_1, Y_2, \ldots . Y_n\}$ which are independently and identically distributed (note they do not need to be normally distributed) with mean μ and standard deviation σ then Z_n defined as:

$$Z_n = \frac{\bar{Y}_n - \mu}{\sigma/\sqrt{n}}$$

will tend to a standard normal distribution as $n \to \infty$ where $\bar{Y} = n^{-1}\sum_{i=1}^{n} Y_i$. We can say that Z_n has an asymptotic normal distribution.

A *log-normal* (or *lognormal*) *distribution* is a continuous probability *distribution* of a random variable whose logarithm is normally *distributed*. Thus, if the random variable X is log-normally *distributed*, then $Y = \log(X)$ has a normal *distribution*.

Appendix: Logarithms

A fuller exposition of the economic uses of logarithms and the rules that apply to them can be found in Chiang (1984, chapter 10). The reason we need logarithms is that they help us measures changes and, as we have argued in Chapter 1, it is changes we need to measure as they produce the levels that we are ultimately interested in. In fact, we can find an expression for the growth rate of y using the concept of logarithms. It requires a number called e which is the limit of a sum. To see why this number e is so useful let us write out the time path for y with some *growth rate*. We will have:

$$y(1) = y(0)(1 + growth\ rate)$$
$$y(2) = y(1)(1 + growth\ rate)$$

$$y(3) = y(2)(1 + growth\ rate)$$

$$y(t) = y(t - 1)(1 + growth\ rate)$$

We can work backwards to see that:

$$y(t) = y(0)(1 + growth\ rate)^t$$

So far so good, but we have not been explicit as to the time period the growth rate is measured over. A growth rate of 10 per cent per month will give a very different path for y than one of 10 per cent per year. Let us assume the growth rate is per month, m, and we want to measure the growth rate, r, over a year. We can now write:

$$y(t) = y(0)\left(1 + \frac{r}{m}\right)^{mt}$$

The quotient (r/m) tells us that over each of the m months only $1/m$ of the annual rate will actually be applicable. The exponent mt tells us, since the growth rate is to be measured m times a year, that there will be a total of mt periods over which growth is calculated in t years. We can now rewrite the equations as:

$$y(t) = y(0)\left(1 + \frac{r}{m}\right)^{mt} = y(0)\left[\left(1 + \frac{r}{m}\right)^{\frac{m}{r}}\right]^{rt}$$

If we write $\frac{r}{m} = w$ then:

$$y(t) = y(0)\left[\left(1 + \frac{1}{w}\right)^{w}\right]^{rt} = y(0)e^{rt}$$

The reason for this final step is that

$$e = \lim_{w \to \infty}\left(1 + \frac{1}{w}\right)^{w}$$

The number e is the limit to an infinite series but it has here an economic meaning as the base for calculating a growth rate which would occur if that growth rate was calculated continuously as $m \to 0$ then $w \to \infty$. In other words, it is going to be the base for a good measure of growth providing our growth rate is not too large.

We now need to introduce logarithms to show how we can graphically represent the growth rate.

Consider two number 4 and 16 then it is true that $4^2 = 16$

We can now define a logarithm, we will always use 'log' for short.

$$log_4 16 = 2$$

We say that the logarithm of 16 to the base 4 is 2, namely the logarithm is that number to which 4 must be raised to get 16. A logarithm can be defined for any base, but for our purposes by far the most useful is to define them to the base e so we have what is termed an exponential function:

$$y(t) = e^{rt}$$
$$log_e y(t) = rt$$

Note that this just uses the definition of the logarithm to base e The logarithm is that number to which e must be raised to get $y(t)$. Our final step requires us to use the rules for logarithms as we want to measure the increase in $y(t)$ from a base period of $y(0)$:

$$y(t) = y(0)e^{rt}$$
$$log_e y(t) - log_e y(0) = log_e y(t)/y(0) = rt$$

We can now see why the difference in logs does not work as a growth rate when the change in y is large. Consider this extract from Table 2.1:

Level of household equivalized incomes	Log Scale	Percentage change in level of incomes	Difference in the log scale × 100
3,100	8.04	8,130/3100 =	
8,103	9.0	2.62 = 161%	0.96 = 96%

We see that the difference in logs, 0.96, is rt which over a period of one year is far too large a growth rate for our formula to work. We need to use $y(t) = y(0)e^{rt}$ and if the growth rate over one year is 96 per cent then the increase will be $e^{0.96} = 2.61$ or 161 per cent as shown in the table.

3

Five Countries

The United States, United Kingdom, Brazil, China, and India

The Richest People in the World

In a widely cited Oxfam report released in February 2017 it was claimed that 'eight billionaires own the same wealth as the 3.6 billion people who form the poorest half of the world's population'.[1] Let us translate that wealth number into income so we can compare with our poor and rich earners in the UK who were our concern in the last chapter. On the basis of the Forbes list of the eight richest people in the world their total wealth in 2016 came to (in round numbers) US$500 billion (say £400 billion).[2] Assuming a real long-run return from the stock market of about 5 per cent, that means our eight richest people have a total income of about £20 billion or an average annual income of about £2.5 billion. Note now why the top 0.01 per cent in the UK with their modest £2 million will feel a bit hard done by. Rich men have some £2 billion in income not a paltry £2 million. Note also if we take £1000 per year as the income of the very poorest of the families we observed in our UK data, we need 'only' 20 million of the poor in the UK to have the same income as the richest eight men (the richest people are all men) in the world, not 3.6 billion. The reason for the discrepancy with the Oxfam number is partly that wealth is much more unequally distributed than income and partly that the poor in the UK are not poor at all by global standards.

The Oxfam report was concerned with inequality between countries, contrasting the very rich in rich countries with the incomes of most in the poorest countries. In addition to such concerns, the extent of inequality of

---

[1] https://www.oxfam.org/en/press-releases/just-8-men-own-same-wealth-half-world (accessed 7 August 2020).

[2] In 2016 there were some 1,700 billionaires. We will present data for their total net worth and how this has changed since the mid-1990s in Chapter 10.

incomes within countries has also moved to the front of the political agenda. Whether those with relatively low incomes in a country are classed as poor depends on whether we have a relative or absolute conception of poverty in mind. Your British or US worker struggling on £20,000 a year is unimpressed by being told they are so much richer than the worker in sub-Saharan Africa (SSA) where a 'rich' person will have an income of £2,000 a year. Poverty clearly has a relative as well as an absolute dimension. Being relatively poor only makes sense in the context of average incomes within a society and the rise in inequality in some countries in the recent past—the ones that have received a lot of attention are the US and the UK—has come to be seen as posing a problem of rising poverty within those countries. Poverty in this relative sense can be increasing even if the incomes of all are rising if it is the case that the incomes of the richer are growing faster than the incomes of the poorer.

Where Do Billionaires and the Poor Come From?

Of the eight richest billionaires in the Forbes list for 2017 six are US citizens (the other two are from Spain and Mexico). None are from the UK so by focusing on the UK, as we did in the last chapter, we will be missing the richest people in the world. So, a good place to start for the search for billionaires will be to look at the US economy and ask how it has managed to produce so much wealth and so many (very) wealthy people. The existence of billionaires from Mexico and Spain alerts us to the fact that there is more to becoming a billionaire than being born in the richest country. However, six out of eight is not a bad proportion so let us look at how the US got so rich and we will compare it with countries which were richer than the US in the past (specifically the UK) and three other very much poorer countries, Brazil, China, and India. Until the very recent past by far the easiest place to find the very poor has been China and India. Thus, in comparing these five countries we will get the full range of incomes across the globe and we will see how both their relative and absolute positions have changed over a long span of time.

The way incomes across countries are compared is by means of a measure termed Gross Domestic Product (GDP) which is a measure of how rich a country is if all the sources of income in that economy are added up. It is sometimes referred to as a value-added measure as it seeks to capture the difference between the outputs of an economy, the cars, televisions, food that is produced and the inputs like steel, electrical parts and fertilizer which are the inputs necessary to produce the outputs.

While we will use the term GDP in our figures to be clear where the data being used comes from we will use the terms aggregate income, or simply income, when the context is clear in the text as that is exactly what GDP is trying to measure—the total income available to all the people in an economy. If we divide this income by the number of people in the country we get its per capita income and—again you need to suspend belief for a while—that would be the income all would get—all means all men, women, and children – if each were given the same income. Now you will object that as many get no income and as we have already stressed the range of incomes that individuals in an economy do get is very wide that this average number is not very interesting. It is true it is not interesting as a measure of what they do get but it is very interesting as a measure of what they could get. It is a measure of potential income and is very important if we wish to understand why so many are so poor and why a very few are so rich. You cannot have billionaires in economies with low per capita incomes and small populations—there is simply not enough potential income for them to capture. Where, and when, you can have billionaires we will consider below when we measure the size of an economy.

We are going to be using a US$ measure of GDP so we need to be explicit as to when we are talking about. As inflation in nearly all economies has occurred at some point in their history it matters the year we are using when talking about dollars or pounds. All our data, in this chapter, will refer to 2011 as that is the most useful year to use for the comparative data we plan to use. However, as any traveller in poorer counties knows, US$1 buys far more in poor countries than it does in rich ones. Why that is so is a very important question. The underlying reason is that unskilled labour is much cheaper in poor than in rich countries and, mostly, such labour is not allowed to migrate. As unskilled labour is much more abundant in poor than rich countries; its price is low relative to the prices of goods that do enter trade which can, at least approximately, be priced by using the actual exchange rate. We have been stressing that this low price of unskilled labour in poor countries is the underlying cause of poverty. This low price for labour gets reflected in the price level, ensuring that converting prices using the actual exchange rate will mislead as to the purchasing power of incomes in poor countries. Low prices ensure that the poor can survive on low wages, they could not survive on those wages in a rich country. A poor worker earning US$200 a month using actual exchange rates would be even poorer if we magically transferred him or her to a rich country still with the same US$200 wage, as prices would be so much higher in the rich country. To enable these comparisons to be done across poor and rich countries it is necessary to establish a set of comparable prices and the measure used in the data presented here is purchasing power parity US$ (termed PPP US$ in the figures) which is based on a set of prices which seek to compare similar goods across countries in a common currency unit. So, given that we are measuring goods at similar prices and the changes we measure are changes in real incomes—that is, changes which reflect the ability of workers in an economy to consume more goods—the data enables us to see which countries are the wealthy ones and when they became rich.

The Economic History of Five Countries—US, UK, Brazil, China, and India

In Figure 3.1 we show incomes for five countries—the US, UK, Brazil, China, and India—to provide a first attempt to find out where billionaires and poor people live. The top panel shows the data from 1500 to 2014 while the bottom panel uses the log scale we introduced in the last chapter. From the top panel, it appears (and we stress appears) that incomes were very similar for all our five countries from 1500 until 1800 when incomes in the US and the UK started to rise, followed a century later by Brazil and then roughly another century later by China and then India. From the bottom panel, we see that by the start of the twenty-first century very large gaps in per capita incomes had arisen with the US by far the richest of the five countries with incomes of over US$(2011 PPP) 50,000, approximately ten times the Indian per capita income.

Now while US$50,000 is clearly a very large income relative to that of your average Indian with US$5,000, it's a long way from the millions or even billions which are the incomes of the richest Americans. The clue to where they come from is that not only is the US very rich on a per capita basis it also has a relatively large population by the standards, that is, of rich countries (Figure 3.2). The combination of high per capita income and high population results as shown in Figure 3.3 of a total income of the US which dwarfs that of our other countries until very recently. Total income in the US by 2014 was some 15 trillion US$ (PPP) (a trillion recall is a million million), a number which it is hard to imagine. However, we can link it to our eight richest billionaires whose average income we estimated (very

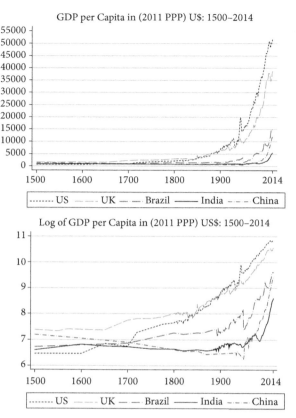

Figure 3.1. GDP per Capita for US, UK, Brazil, India, and China 1500–2014

Note: Details of these sources can be found in an Appendix to this chapter.

Source: The Maddison-Project, http://www.ggdc.net/maddison/maddison-project/home.htm, 2013 (accessed 7 August 2020) and PENN World Tables 9.0. Updated from Angus Maddison, *Historical Statistics of the World Economy, 1–2006 AD*.

roughly and possibly too high) at $2.4 billion (that is income remember not wealth). The population of the US in 2014 was some 320 million so these eight billionaires capture 'only' 0.13 per cent of total income or, as Oxfam would probably wish to report it, eight people have average incomes of 2.4 billion dollars while the other 319,999,992 people have average incomes of US$47,000 an income gap of some 50,000 times.

These numbers might appear to indicate an absurd degree of inequality but remember that incomes on average of US$ (PPP) 50,000 are among the highest in the world. So, once we start comparing rich and poor across

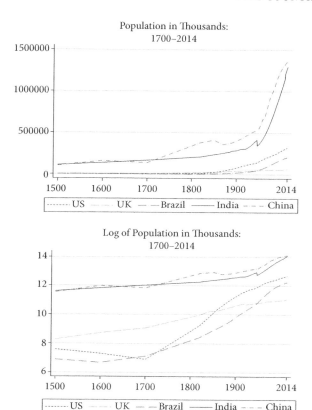

Figure 3.2. Population for US, UK, Brazil, India, and China 1500–2014
Source: As for Figure 3.1.

countries, as distinct from within countries, we will observe much higher degrees of inequality. Indeed, that is the central point of the Oxfam report we have already cited. The GDP per capita measure we have been using to indicate income differences across countries is a measure of average incomes and, as our illustration with US billionaires has shown, such averages are very misleading as to how much income individuals actually receive in a society. While averages may be uninformative as to an individual's income—indeed, it is perfectly possible almost nobody earns the average—they are highly informative as to the potential incomes in a society. That is what we see with billionaires. You need a certain level of total income to make them possible or at least to make them as numerous as they are today. It is the truly staggering rises in income in the US—from 0.5 trillion (PPP) dollars in 1900 to 15 trillion

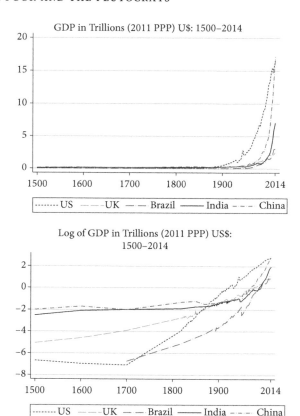

Figure 3.3. GDP for US, UK, Brazil, India, and China 1500–2014
Source: As for Figure 3.1.

in 2014—that has made billionaires possible. The question to which we want to know the answer is whether it has made them inevitable.

However, first things first. Creating the income necessary for our billionaires requires some explanation. How did the US, and indeed the other countries in our data, increase their incomes so remarkably, albeit at different times? As a first step to answering that question we need to look at our charts using the log scale we introduced in the last chapter. From our charts in levels it appears that nothing much happened to either per capita or total incomes from 1500 to 1900. So why not start in 1900? Well the answer is that the charts are very misleading as they are hiding a lot of important detail. You might also think from looking at the charts that the countries, once they started to grow, grew at a faster and faster rate. The plots for the US and China look almost vertical by the end of the period. As with the absence of any action before 1900 this too is very misleading.

The problem with the charts is that, taking Figure 3.1 with per capita incomes as an example, if incomes in 1500 differed between US$ (PPP) 600 (that for the US) and US$ (PPP) 1000 (that for the UK) it is completely invisible as the scale has to get from 600 to 50,000 to encompass the changes from 1500 to 2014. Now using our log scale, we can see this difference. Starting with the long run of data in Figure 3.1 we see immediately, once a log scale is used, that by 1700 the UK was much richer than the other countries in the comparison. However, on a per capita basis it was not richer than many other European countries. Also, by 1700, Europe as a whole was not much richer than some other parts of the world (see Figure 4.4). The use of log scale to view growth is particularly important as the chart shows for both the UK and the US a kink about 1700 when the slope of the line increases. That increase in slope is the increased growth rate usually referred to as the industrial revolution in UK economic history. The UK slope is slightly lower than that for the US and the result is that the US overtakes the UK in terms of per capita income by 1920. The gap between the US and the UK really opened up during the Second World War which saw a very substantial rise in per capita income for the US relative to the UK.

The growth of the US appears—in the long-time span considered here—to be remarkably stable. It has produced a high level of income by a relatively low, but very long run, rise in per capita incomes with a high rate of population growth. However, that stability is misleading. In Figure 3.4 we compare the growth rates for the US and the UK over the epochs we have identified in the data. Table 3.1 shows the growth rates which underlie Figure 3.4. The collapse of the US economy at the time of the Great Depression from 1929 to 1934 is well known; less well known is the speed of the recovery and in particular the rapid growth in the US over the period of the Second World War. Since 1950 the growth rates of both have been far more stable than before 1950 until the financial crash of 2008–09 which saw large declines in growth in both countries. It might also be noted that since the UK joined what was then the EEC the UK economy has grown more rapidly than the US. As we will see in later chapters it has also been much more successful than the US in increasing the incomes of the relatively poor.

Our three other countries each have their kink in the growth rate. For Brazil this occurred at the turn of the twentieth century; for China and India

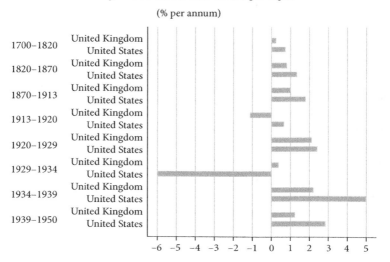

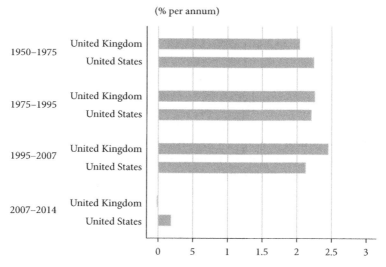

Figure 3.4. Average Annual Growth Rates of GDP per Capita for the UK and US 1700–2014

Source: As for Figure 3.1.

Table 3.1. Average Annual Growth Rates of GDP per Capita for the UK and US 1–2014

	Average Rates of Growth of GDP per Capita (per cent per annum)	
	United States	United Kingdom
1–1700	0.02	0.08
1700–1820	0.72	0.24
1820–1870	1.33	0.80
1870–1913	1.80	1.01
1913–1920	0.66	−1.12
1920–1929	2.41	2.12
1929–1934	−5.99	0.38
1934–1939	4.98	2.21
1939–1950	2.84	1.2
1950–1975	2.24	2.04
1975–1995	2.21	2.26
1995–2007	2.12	2.45
2007–2014	0.19	−0.2

Source: As for Figures 3.1–3.3.

we see clearly the change in their growth profiles in the 1970s. So, a common factor across all five countries is the kink, however the timing is different for each. And not only the timing. We see that Brazil for the first three quarters of the twentieth century grew faster than the UK and the US (its log curve is steeper) but after 1975 sustained growth ended. The two late comers to modern economic growth, China and India, seem to be making up for lost time. The Chinese growth rate is unprecedented, the slope of its log curve being much steeper than any of the other countries shown. Indeed, it is faster than any other country in the economic history of the world. India's growth is less dramatic but it is the only one of our five countries that may be seeing an acceleration in its growth rate, its line in the bottom panel has a slight curve to it.

While as we have noted the common factor across the countries is the kink, there is little else in common. The kink occurred at very different times, the resulting growth rates were very different and Brazil saw a slowdown in its growth rate while India is seeing some acceleration. Thus, we need to explain not simply the kink but also the variety of outcomes afterwards. The experience of the UK and the US, shown in the figures, is not typical of the growth experience of most countries in the world. When it comes to their growth of total incomes, as distinct from incomes per capita, the US and the UK experiences are also very different from each other. The reason is their radically different rates of population growth shown in Figure 3.2.

Population growth, driven in substantial part by migration, is far higher in the US than in any of our other countries. The US growth experience is unique not primarily for its long-run growth rate but that it has combined a sustained growth in per capita incomes while absorbing large increases in population. A process that has clearly not been without its strains but points to a key feature of international patterns of growth from the eighteenth century onwards that they were, on occasion, accompanied by major shifts in population. The combination of these different patterns of per capita income growth and population growth can be seen in Figure 3.3 which presents the patterns of changes in total income across the five countries on which we are presently focusing.

The Size of an Economy and the Location of Billionaires and the Poor

We noted above that with a total income of some 15 trillion US\$ (PPP) in 2014 the income of its eight richest citizens is a drop in the bucket at only 0.13 per cent of total incomes. We see here how the contemporary world economy can give rise to radically different perspectives. Do we focus on the fact that the dramatic increase in total incomes has made the income of the wealthiest in society a relatively small percentage of total incomes or, as most do, are we transfixed by the enormous differences across the population in incomes? We have so far presented the differences within the US that the existence of billionaires creates. What though of China with a total size similar to that of the US, by 2014, but with per capita incomes a quarter as high. In October 2017 the Forbes report estimated there were about 300 billionaires in China, although as they also estimated that one more was being created every week that number would now undoubtedly be higher. They also noted the average wealth that a billionaire holds stands at \$2.5 billion, which is the lowest among its Asian peers. Using the same stylized calculations as we did for our eight richest billionaires, the average income of Chinese billionaires would be some US\$125 million—very modest it will be noted relative to the richest eight. Again, doing a similar calculation to the one we did for the US, we find that the percentage of total income these 300 billionaires will absorb is some 0.23 per cent of total incomes. Is that a big number or a small one? In China the poorest incomes are a few hundred dollars a year. Compare that with the tens of millions of the billionaires and the inequality in the US starts to look relatively benign.

The point of these calculations is that in 2014 the size of the US and China economies are such that the super-rich can easily fit but it does require an economy of that size. As Figure 3.3 shows the Indian and Chinese economies have for most of the period of our data been the dominant economies in terms of size. It is just that their large size was a function of large populations and low incomes. While billionaires need large economies, the poor do not. Poverty indeed has been the lot of almost all of the world's population until very recently and it is the failure of China and India to grow that explains why, again until relatively recently, that most of the poorest people in the world were in Asia.

As a result of the rapid changes of income in Asia the locus of where poverty is concentrated shifted from Asia to sub-Saharan Africa in the 1980s and 1990s. The even more recent revival of growth in SSA has been the backdrop to a fall in absolute poverty in that region. It is though in China where the largest falls in poverty have occurred and where its emergence as a major exporter of manufactures has been viewed as a threat to the jobs and prosperity of the richest countries, particularly the US. Indeed, a direct link has been made between the rise of Chinese exports and the failure of wages in the US to rise for a sustained period of time. We will return to this possibility in Chapter 8.

Wages and GDP per Capita in the US for the Last 200 Years

So far in this chapter we focused on the aggregate income of an economy. Again, we stress that aggregate income should be seen as a measure of the *potential* income for those living in the country. It is, by itself, uninformative of whose incomes in an economy have been rising. In this section we are going to be looking at how the wages have changed over the last 200 years in the US and how these changes are linked to changes in the level of GDP per capita. The poor will be those on low incomes and in a society where most work for wages poverty and the wages of unskilled labour will be closely linked. Over the course of the last 200 years the US has become increasingly a society in which incomes depend on wages, so in tracing the path of the wages of the unskilled we are tracing out the possible income paths of the relatively poor. Our ability to do this is thanks to the work of economic historians who have collected comparable data on wages for both the unskilled and for production workers in the manufacturing sector, which includes both the skilled and the unskilled, over this long period. The data for unskilled labour is in the form of a cost index where a range of occupations have been used all having the feature that little or no skill is required for the job. The data for production workers is in the form of hourly wage rates which have been scaled up in the graph to annual earnings so they can be compared with GDP per capita below (the sources for the data are given in the notes to the tables).

In Figure 3.5 we present these two series where the data has been deflated by a price index based on 2011 prices so that these wages can be compared directly with GDP per capita. As we have done above, we present in the top panel the level series and in the bottom panel the data in logs, recalling that the slope of the log curve can be interpreted as a growth rate.

As can be seen from Figure 3.5 the prices for production workers and for the unskilled appear to follow each other closely. However, appearances can be deceptive. Production workers in fact do twice as well as the unskilled over the long time period shown in Figure 3.5. Production workers between 1820 and 2015 see a 40-fold increase in their wages while the unskilled slightly less than half of that at 17 times. The slopes of the lines in the bottom panel, which remember are growth rates, look similar but the trend growth rate for production workers is 1.9 per cent per annum while that for the unskilled is 1.48 per cent per annum. A difference of only 0.4 per cent but over the 195 years shown in the figure that difference matters a lot.

While in the long-term production workers have done much better than the unskilled, clearly the rise for both has been dramatic. However, that long-term perspective misses a crucial feature of the figure for both the unskilled and for production workers. Between 1920 and 1970 the rate of growth of wages for both was almost identical at 3.0 per cent per annum, after 1970 it was virtually zero for both, indeed mildly negative for the unskilled. The long-run average hides a period of very rapid real wage growth and then stagnation for more than four decades. While the calamity in terms of employment which overtook the US in the 1930s is firmly entrenched in the popular mind, that this was a period of very rapid real wage growth for those lucky enough to retain their jobs is less well known. The collapse in the growth of these wages from the 1970s onwards is also

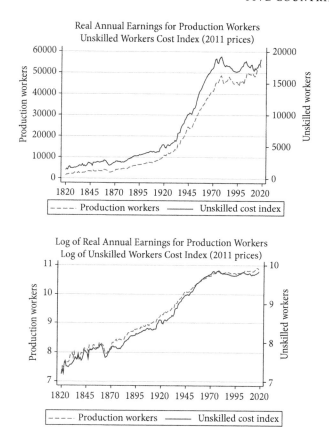

Figure 3.5. Earnings for the Relatively Unskilled in the US 1820–2018

Source: Earnings from Lawrence H. Officer and Samuel H. Williamson Annual Wages in the United States, 1774–Present, URL: http://www.measuringworth.com.

well known and its causes and consequences are central to any investigation of the sources of inequality and discontent in the US. In Figures 3.6 and 3.7 we link these wages to GDP per capita.

The levels data is in the top panel and the log data in the bottom one. In both we see the dramatic difference between the period from 1920 to 1980 and the period after 1980. In the earlier period wages rose faster than GDP per capita—you can see this from the log curves which are steeper for wages (either production wages or the wages of the unskilled) than for GDP per capita. While the period after 1980 sees a lower rate of growth of GDP per capita (the trend growth rate from 1920 to 1980 is 2.2 per cent per annum

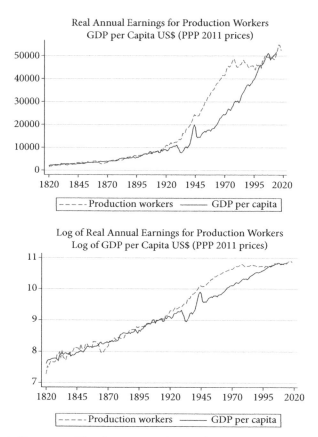

Figure 3.6. Earnings of Production Workers and GDP per Capita in the US 1820–2018

Source: Earnings from Lawrence H. Officer and Samuel H. Williamson Annual Wages in the United States, 1774–Present, URL: http://www.measuringworth.com. See US Wages and US GDP files. GDP from Louis Johnston and Samuel H. Williamson, 'What Was the U.S. GDP Then?' MeasuringWorth, 2020.

while after 1980 it is 1.7 per cent per annum) real wage growth ceases. Indeed, for the unskilled shown in Figure 3.7 there is a sustained fall in real wages from 1980 onwards an event as the figure shows without historical precedence.

Much public discussion of the problems in the US labour market sees the financial crisis of 2008–09 as central. To see how important was this

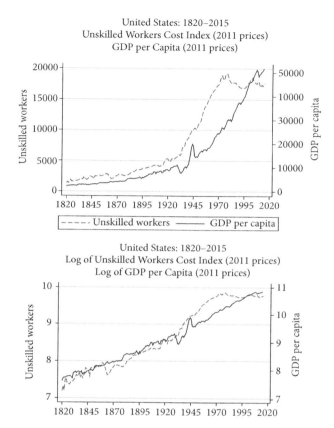

Figure 3.7. Unskilled Labour Costs and GDP per Capita in the US 1820–2015
Source: As for Figure 3.6.

recession we show in Figure 3.8 the data for production workers since 1980 which allows the contrast to the growth of GDP per capita and the lack of growth in production wages to be seen even more clearly.

While the financial crisis was clearly a major downward shock to the economy, it was, equally clearly, not the cause of the problems for the growth on wages for production workers shown in the figure; their growth stopped in 1980. A point to which we will return to below is that while there is no growth in these wages, they are both by historical standards within the US, and even more so by standards across the world, very high wages. It is

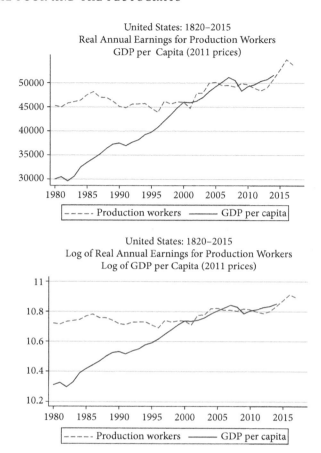

Figure 3.8. Earnings of Production Workers and GDP per Capita in the US 1980–2015

Source: As for Figure 3.6.

the size of this collapse in the labour market for the less skilled workers in the US that has sent shock waves through that country and now, with the political dissent it has generated, shock waves throughout the world. The collapse is well known and its possible causes the subject of much debate. We now ask how similar has been the experience for the UK.

Wages and GDP per Capita in the UK for the Last 200, and Last 20, Years

We have already presented the data for wages in for the UK in Chapter 2 so here we carry out a similar exercise as we have just done for the US and compare these wages with GDP per Capita. The pattern is quite different to that which we observed for the US in two respects. The first is that there is no evidence for the UK of more rapid rises in the price of labour than in GDP per capita before the 1980s. The second contrast to the US is that the two series remain closely linked until the financial crisis of 2007/08. Figure 3.9 shows the long run of data from 1820 to 2015. While the data series is not quite comparable with that for the US, which is confined to production workers in manufacturing, there is no sign of a break in 1980. In Figure 3.10 we show the data from 1997 which shows clearly that there has been a break at the time of the financial crisis.

After 2007–08 we see a sharp decline in both average and median wages. In particular we see that after the financial crisis the GDP per capita and wages series become delinked, in a similar manner to what happened in the US after 1980. After a relatively short contraction growth in GDP per capita continues while real wages fall for a much longer period than any experienced since the Second World War.

Delinking GDP per Capita and Wages

We have seen periods when GDP per capita and wages get delinked for both the US and the UK. Such delinking has profound implications for an economy. Implications which clearly underlie the rise of populist political movements in both countries. So the question the data for the US and the UK pose is: when is real wage growth linked to GDP growth? Until the 1970s few would have thought that an interesting question—the two were obviously linked, just look at Figures 3.6–3.10. However, it was exactly this question— as to how GDP and wages are linked—that was the subject of fierce political debate in the UK in the Victorian period, with Marx seeing the immiseration of the masses as the inevitable outcome of a capitalist system that concentrated more and more power into the capitalist class. It is the rise in wages for the relatively unskilled from the mid nineteenth century that proved Marx wrong. It is probably no accident that the socialist rhetoric of that period has emerged anew in the twenty-first century when that rise has ceased.

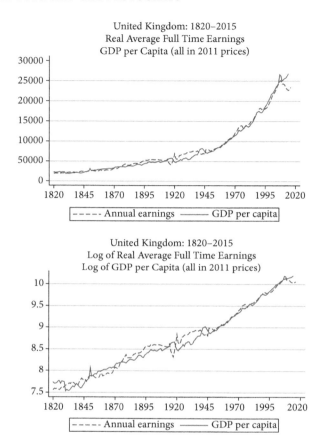

Figure 3.9. Real Average Full-Time Earnings and GDP per Capita in the UK 1820–2015

Sources: GDP data from Samuel H. Williamson, What Was the UK GDP Then? MeasuringWorth, 2016 Earnings data from Gregory Clark, What Were the British Earnings and Prices Then? (New Series) MeasuringWorth, 2016, URL: http://www.measuringworth.com.), Updated from ONS data.

Such delinking has been much longer term in the US, at least so far, than what has occurred in the UK. Further, in the case of the UK after the financial crisis the problem is not simply that unskilled wages fall but that all wages have fallen, suggesting that the share of labour in GDP is falling. This too has a distictly Marxian ring to it. If technological change is driving up labour productivity and driving down the demand for labour then does the immiseration of the masses become a real prospect?

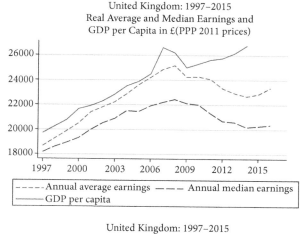

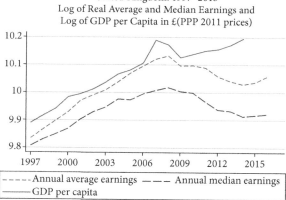

Figure 3.10. Real Average and Median Earnings and GDP per Capita in the UK 1997–2015

Sources: As for Figure 3.9.

Manufacturing Wages in the Rest of the World

Now of course the 'masses' in rich countries are very different from the 'masses' that were part of socialist rhetoric of the nineteenth and early twentieth centuries. They are, by the standards of those times, very well off indeed. The countries with labour with low prices are now where the contemporary 'masses' are located. Just how low those prices are can be seen

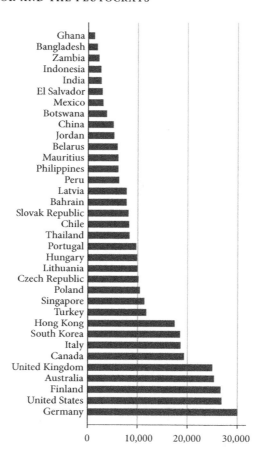

Figure 3.11. Average Annual Manufacturing Wages for Labourers in (2011 PPP) US$: 2005–2008

Source: Occupational Wages around the World (OWW) Database: http://www.nber.org/oww/' created by Freeman and Oostendorp (2013).

in Figure 3.11 where we show comparative data for manufacturing wages in occupations which can be classed as unskilled. The data is in terms of PPP exchange rates so allows for the differences in prices across these countries. Among the countries for which comparisons are made in the figure Ghana has the lowest annual wages at US$ (PPP) 1,279. Even China, whose success in raising per capita GDP we have documented, has wages of only US$5,125, some one-sixth of the level of the US and Germany. We have already noted that the rise of China as a manufacturing exporter has been seen as a threat to the wages of the relatively unskilled in the rich countries, particularly the US. What Figure 3.11 alerts us to is the problem from the perspective of the absolutely poor. Yes China has grown very rapidly but its wages, even by the first decade of the twenty-first century, remained far below those of rich countries. Further, China's wages were by then by no means the lowest.

While for the US the decoupling of wages from GDP per capita growth dating back many decades provides the economic basis for the rise of populist discontent, the failure in many poor countries for their GDP growth, which we are going to document more fully in the next chapter, to match into the wages of the unskilled, and thus the poor, is the basis there for populist discontent. We appear to be observing a world where GDP growth and wages have got more broadly disconnected.

However, wages are clearly only one element in the determination of incomes so in the chapters that follow we will investigate how incomes have changed and then return to how those changes link to wages and the incomes of both the relatively and the absolutely poor.

Appendix: Notes on the Country GDP Data

This chapter draws on a range of data that is going to be used throughout the book. The data describing the size of the world economy and the incomes of different countries and regions is based on two data sources. The definition of country is their current geographical area. The first is the work of Angus Maddison who set out to measure incomes of the world going back to the beginning of the Millennium. This work is reported on in:

The World Economy
Volume 1: A Millennial Perspective
Volume 2: Historical Statistics
OECD Development Centre Studies, OECD 2006.
Angus Maddison
http://www.ggdc.net/maddison/oriindex.htm (accessed 7 August 2020).

This work, which covers the period until 2001, has been updated by a group of researchers at the University of Groningen—the Groningen Growth and Development Centre—and can be found on the web under the title 'The Maddison Project'.

The Maddison Project launched an updated version of the original Maddison dataset in January 2013. The update incorporates much of the latest research in the field, and presents new estimates of economic growth in the world economic between AD 1 and 2010. The new estimates are presented and discussed in:

Jutta Bolt and Jan Luiten Van Zanden (2014) 'The Maddison Project: collaborative research on historical national accounts', *Economic History Review*, 67(3): 627–51.

https://www.rug.nl/ggdc/historicaldevelopment/maddison/releases/maddison-project-database-2013 (accessed 7 August 2020).

This data is being regularly updated and the version used in this book is the 2013 update which takes the data to 2010. In both the update and the original Maddison data incomes are measured in US$1,990 purchasing power parity. This has been converted to 2011 purchasing power parity prices.

As well as these sources the data used in this book has also incorporated revisions to historical national accounts which, for the UK, can be found in:

Stephen Broadberry, Bruce Campbell, Alexander Klein, Mark Overton, and Bas van Leeuwen (2014). *British Economic Growth, 1270–1870*. Cambridge: Cambridge University Press.

The data used here also incorporates revisions to the GDP numbers for Italy, the Netherlands, and Spain from

Stephen Broadberry, Hanhui Guan, and David Daokui Li (2017). 'China, Europe and the Great Divergence: A Study in Historical National Accounting, 980–1850', Discussion Papers in Economic and Social History Number 155, April 2017, University of Oxford.

Again, work on historical national accounts has been contentious. The most recent work by economic historians, seeking to compare different countries in the past, has concluded that Northern Europe was very significantly richer than the rest of the world by 1700. In other words, what has been termed the great divergence between 'West' and 'East' pre-dated the conventional timing of the industrial revolution as beginning in the late eighteenth century.

The second source of aggregate macro data is the PENN World Tables 9.0 which is also currently hosted at the University of Groningen:

https://www.rug.nl/ggdc/productivity/pwt/ (accessed 7 August 2020).

The PENN World Tables have become the standard source for work on global aggregate measures of national income. They have not been uncontroversial and the most recent version, which is 9.0 at the time of writing, has taken significant steps to address earlier concerns. One of the most basic problems such data face is that the prices needed to compare real income growth over time within a country may differ from the prices needed to compare across countries. When we are interested in changes over time, we have used the PENN data based on national accounts. When the interest is in comparisons across countries, we have used their data intended for that purpose.

4

The Rise (and Rise) of the World Economy

The Relentless Rise of the World Economy

In the last chapter we showed the long-run economic history of five countries—the US, the UK, China, India, and Brazil—and, for the US and the UK, linked the data for aggregate incomes to the earnings of relatively unskilled workers. That link we are going to argue is crucial for understanding when growth in aggregate income for a country leads to a decline in relative poverty within that country. In the US that link has been broken since the 1980s, in the UK it appears to have broken since the financial crisis of 2007–08. To understand the sources of political discontent in these two countries requires understanding the reasons behind that broken link.

A well-publicized claim of the World Bank is that for the first time in history the numbers of the absolutely poor in the world has been falling. A claim which, not surprisingly, has been challenged and, indeed, conflicts with the widespread view that world inequality is rising with the numbers of poor increasing. There are two major reasons for disagreements on the World Bank claim. First, that it rests on a particularly low level for defining the poor and, second, that much of the data is open to dispute. This issue needs to be seen in context. As we will show, most of the world, for most of human history, has been very poor. If population in poor countries is growing but their incomes are not poverty will be rising. So, to reduce the numbers in poverty requires that poor countries grow and that the income of the poor within those countries grows faster than their number. That is a tall order which most countries in the past have failed.

We will show in Chapter 6 that it is correct that whether or not the absolute number in poverty has been falling does depend on the poverty line chosen. The World Bank poverty line is US$ (PPP) 1.9 per day which is indeed dire poverty. However, even if we take a poverty line more than three times higher at US$(PPP) 7 per day, poverty in absolute terms since 2003 has been falling. The scale of this achievement is considerable. It is not that the growth of world population ceased, indeed there has been only a modest decline in the growth rate, it is that income growth in the poorest countries has been rapid enough to enable more people to climb out of poverty than ever before. In particular, and contrary to what is widely believed, the growth in incomes of the poorest within poor countries has been, by historical standards, remarkably high. That, of course, does not mean that there are not a lot of very poor people, there are. How to get those numbers down more quickly is one of the key questions we seek to answer.

This success in alleviating poverty has been combined with a revolution in health documented by Angus Deaton in his book *The Great Escape: Health, Wealth and the Origins of Inequality* showing that longer, healthier lives, with higher incomes, are available to an increasing proportion of the world's population. Indeed, in many rich countries the problem of ill health caused by poverty has been replaced by the problem of being rich and poor choices of diet and lifestyle. Deaton also notes the qualifications that are required regarding the data to be used.

While Deaton celebrates this success, noting that progress has been far from uniform and that there have been setbacks such as the AIDS epidemic, his perspective is one from that of the poor. From the perspective of the now-rich countries the picture looks very different. Rather than these sources of success being seen as causes for celebration there is across many, if not most, rich countries deep disquiet at the perceived failure of rich country governments to address the problem of stagnating wages, high levels of inequality and the fact that, in some, the young face lower prospects of lifetime income increases than their parents. This disquiet at inequality within countries runs in parallel with the implications for migration of inequality across countries, with widening gaps between rich and poor, such that the incentives for the poorest to migrate, whatever the risks, appear to grow by the year. Threatened by stagnating wages and high levels of migration the political atmosphere is breeding a nationalism last seen in the 1930s.

How to explain the co-existence of such success with such unrest? In this chapter, and the next two, we tackle that question. In the following sections we describe the growth of the world economy and how that growth has varied over time and across regions of the world. It will be shown that the differing patterns of regional growth explain the evolving pattern of the geographical location of the poorest of the poor. In other words, we seek to justify the assertion in Chapter 1 that to understand who is poor we need to understand why some countries are so poor. The second element to justify that assertion depends on inequality in poor countries being greater than in rich ones. That we will consider in the next chapter. The result for how inequality and poverty have evolved will be set out in Chapter 6. We will still not have got to the plutocrats, who it might well be argued are a key part of the unrest, but they will appear in Chapters 7 and 8 when we examine the incomes of the top 1 per cent and those even higher up the scale, reaching eventually to those rich enough to qualify as plutocrats.

The Size of the World Economy and the Sources of Absolute Poverty

Only sufficiently rich countries will be big enough economically to house plutocrats, while countries which are poor will house most of the absolutely poor people in the world. That is the central argument of this book which this chapter, and the ones that follow, will seek to justify. The implication is stark. Contemporary absolute poverty is a choice of governments.

We are going to begin, not with any particular country, but with the whole world and then ask which countries have been rich enough to produce the very rich and when they achieved a sufficiently high level of income to do so. The size of the world economy depends on only two factors—the size of its population and the average income of those people. In this section we show both factors and how they have changed from 1700 to 2014. Figure 4.1 shows in both a level and a log scale these two ingredients for understanding the size of the world economy.

In order to understand changes in the patterns of growth of world GDP we have divided the period from 1700 to 2014 into a number of epochs capturing different time periods of the growth of the world. These epochs are used in Figure 4.2 to report the differences over these two centuries in the patterns of per capita and total GDP growth. As the slope of the curve in the log graph is the growth rate the data in Figure 4.2 is reporting on how those slopes translate into annual growth rates.

For most of the last two millennia there has been very little sustained growth in per capita incomes. By 1700 the average GDP per capita in the world was some US$ (PPP 2011) 970 which, while higher than the average at the start of the millennium when it was some US$ (PPP 2011) 734, was clearly not much higher. While historians would no doubt be (justifiably) horrified by being told that nothing of much interest happened before 1700, in terms of our search for the co-existence of plutocrats and the poor we need to start our search after 1700. Incomes before then were simply too low to support the lifestyle required by those of middling incomes, never mind the contemporary super-rich.

From US$970 in 1700 the average global income is now close to US $15,000 as can be seen in the middle panel of Figure 4.1. This rise in average incomes has occurred as the world population has also exploded, rising from less than half a billion in 1700 to over 6 billion by 2014. The result—shown in Figure 4.1—is an increase in the size of global income from US$0.43 trillion (a trillion recall is a million million) to US$109 trillion in 2014—a rise of 235 times, demonstrating the truly staggering rise in the size of the

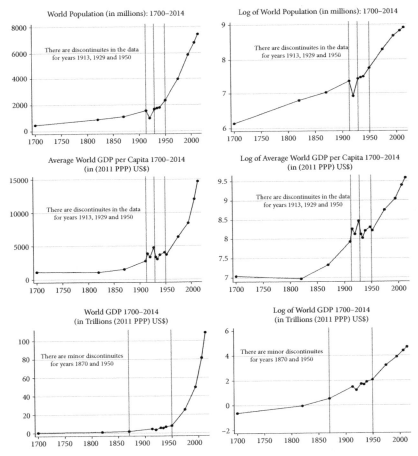

Figure 4.1. The Size of the World Economy

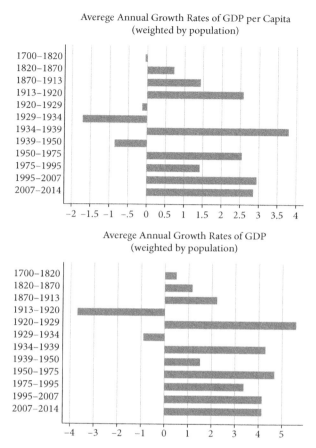

Figure 4.2. The Growth Rate of the World Economy 1700–2014

Source for Figures 4.1 and 4.2: The Maddison-Project, http://www.ggdc.net/maddison/maddison-project/home.htm, 2013 (accessed 7 August 2020) and PENN World Tables 9.0.'Updated from Angus Maddison, Historical Statistics of the World Economy, 1–2001 AD.

world economy. There is no indication of any slowing in this growth. The size of the world economy doubled between 1975 and 1995 and doubled again by 2014.

However, we want to know how smooth this growth was and, even more important, which countries participated in this growth and when they participated. We already know that this growth was far from uniform across the countries of the world, it was also far from uniform over the centuries.

That is what is shown in Figure 4.2. The story told by that figure is really rather dramatic. Growth rates rise from low levels and start to accelerate from 1700 to 1913. The word accelerate in that last sentence is important; it is not simply that levels of income start to rise, it is that the rate at which they are rising increases. The first setback to this pattern of rising growth rates was the First World War when over the period 1913 to 1920 growth was negative across the world for the first time since the beginning of the growth path we have been tracing since 1700. The second major setback to world growth was the catastrophe that was to overwhelm the world in the Great Depression. For the five-year period from 1929 to 1934 the average rate of fall of per capita GDP was just over 1.5 per cent per annum—the largest fall in the epochs we have identified in the data.

While the drama of the Great Depression is well embedded in the historical mind, the speed of the recovery from 1934 to 1939 is less so. Average growth rates were only marginally below the average for the period from 1920 to 1929. While the Second World War was much less of a setback for growth than the first, it nevertheless brought the rapid recovery apparent over the period 1934 to 1939 to a halt. The period since 1950 has seen a pattern of long periods of sustained growth. While there is no evidence of a pattern of accelerations as was seen over the period from 1700 leading up to the First World War, and some evidence that more rapid periods are followed by slower ones, the overall outcome from the mid-1930s onwards is of rapid and sustained global growth. Moreover, the period since 1950 has seen faster growth of world GDP than for any of the periods before 1913. In Figure 4.2 we showed that growth had varied dramatically, on average, over our epochs. In Figure 4.3 we show how it has varied over the countries for particular epochs since 1950.

Before 1950 the average rate of growth for countries for which we have data was only 0.6 per cent per annum and this is an over-estimate of average growth rates as many countries are missing from the data and will have had no, or negative, growth. So, we focus on the period since 1950 when the data becomes reasonably comprehensive. What is shown in Figure 4.3 is the key to understanding the increasing dispersion in incomes across the world. The figure shows how country-level growth rates have varied over the epochs we have identified since 1950. This range of growth rates was much greater after 1950–70 than it was during the 1950–75 period. In particular in the period 1975–95 far more countries had negative growth rates than had been the case in 1950–75, while after 1995 far more countries had higher growth rates than ever before. In summary both average growth rates were rising and the

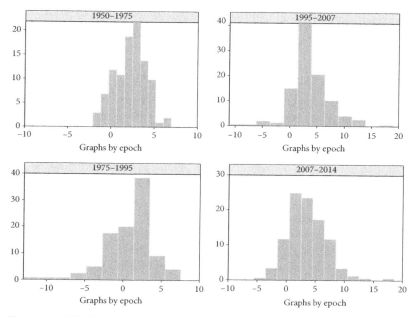

Figure 4.3. The Distribution (in percentages) of Growth over Epochs since 1950
Source: As for Figures 4.1 and 4.2.

range—the difference between high and low performers—was increasing. The world was getting richer faster but at such different rates that what we are observing is an explosion of inequality at the country level—driven essentially by the differences in the success of governments in generating growth.

The Rise of the 'West'

So far, we have focused on global averages of growth over time and noted that growth rates have varied a lot across countries. But which parts of the world saw growth in their incomes and when? In this section we consider the consequences of the first wave of globalization which began in the early nineteenth century, peaked in 1913, and by 1950 had emerged from two major wars. The world of 1950 was unimaginably different from the world of 1700. This period saw the rise of the 'West' to dominate the world economy for which Ian Morris (2011) in his book *Why the West Rules for Now* seeks an explanation, which we will consider below. As we will see both when the 'West' overtook the 'East' is contentious as is how the evolution of patterns of relative wealth and relative poverty are linked. We begin by documenting the extent of the change which is shown in Figure 4.4 for seven countries or regions for which we have data for both 1700 and 1950. Sub-Saharan Africa is the big missing region as there is only data for South Africa for 1700. We will come to sub-Saharan Africa below as it is a key part of the changing location of poverty across the world after 1950.

If we want to locate the poor, we need to find which regions were poor and then look within the region to find which countries were poor. So, we begin in the top panel of Figure 4.4, by looking at per capita incomes across the regions and countries we have identified. Already by 1700 there was a gap between the richer regions—Europe and north America and China and India in particular—with per capita income differences of just under 2:1. By 1950 (shown in the right-hand panel) these differences had risen enormously. Note that the scale in the left- and right-hand parts of Figure 4.4 are not the same. It is not that India's income per capita fell, it is that it failed to rise so that the gap between Europe and North America and the rest of the world raced ahead, with the exception of Australasia where, as the second row of Figure 4.4 shows, very few people lived, so its importance in the world economy was very small.

In fact, the second row of Figure 4.4 shows that in 1700 the large populations in the world were concentrated in areas of relatively low incomes. The result, shown in the bottom row of Figure 4.4, is that in 1700 Europe and North America, China, and India are roughly equally important in terms of their size in the world economy. Low per capita incomes matched with high population. By 1950 this level pegging in terms of economic size between the 'West' and the 'East' had been transformed. This had come about through four key aspects of growth over this period. Growth in Europe and North America had accelerated from its pre-1700 level, China's per capita income had halved, India's had stagnated and, a fact less widely appreciated, population growth in Europe and North America had outpaced that in China and India. By 1950 the 'West' did appear a colossus.

Those key facts describe what happened, they do not explain why and that why question is at the centre of both historical debates as to the causes of the 'rise of the West' and what policy options currently poor countries need to pursue. However, before we can turn to those issues we need to extend our data to the period beyond 1950, when the scale of the expansion of the world

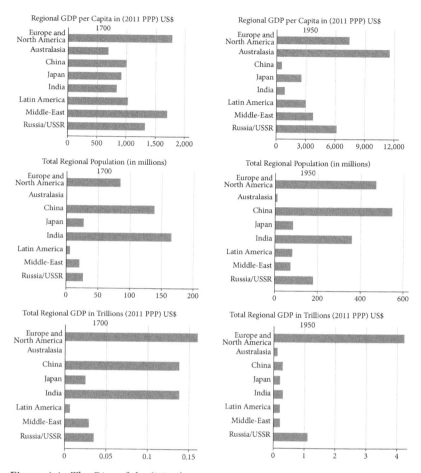

Figure 4.4. The Rise of the 'West'
Source: As for Figures 4.1 and 4.2.

economy would dwarf what has occurred up to that point, and introduce sub-Saharan Africa into our data.

The Changing Geography of Poverty in the Second Wave of Globalization

Figure 4.4 has two important omissions. The first is that SSA is not shown at all as we only have data before 1950 for any except a handful of SSA countries. The second is that other countries in Asia besides China and India, are not included. In Figure 4.5 we remedy these omissions and provide a map of income changes from 1950 to 2014. As we want to find out where the poor are located, we separate the rich regions of Europe and North America and Australasia and the poorer parts of the world, so we can see more clearly the progress made since 1950 in both regions. The figure shows two sub-periods, the first from 1950 to 1975 and the second from 1975 to 2014, the most recent year for which we have data.

The first and possibly most striking aspect of Figure 4.5 is that, if we consider the poorer parts of the world in 1950, SSA is not the poorest. Indeed, its GDP per capita is about twice that of China and India (we exclude South Africa which is shown separately in the figure). Growth over this period from 1950 to 1975, which we showed above was a period of rapid growth for the world economy as a whole, saw negligible progress for any of the poorest parts of the world. The period from 1975 to 2014 saw a remarkable transformation with all the poorer regions of the world seeing a rise in their average incomes with the conspicuous exception of SSA.

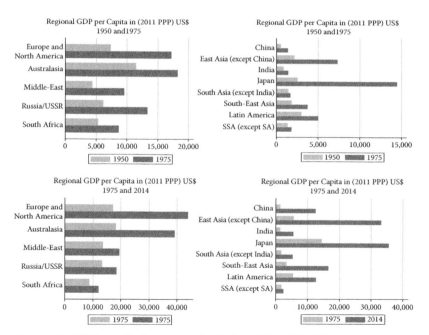

Figure 4.5. GDP per Capita Across the Rich and Poor World 1950–2014
Source: As for Figures 4.1 and 4.2.

What has been happening since 1975 is that the two most populous countries in the world, China and India, have started to grow and grow rapidly for the first time in their history. We knew this from Chapter 3 but Figure 4.5 confirms that these countries have changed the pattern of world growth. Indeed, their growth rates have exceeded 8 per cent per annum and with 8 per cent growth your income can rise from US$600 to US$30,000 in fifty years, one sixth of the time it took the US to reach its current income from its base at US$600. Countries can go from very poor to very rich within the space of one lifetime. The trick is to know how. This change, the effect of which across the whole world we show in Figure 4.6, is associated with a

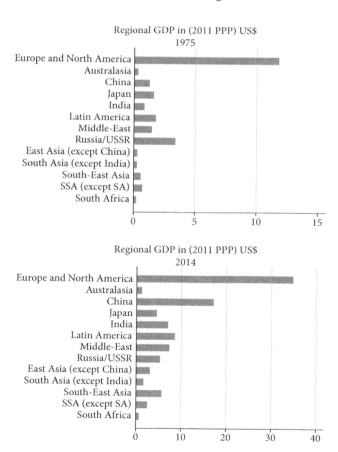

Figure 4.6. The Rise of China
Source: As for Figures 4.1 and 4.2.

reshaping of the contours of the world economy as radical as that which occurred in the early stages of the industrial revolution in the late eighteenth and early nineteenth century.

If we compare the world economy in 2014 (the bottom panel of Figure 4.6) with the world of 1950 (shown in the bottom right of Figure 4.4) we see that the 'West', while still the biggest part of the world economy, is very much less dominant than before. China alone now is half the size of the Europe and North America region. Further, Figure 4.6 alerts us to the fact as to how recent is this transformation. In 1975 there had been little change from 1950 in the dominance of the 'West'. We need to try and understand what generated this transformation but we have in large part ended our search for the absolutely poor—they are in countries which have failed to grow.

The Pattern of Global Growth Rates from 1700 to 2014

So, we now need to investigate the patterns of global growth rates that the countries of the world have achieved since 1700. The first, and most obvious, question we can ask is whether being rich helps. It might seem obvious it does and indeed one of the first economists to write about development, Gunnar Myrdal, saw a cumulative process by which markets left to themselves would ensure a steadily widening gap between rich and poor countries. He argued for the need to replace a 'soft state', which was largely powerless in enforcing its wishes, with a 'strong' one able to do so.[1] The laissez-faire approach was argued to have led to decades, indeed centuries, of economic stagnation in India. China was different; there a combination of internal conflict, and outside interventions, combined to produce its catastrophe. However, surely the opposite view is equally plausible. If your country is very poor, and poor because it is a low productivity economy, then the possibility of emulating the more productive techniques of the now-rich should make it possible to grow much more quickly and catch up with the now-rich.

---

[1] The problem posed for development by a 'soft state' was a prominent theme of his major work *An Asian Drama: An Enquiry into the Poverty of Nations* (1968). Two of its major themes—the need to consider institutions in understanding development and the inadequacies of laissez-faire economics, now summarized as neo-liberalism— have a strong resonance in current development discussions.

So, which is it? We start by bringing together all the different growth rates across the epoch we have identified in Figure 4.2 and pool them in Figure 4.7. We use unweighted data as it is growth at the level of the individual country that matters for the dispersion of growth rates across countries. We have already shown that once weighted by population aggregate growth is very different as after 1970 more populous countries started to grow more rapidly.

Figure 4.7 shows that growth is remarkably close to a normal curve that is the bell-shaped curve also shown in Figure 2.6. This suggests a possible answer to the puzzle of the diversity we observe. The normal bell shape curve arises because the factors that impact on the variable of interest are numerous and independent of each other.

Now what would make growth rates follow approximately a normal distribution? If growth is unrelated to the level of income that means that it is equally likely that a poor country grows faster or slower than a rich one, then for rather similar reasons to our height example, growth will follow a normal distribution. That suggests that looking for 'a' cause of growth may be a mistake. There is not 'a' cause but numerous factors which arise, if not by chance, then at least in an unpredictable way, and which may vary a lot over time and across countries. We now want to consider if that inference is supported by the data for how the level of income is related to the growth rate. It might seem we could do this with a simple chart showing how the

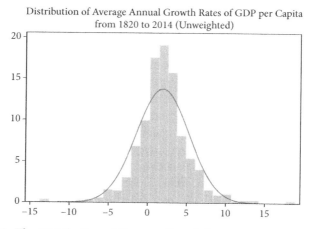

Distribution of Average Annual Growth Rates of GDP per Capita from 1820 to 2014 (Unweighted)

Figure 4.7. The Distribution of Country Growth Rates 1820–2014
Source: As for Figures 4.1 and 4.2.

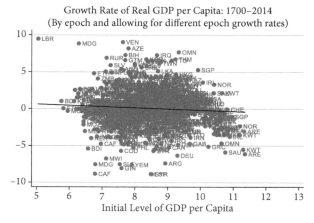

Figure 4.8. Growth Rates and Initial Income Levels 1700–2014
Source: As for Figures 4.1 and 4.2.

growth rate compares for countries at different levels of income, which we do in Figure 4.8. There are two important reasons why it's not as easy as doing that. The first is a measurement problem, the second is a problem of interpretation.

Let us consider the measurement problem first. The level of income is mechanically linked to its growth rate. In fact, if we measure growth rates in logs, as we have done, then our chart of growth rates against levels would be a plot of the change in the log of income on one axis and its initial level on the other axis. Now we have stressed that all incomes, particularly incomes at the level of the whole economy, will be measured with error. So, if we erroneously think the level of income is higher than it actually is we will mechanically show a slower growth rate. In other words, if our variables are measured with error we will mechanically set up a negative relationship between the level of initial income and the growth rate which will lead us to conclude, erroneously, that richer countries grow slower.

The second problem arises from interpreting what we see in the chart. Let us abstract from measurement issues and graph the growth rate (remember that is the change in logs of income) on one axis and its initial level, again in logs, on the other axis and we find that there is a negative relationship between the variables. Are we home, have we shown that richer countries grow more slowly? Well in one sense yes. It appears there is a negative relationship between the growth rate and its initial level. But think about what happens over time. As its incomes grows its growth rate will decrease. At some point it will stop growing and it will reach its final level of income. Now what determines the growth rate once it's there? We don't know that from the relationship between the change in income and its level. What we know is that countries with different initial levels of income approach this final resting place at different rates. It may well be the case that this final resting place is not the same across countries. It may also be the case that the growth rate at his final resting place may be very different across countries.

That final sentence of the last paragraph may sound puzzling. We are looking for determinants of the growth rate and we are talking about a final resting place when growth has stopped. That sounds contradictory but it is not once we realize that growth can be seen as having two elements. One is when economies are shocked by some event and then get back—at different speeds—to where they were before and how, in the long run, their level of income changes.

Let us look at how growth is related to income but we will allow for the possibility of measurement error setting up a mechanical link between the initial level of income and the change by comparing that chart with one where we use the average of incomes at the beginning and end of the period. Figure 4.9 below shows both charts.

We see that once we allow for measurement error it appears that the growth rate of incomes is unrelated to the level. In other words, the growth

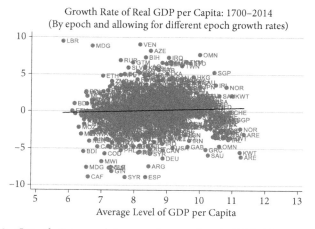

Figure 4.9. Growth Rates and Average Income Levels 1700–2014
Source: As for Figures 4.1 and 4.2.

rate of income we should see would be equally likely to be high or low whatever the level of income. Let us see why random growth in the sense we have just defined the term may give rise to the patterns we are seeing in the data. First if the change in income is not related to its initial period then what happens to growth depends on what shocks GDP in the current period. This might be a collapse of the stock market, the sub-prime crisis in the US or anything else that comes out of the blue. But note what happens now. If growth does not depend on the level of income there will be no tendency to get back to where it was, it could go anywhere depending too on the shocks that occur next period. We will see just the kind of pattern we have seen in our charts.

Indeed, we can go further. If the factors that shock the economy are many and independent of each other, then the growth rates will have a normal distribution, rather similar to the pattern of growth rates we saw above. Growth will indeed be very hard to predict but this, far from showing how useless economics is, shows us the process by which growth occurs. It is one independent of the level of income.

The Fall of the 'West'

We have presented evidence showing several striking facts about patterns of growth across the world since 1700. The first is that they have varied enormously and follow close to a normal distribution, the second that they seem independent of the level of income and, third, that since the 1980s poorer countries have grown at what are, by historical standards, unprecedented rates. This last fact has led to speculation as to the potential decline of the 'West' mirroring its rise which we documented above.

Underlying all these facts is a question we have not answered, namely what does drive the long-run rate of growth of the economy? The evidence very clearly seems to support the view of those who think that poor countries can, if they adopt relevant policies, 'catch up' with now-rich countries. It is rare for a rich country to sustain rates of growth of more than 2–3 per cent per annum for any sustained period of time. For those who are rich this may be about the rate at which technological change allows economies to grow. Those far poorer than the rich can grow much faster by adopting the technology and knowledge that are currently used by the rich. If that process continues for much longer there will indeed be a 'fall' of the West but this will be driven by the same factors as its rise, namely the decisions different countries take as to whether they wish to grow.

So Why Do Economies Grow?

That question is the one posed by Morris (2011). His answer as to what explains long-run differences in outcomes across the world is in terms of different rates of social development. Rather than that being a vague term covering lots of possible elements of success, Morris measures and identifies three components of social development. The first of these is energy capture; the second urbanization, which is used as a proxy for organizational capacity; and third is the capacity to make war. The last is critical as conflict between countries or regions is the norm of human history. Without the ability to withstand outsiders and impose your own wishes any form of development is impossible. Morris argues that these three elements capture the key to the very long-run development of different regions summarized in his book as the 'East' and the 'West'. The period Morris covers is from 14,000 BC to the year 2000, a time span that dwarfs that presented above.

Morris is concerned to understand both how, and when, the 'West' overtook the 'East'. In the first millennium from 300 to 1100 AD his measure of social development for the 'West' falls decisively below that of the 'East' (his figure 7.1). From then until 1700 CE the 'West' catches up (his figure 9.1). By 1700 they are level pegging, after that the 'West' not only pulls ahead but its rate of social development explodes (his figure 10.2).

While historians are agreed that there was this 'Great Divergence', they are not agreed on when it occurred or why. Morris's measure of social development implies it began about 1500. At that date the 'East' was ahead but, from that date, growth was much higher in the 'West'. This dating is controversial as earlier historians dated the divide to the English industrial revolution, seeing that as the start of what Kuznets (1966) termed 'Modern Economic Growth'. The causes are even more controversial than the timing as with the 1500 date coinciding with the opening of the Americas and the beginning of European colonial expansion Marxist historians have seen the success of the 'West' as being due to the impoverishment of the 'East'. Poverty, in other words, was created in the 'East' and underlies the success of the 'West'.

The data presented in Figure 4.1 imply that if our question is 'When did the world economy start to grow much more rapidly?', then Kuznet's dating is much more accurate than a dating back to 1700. It is after 1800 that we see a marked kink in the log graph of world per capita GDP. It is that kink which shows an acceleration in growth rates. If we go back to Figure 3.1 which looks at the UK, the US, Brazil, China, and India, we see similar kinks, albeit at very different times. Indeed, this kink was, in what is now a very dated approach to discussing the causes of growth, termed a 'take-off' (clearly a much more engaging term than kink) used in W.W. Rostow's (1969) *The Stages of Economic Growth: A Non-Communist Manifesto*. Whatever it is called, it is clearly an important event in the economic history of any country. It is indeed the dividing line between poverty being the inevitable lot of almost all to the possibility that poverty, in an absolute sense, can be eliminated.

So, in addressing the question as to why economies grow, the answer must differ before and after 1800. Before 1800 the knowledge and technology did not exist, or insofar as it did was not used, to enable the productivity of an economy to grow. After 1800 it did and its successful use was confined to a relatively small number of countries. As we can see from Figure 4.2, the growth rate of the world economy, in the second great wave of globalization after 1950, was more than twice that during the first from 1700 to 1913. Indeed, it is the very scale of that success that threatens its sustainability due to its effect on the climate. The question our data throws up is to explain the extraordinary diversity across countries in their ability to take advantage of the tools made available for their increased incomes.

Economists have provided good evidence for what might be termed the proxy sources of growth, in terms of increases in the capital stock of the country, both in terms of capital, technology and skill. However, as we reported in Chapter 1, all the work linking such inputs to outputs has revealed a puzzle, namely that in some countries the same measured inputs produce much more output than in other countries—which we named as Total Factor Productivity (TFP). That is a level effect. Further, when measuring growth rates it has turned out that it is the growth of TFP which is the most important source of growth. Now, of course, it is not being suggested that TFP growth can proceed without the knowledge and technology which gets embodied in the capital stock of a country—they are inextricably linked. It is simply that it matters of lot when, and where, that investment occurs and the factors that enable that investment to increase output by such differing amounts across countries are not well understood.

Suggestions include what economists term the externalities due to human capital; in other words having a more skilled population benefits everyone in that society, not simply those who have the skills (Lucas, 2002); a second is that TFP depends on the social capital of an economy (Hall and Jones, 1999); a third that it is the existence, or creation, of inclusive institutions (Acemoglu and Robinson, 2012). With the possible exception of the first of these suggestions, what they all have in common is that they are not easy to replicate. Our normal curve of growth rates suggests that luck, or chance, plays a big role. A view that economists do not have much idea as to what generates successful growth can be found in Easterly (2002). As we will report in Chapter 6 (Figure 6.8), the fastest-growing economies during the first wave of globalization, from 1700 to 1913, were, in order, Australia, New Zealand, Canada, and the United States. And, before you think it has something to do with being White, Anglo-Saxon or Protestant, the fastest-growing economies over the second period of globalization, 1950 to 2014, were, in order, South Korea, China, Hong Kong, and Singapore. These economies grew at over 4 per cent per annum on average, nearly four times faster than the fastest-growing ones in the earlier period of globalization.

Three of these economies—South Korea, Hong Kong, and Singapore—were part of the 'gang of four' Asian economies, termed 'the Asian tigers' at the time. The fourth, Taiwan, also grew equally rapidly but our data for it does not go back to 1950. Their success set off a major policy and academic debate as to the causes of their growth. Those on the left pointed to the role of industrial policy in South Korea, those on the right the success of free market capitalism in Hong Kong. Possibly what is most striking about their growth experiences is the diversity of the institutions and policies which proved successful. Stepping back from the economic perspective on the question, Fukuyama (2014) argues that what they all did have in common was a strong state. He does not argue that that is all that is required, but he does think it is an essential element.

Our objective in this book is not to say what will promote growth for a particular country; even if we could it would take us too far from our central theme. However, without growth in poor countries poverty is inevitable and those countries who have managed, by whatever means and policies, to grow have created a path, indeed the only path, out of poverty. Those who wish to argue that poverty was 'created' in the 'East' and this underlay the success of the 'West' need to show that the 'West' lowered their productivity. It is that low, and in some cases declining, productivity that underlies poverty and what makes absolute poverty inevitable without growth. We will elaborate on this theme in Chapter 6.

5

The Growing Equality across Countries and Inequality within some Countries

Inequality

Just as unemployment dominated the political agenda of the 1930s so inequality has come to dominate the concerns of rich countries in the twenty-first century. In our search for the co-existence of contemporary plutocrats and the very poor, inequality both across, and within, countries matters. If rising national incomes go with rising inequality there will be a race. Will the incomes of the poor grow so that, even with rising inequality, absolute poverty falls while relative poverty increases? An increase in relative poverty in such countries is inevitable, that is what rising inequality means. If, in contrast, as national income grows inequality falls then the poor will gain more than the rich. We need to know which pattern dominates and why and, in particular, whether this pattern differs systematically between rich and poor countries.

We are going to begin where we left off in the last chapter, with national incomes, and ask how inequality across countries has changed since 1700. The implication of the data we have already presented is that since 1700 there has been a steadily widening gap in national incomes across countries, with some in 2014 poorer than most countries were in 1700. At first sight such a widening gap would seem to imply increasing inequality over the three centuries as well as since 1700. However, countries are very different in their populations, so it matters which countries grew and which did not. In allowing for that we will see that it alters, rather radically, this pattern of global inequality across countries and it can be, indeed has been, argued that the world has become a strikingly more equal place over the last three decades. Such a view contrasts, rather strongly, with popular perceptions. We need to understand what is the basis for these very different perspectives.

Now, of course, such national data only tells us about average incomes. Much of the focus of the concern with inequality is on the changing income distribution within countries, in particularly those of rich countries, of which the UK and the US have been prominent examples. So, after viewing the national averages, we return to the Gini coefficient, introduced in Chapter 1, as the most widely available measure of inequality within countries. Here we will encounter what may appear to be a paradox in the light of current rich country concerns. Across both the data sources we use—one from the World Bank, the other from the *Chartbook of Inequality*—on average rich countries have much lower Gini values than poor countries. A higher Gini value means more inequality in the sense we defined it in Figure 1.1—the proportion of incomes going to the poor is lower as the Gini goes up. This association of high Gini values, that is high levels of inequality, with low incomes has led many to impute a causal connection between the two, so reducing inequality will lead to higher average incomes. A way, in other words, to set up a virtuous cycle, of increases for all, but increases most for the poorest.

The problem clearly is that if high inequality does cause lower incomes, we are hard pushed to explain why we observe rising incomes and rising inequality as, at least for some countries, we clearly do. The underlying reason from which these apparent problems arise is that we are relating a Gini value, which can vary at most between 0 and 100, and in practice varies between 25 and 75, with income which has, as we have shown, risen in some countries more or less continuously for 300 years. If there was either a positive or a negative relationship between the level of income and the level of inequality we would have had to see either a continuous rise or fall in inequality. What we will show is that is certainly not what we observe. If we are to find any relationship between inequality and income, we must look for how the Gini is related to the growth rate of incomes. Do countries which have faster growth in income see an increase in the Gini? We will find that the answer to that question is yes, but the effect is small and the relationship rather weak.

When looking at inequality within countries we want to know the effect of inequality changes within both poor and rich countries. For poor countries does the Gini capture changes so that we can see whether increasing inequality there has led to an increase in poverty? The answer to that question is not as obvious as it seems. If higher inequality goes with higher growth you may observe higher inequality and lower poverty—indeed we will argue that is exactly what has happened in China. For rich countries we want to know if the rises in inequality, where they have occurred, as measured by the Gini value can explain the rise of the plutocrats. We will argue that the answer to that question is no. First though we want to look at country-level averages.

The Distribution of Total Incomes at the Country Level

Figure 5.1 provides us with a picture of how the spread of average incomes of countries has changed in the three centuries since 1700. This is an average so you can think of it as telling you what has happened to the 'average' person in the country or, more fancifully that, if all have the same income, then you are seeing the distribution of income of all the peoples in the world. In the top half of the figure we show 1700 and 1913, in the bottom half we show 1950 and 2014. The black bars in the top chart show you the range of incomes in 1700. The chart uses logs but the scale on the horizontal axis translates the logs into actual incomes. That is important. When we use logs a one-unit change in the log is a nearly threefold increase in the actual income. So, looking at the horizontal axis we see that a one-unit change in the log at the bottom of incomes raises them from US$403 to US$1,097, then the one-unit change in log translates into a rise to US$2,981 until, after a change in logs of 6, we get to US$162,755 which is the highest income we observe in 2014. It is that increase in the spread of incomes, which we have already discussed in the last chapter, which underlies the increasing spread of country-level incomes across the world. Our use of logs enables this rise in income inequality to be seen very clearly.

The heights of the bars show you how many countries were at the levels shown so, for example, the most common income around which some 35 per cent of countries clustered in 1700 was US$1,500. Less than 20 per cent of countries had incomes higher than US$2,000 which you can read off from the height of the bars. In 1700 the two richest countries in the world on a per capita basis were the Netherlands and Iraq (we give a full listing of countries in the next chapter). They were both over twice as rich as the UK and France, two countries which were about to set off on a century of, more or less, continuous conflict. In 1700 the total GDP of France was by far the largest in Europe, about twice that of the UK, so wars could only be fought with allies which made inevitable the shifting alliances among the European powers over the century if the wars were to be sustained.

The bars outlined in green in the top part of Figure 5.1 show the distribution of incomes per capita for 1913. A much larger number of countries is included than for 1700 and incomes per capita range from nearly US$10,000 to US$650, a ratio now of 15 times. Further less than half the countries included in the data in 1913 had higher incomes than the highest incomes in 1700 so the first wave of globalization had a modest impact on global incomes. In contrast by 2014 more than 50 per cent of countries included

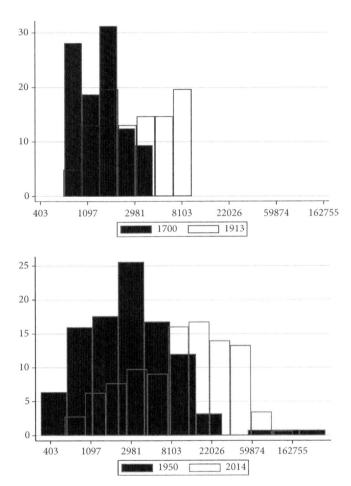

Figure 5.1. Distribution (in percentages) of Log of GDP per Capita in (2011 PPP) US$ from 1700 to 2014 (unweighted)

Note: The distribution is of the log of incomes. The horizontal axis has converted the logs to actual incomes.

Source: Updated Maddison data and Penn Data 9.0.

in the data had higher incomes than the highest income in 1913. Of course, some, as we know, had not grown so by 2014 incomes ranged from US $160,000 to US$570—a ratio of 280 times!

We may now be closer to understanding where we can find both the plutocrats and the very poor. While average incomes of US$160,000 are still a long way from the millions, indeed billions, we need to find the plutocrats, they are nonetheless a good start. We are also zeroing in on where those in extreme absolute poverty will be living. They are rather likely to be in countries which, in 2014, have lower incomes than many countries did in 1700. As most, although by no means all, the richest countries in the world are in Europe and North America, and virtually all the poorest are in sub-Saharan Africa (SSA), we present in Figure 5.2 the distribution of incomes in those two regions in 1950 and 2014.

The striking success of the countries within Europe and North America and the equally striking failure of the countries of SSA can be seen from the figure. Two aspects of the distributions shown are important. The first is its location in the sense of where in the range of incomes most countries are located. The second is the shape of the distribution as that tells us how many of the countries are in any particular range.

So, for Europe and North America we see that about 65 per cent of countries lie between US$4,900 and US$13,400 in 1950. By 2014 about the same percentage of countries had incomes of at least US$36,300. You can see that from how high are the bars in the figure. For Europe and North America not only has the entire distribution of incomes shifted to the right but its range in logs has narrowed. The extent of the shift to the right in the distribution means that virtually all countries in this region in 2014 were richer than the richest European country in 1950. Note that this narrowing in range in logs (the spread of the distribution in logs gets more squashed) is consistent with an increase in the spread of actual incomes. This is something that is going to recur throughout this chapter. Equal percentage increases in income imply a widening gap between the incomes of the richest and the poorest. A ten-percentage increase in an income of US$10,000 is US$1,000 while a ten-percentage point increase for an income of US$100,000 is US$10,000.

For SSA the picture shown in the bottom panel of Figure 5.2 is very different. As we know from Figure 4.5 in 1950 the SSA region was not the poorest part of the world, per capita incomes in both India and China were lower but over the period since 1975 (although not prior to that) its growth rate was by far the lowest. There we were looking at regional averages, in

Figure 5.2 we are looking at what happened within that region so we are looking behind the average to see if there were some successes. The answer is a qualified yes. In 1950 the average hides a very large range in incomes from US$403 to US$13,360 and by 2014 the range was from US$665 to US $36,315. However, the much higher incomes were the exception. Looking at the shape of the distribution we see that even in 2014 substantially more than half the countries had incomes lower than US$4,914 which, as we already know from Figure 4.5, had by 2014 ensured SSA was by far the poorest region of the world. The distribution of incomes in SSA did shift to the right but the shift was nowhere near as complete as that for Europe and

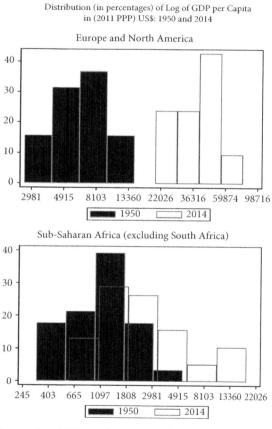

Distribution (in percentages) of Log of GDP per Capita
in (2011 PPP) US$: 1950 and 2014

Figure 5.2. Comparing GDP per Capita in Rich and Poor Countries 1950–2014
Source: As for Figure 5.1.

North America with the result that there is a substantial overlap in the two distributions. Indeed, the most common bar in the figure, indicating where the most countries were located, was for SSA the same in 2014 as it had been in 1950. We have here the key to where the poorest are to be found as the spread of incomes has increased with very limited growth.

We now look at the overall picture across the world. Most SSA countries are ones with relatively small populations so looking at the distribution of incomes at the country level misses the important fact that the growth of a country with 1 billion people is a very different event for a similar growth rate with a country of 1 million. To allow for that we are going to introduce the standard deviation in our log measures. This is simply a measure of spread of how far the countries are from the average—we have already met it with the special case of the normal curve. In the case of the normal curve we know that 95 per cent of incomes will be within 1.96 standard deviations around the mean. The larger the standard deviation the larger the range of incomes. We can see from Figure 5.1 that the range of incomes has been increasing across the years shown. The advantage of the standard deviation is that we can summarize this spread for each of the epochs we have identified in Chapter 4. More importantly, if we weight this standard deviation by the population of countries, we can show what happens when rapid rates of growth are concentrated in more populous countries, which has been the case since 1980. We show the results in Figure 5.3.

The top row of Figure 5.3 shows the standard deviation of the log for all the countries we have in the data. The lines indicating discontinuities in the data are due to the increase in the coverage of countries over time. In particular the increase in the standard deviation in the left-hand panel for 1950 is due to the inclusion of many SSA countries for the first time. It will be noted that this increase is much less apparent in the weighted numbers shown in the top row right-hand panel as while a large number of countries were included for the first time in 1950 many had relatively small populations.

Now the results in the top panel of Figure 5.3 enable us to claim that country-level inequality has risen consistently since 1700 with the highest ever level in recent decades. Or, we can claim that since 1980 inequality across countries has fallen rapidly for the first time in economic history—a claim made by those who wish to celebrate the successes of the second wave of globalization. Both claims can be true. The first claim is looking at the left-hand top row of Figure 5.3 and the second claim the right-hand panel, the

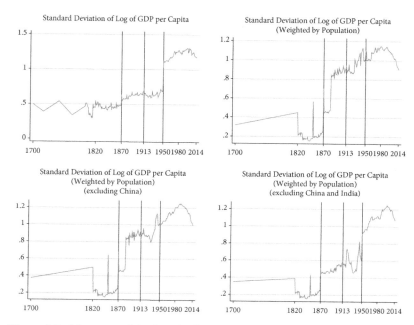

Figure 5.3. Measures of the Standard Deviation of Incomes (in 2011 PPP US$) across the World

Note: The vertical lines indicate discontinuities in the data.

Source: As for Figure 5.1.

difference being whether or not we weight for population. If we do, and clearly we want to, if we want to know how people, rather than countries, have fared, then the news in the top right panel of Figure 5.3 looks rather dramatic. This measure of country-level inequality has fallen so rapidly since 1980 that by 2014 it was below the level of 1950.

But, it will be objected, that is just another way of saying that China's growth has been uniquely rapid. That objection is allowed for in the bottom left-hand panel of Figure 5.3 and, to some extent, it is correct. If we exclude China from our data this measure of inequality is still down, not to below the level of 1950, but still back to that level. In the bottom right-hand panel we exclude both China and India which makes the decline less but there is still a sizable reduction in the measure. However, these are all measures using country averages; we now turn to consider what was happening to inequality within countries.

From Countries to Households

There is much scepticism regarding GDP numbers, particularly for poor countries. By their nature GDP numbers are adding incomes from very different sources and much estimation may well be used. Even more important the GDP number is for total incomes in a country, they tell us nothing about who in the country is getting the income. So, our next step is to go inside the GDP numbers and ask whose incomes have been changing. Just as there are problems in measuring the incomes of countries so there are problems, albeit different ones, for measuring incomes within a country. Many individuals do not have incomes for a range of reasons, some aged one are a bit young, some choose not to work as they can depend on someone else to give them some of their income. However, all individuals have access to incomes, even if they themselves do not earn any, and all individuals consume. Consumption is a more natural measure to assess how well off an individual is than their income not only because all consume but for the more important reason, from the point of view of measurement, that consumption will be a much better measure of their long-term income than their current income. Incomes fluctuate much more than consumption as individuals smooth out their incomes over time. Economists make a distinction between current and permanent incomes and consumption is often used as it is a better measure of their permanent income.

Consumption has another benefit from the point of view of assessing how well-off individuals are in a society, namely that it can be measured for the household and that ensures our one-year-old, with no income, stays alive. Households are indeed a rather natural unit in which to measure incomes as within households incomes are, at least to some extent, pooled. Households are indeed the unit which is used for many poverty comparisons.

Inequality within Countries: Mostly Poor Countries

The measure of inequality we are going to use first is the Gini coefficient which we introduced in Chapter 1 to show the range of incomes in Ghana and the world. Our reason for the choice of the Gini (there are in fact many measures of inequality and we will also consider some of these alternatives) is that it is the one that is most widely available across a diverse range of countries. However, while the Gini is widely calculated it is done using a different measure of income and consumption so we need to be careful when comparing the Gini across countries that they are in fact comparable. Before we consider those different measures, we need to be clear how the Gini allows us to move beyond averages and say something as to how incomes are distributed within a country.

In Figure 5.4 we use one of the most comprehensive datasets for the Gini which has been collated on a common basis. This is the PovCalNet dataset created by the World Bank which is based on household survey data for a large number of countries over the years from 1981 to 2014. We present in Figure 5.4 the average value of the Gini for these countries and their average level of GDP per capita again measured in US$ (PPP) 2011 prices. In the figure you can see the World Bank code names. The Appendix to this chapter shows the country names and the value of the Gini when the country is first observed in the data.

It appears from Figure 5.4 that there is clear inverse relationship between inequality and the level of national income. The fitted line shown in the figure is an indicator of how this relationship looks on average. The countries with the highest level of inequality shown in the figure are South Africa

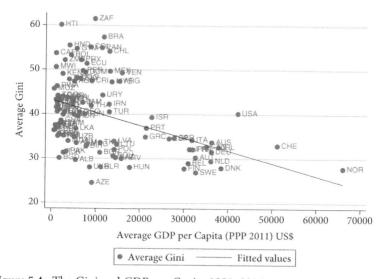

Figure 5.4. The Gini and GDP per Capita 1981–2014

Note: The Gini is as reported in PovCalNet and uses Consumption per Capita. It, and GDP, are averaged over the period 1981 to 2014. The sample is confined to countries with a population greater than 2 million.

Sources: World Bank PovCalNet (Accessed August 2017) and Maddison updated with PENN World Tables 9.0.

(ZAF), Haiti (HTI) and Brazil (BRA). We can see from the figure the large range of the Gini, that for South Africa is over 60 as compared with less than 30 for Norway, and a cluster of middle-income countries (in the sense of where they are on the chart). We now need to clarify how we can interpret these Gini values.

In Chapter 1 we gave an interpretation of the Gini in terms of the Lorenz curve. There we noted the important distinction between inequality as reflecting the shares of incomes going to different parts of the population and the spread of incomes that results from increasing income for any given level of inequality. This distinction can also be seen in another way as we can give the Gini an interpretation in terms of the differences we will observe on average between two households chosen at random in the country. What this mental experiment consists of is choosing two households at random and comparing the difference in their income. We then repeat this many times and average the resulting differences. It turns out this average difference is expected to be 2G per cent of the mean income where G is the value of the Gini coefficient.

To see what this means in practice let us consider Brazil (BRA) which has a Gini of 57 and a GDP of some US$11,733 (PPP 2011 prices) (those are averages over the period 1981–2014) with Bulgaria (BGR) which has about the same income (10,939) but a Gini of 31, nearly half that of Brazil. So if we carry out our experiment in Brazil we would expect the difference between the incomes of two households selected at random to be $(2 \times 57/100) \times 11,733 = 13,375$. In Bulgaria we would expect to find a difference of 6,782, about half that for Brazil. Clearly the average level of income of the economy is not a very useful measure as to what to expect household incomes to be in Brazil.

There is an important distinction between proportions of incomes going to different parts of the population and the spread of incomes. If we take the level of inequality of Norway (NOR), at 28 even lower than that of Bulgaria, with an income of some US$66,021 our mental experiment would predict a difference in two households of $(2 \times 28/100) \times 66,021 = 36,971$, a much larger number than the difference in consumption in Brazil. While as average income is nearly six times higher in Norway such a difference is much less remarkable than is the difference of 13,375 in Brazil, nevertheless the spread of incomes will be greater. The measure here of inequality is inherently a relative concept in the sense that any given level of inequality, as measured by the Gini statistic, will produce a different range of incomes dependent on the average level of income.

Now if Brazil could move its income towards the level of Norway and reduce its inequality to Norway's level the gain for the relatively poor within Brazil would clearly be very substantial indeed. The data we have plotted in Figure 5.4 certainly seems to show that richer countries tend to have much lower levels of inequality than poorer ones.

One rather obvious way of reading Figure 5.4 is that inequality is bad for the growth of income. In other words, a key part of increasing income is to address inequality in a country. Such an argument is often made on the basis of the strong inverse relationship between inequality and the level of income. However, such an inference does not follow from the figure. The data has been averaged over more than three decades. What we need to know is how the Gini and changes in income are linked, if indeed they are. In measuring changes in income, we have a choice. We can use either use the difference in the levels of income or we can look at the growth rate. These are not the same for reasons we have emphasized. An increase of US$1,000 is a much bigger growth rate for a country with US$10,000 at the start than for a country with US$50,000. As it is growth rates that matter, we are going to be showing how growth rates and inequality are linked.

To answer questions about growth rates we have to move from averages over the period from 1981 to 2014 to measuring how inequality and incomes have changed over this period. To do that we are going to average the Gini and the levels of income for the period from 1981 to 1990 and compare it with averages for the period 2011 to 2014. The reason for this procedure is that the PovCalNet data does not have annual observations for all the countries it covers so to look at a reasonably large number of countries we need to look at averages over a period. So, what we are now doing is creating a data set that will enable us to compare incomes and the Gini in the 1980s with their outcomes in 2011 to 2014.

So far we have asked if the *level* of the Gini is related to the *level* of income. We have already noted in previous chapters that the level of income and its growth rate are not closely related. The reason for this is simple—growth proceeds in a random manner in that it is subject to a whole range of different shocks. We argued that such a pattern of growth would produce a log normal shape for the distribution of income. One implication of such a pattern of growth is that the range of incomes would steadily increase. That would imply that we should see not a relationship between the Gini and the level of incomes but between the Gini and the growth rate of income which should be positive.

In Figure 5.5 we investigate if indeed changes in the Gini are related to changes in inequality. This relationship has been the subject of much dispute within economics and the perceived political implication of this relationship is very apparent. If high inequality is the cause of low growth then there is a double case for attacking inequality if one wishes to reduce poverty. Lower inequality not only directly lowers poverty but, by promoting growth, enables further reductions in poverty. Such a 'left-wing' interpretation of the relationship can be contrasted with a 'right-wing' one, where higher

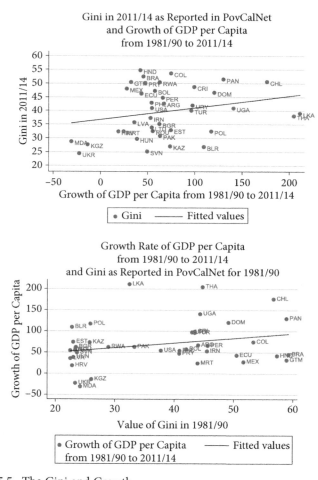

Figure 5.5. The Gini and Growth

Source: World Bank PovCalNet (Accessed August 2017) and PENN World Tables 9.0.

inequality promotes growth by giving all an incentive to work hard and strive for higher incomes.

Once we have measures of the Gini and growth at different points in time we can ask the data about the associations. We have to be careful not to call them causes as there may be other factors producing what we see in the data. In the top panel of Figure 5.5 we show how the value of the Gini in 2011/14 is related to the growth rate in the period from 1981/90 to 2011/14. In rather dramatic contrast to the downward sloping relationship we saw in Figure 5.4 we now see a mildly upward slopping relationship. The reason for the difference is that we are now asking if growth (not the level of income) in the past is related to the Gini later. In the bottom panel of Figure 5.5 we ask how the past Gini is related to future growth. Again, we see an even more mildly positive relationship.

So, who has won? The 'right-wingers' with their belief that inequality promotes growth or the 'left-wingers' who see it as a drag on growth? Well it does look as though the relationship is positive but surely the most striking aspect of both charts in Figure 5.5 is how unrelated are the Gini and growth.

Inequality within Countries: Mostly Rich Countries

Before we conclude that rich countries all have a low value for the Gini we need to remember that Figure 5.4 did not include very many high-income countries and among those that are included the US is clearly an outlier in its level of inequality using the consumption per capita measure of income. So, we need to use another data source which has been compiled for Gini values in mainly rich countries and we will draw on that assembled in *The Chartbook of Economic Inequality*. Once the focus is on richer countries it is possible to measure inequality based on incomes and that is what is done for most of the data presented in the Chartbook. Further the data sources on which the Chartbook draws go back much further than do the sources so we can see how inequality has changed over time within a country—remember the comparisons in Figures 5.4 are averages and the changes shown in Figure 5.5 are only over recent decades.

While consumption per capita is a relatively straightforward measure of how well-off households are it is clear it misses important elements. Dividing household consumption by the numbers in the household which is what we have done so far misses out that children are not the same as adults. A household of one adult and two children has very different consumption needs from one with two adults and one child. In the Chartbook data this is recognized by using what is termed an equivalent scale which recognizes that children consume less than adults. Once the measure for inequality assessment is income it becomes important in rich countries to distinguish gross income, namely income before taxes and credits, from disposable income. Insofar as governments seek to change the level of inequality, disposable income may well differ in important aspects from gross or before tax income. These differences in definition are going to be important when it comes to comparing Gini values across countries.

Table 5.1 classifies the data available from the Chartbook based on whether the measure is based on disposable or gross income or consumption. Within each of these categories there are important differences which may affect our ability to compare across countries.

The researchers who have compiled *The Chartbook of Economic Inequality*—Tony Atkinson, Joe Hasell, Salvatore Morelli, and Max Roser—say that

in the case of overall income inequality, our preferred income concept is equivalized (using a scale to allow for differences in household size and

Table 5.1. Measures of Incomes Used for the Gini in *The Chartbook of Economic Inequality*

Equivalized disposable household income			
France (24), Germany (34), Iceland (12), India (2), Japan (33), Netherlands (31), New Zealand (20), Portugal (20), Spain (23), Sweden (36), Switzerland (8), UK (54), Norway (30)			
Equivalized gross household income	**Household equivalized income**	**Per capita income**	**After tax income of tax units**
US (74)	Argentina (33) Brazil (29)	Italy (36) South Africa (8)	UK (19)
Disposable household income	**Household income**	**Per capita Expenditure**	**Household per capita expenditure**
Mauritius (8)	Malaysia (19)	India (35)	Indonesia (25)
Equivalized disposable household (weekly) income		**Equivalized after-tax family income**	
Australia (16)		Canada (39)	

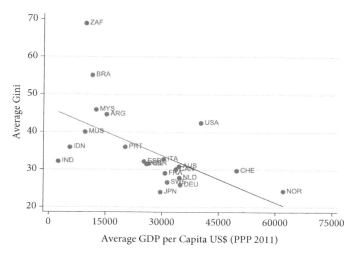

Figure 5.6. Average Gini and GDP per Capita from *The Chartbook of Economic Inequality*, 1975–2014

Note: The various Ginis have been combined to ensure as large a cross section as possible. However, it needs to be noted that in this chart definitions differ across the countries.

Source: Gini from *The Chartbook of Economic Inequality* (accessed August 2017); GDP per capita from PENN World Tables 9.0.

composition) household disposable income, defined as income from all sources, including transfer payments, minus direct taxes and social security contributions. The equivalence scale used in most cases is the 'modified OECD scale', which gives a weight of 1 to the first adult, of 0.5 to each additional adult, and of 0.3 to each child. This means that the income of a family of 2 adults and 2 children is divided by 2.1. In some cases, other scales are employed, such as the square root scale, where income is divided by the square root of the household size (2 in the example just given). The distribution is among persons: each individual appears in the distribution with the equivalized income of the household.

Atkinson et al. (2017, p. 3)

In order to provide a comparison with our earlier charts we present in Figure 5.6 all the values of the Gini available from the Chartbook over the period from 1975 to 2014.

As was the case with the PovCalNet data there is a clear inverse relationship between the level of the Gini and the level of income. However, one of the advantages of the Chartbook data is that for some countries we have a

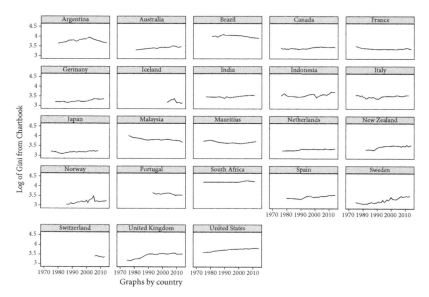

Figure 5.7. The Changes in the Gini Across Countries 1970–2012
Source: The Chartbook of Economic Inequality (accessed August 2017).

long time series and we show the Gini over the longest time period for which we have data in Figure 5.7.

In Figure 5.7 we use the log of the Gini. As we know that means we can interpret the slope of the line as a growth rate. There is a very striking difference between these plots of the Gini over time and our charts for income in previous chapters. While income grows in a sustained way over the period from the 1970s for all these countries, there is remarkably little change for most in the value of the Gini. We see that the high-inequality countries included in the data, Brazil and South Africa, have been highly unequal countries over the whole period. There has been, it is true, some decline in inequality in Brazil, but modest relative to how high it is in comparative terms across countries.

It is possible the charts convey a misleading impression as they are structured to cover both the very high and very low inequality countries; by the standards of other countries both South Africa and Brazil are off the map. There has been much interest in the notion that there is an Anglo-Saxon model of liberal labour markets, low taxes and poor public service with high inequality to be contrasted with the Nordic countries which have

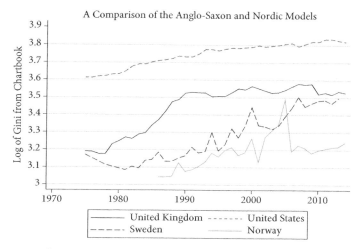

Figure 5.8. The Gini for Anglo-Saxon and Nordic Countries

Source: Gini from *The Chartbook of Economic Inequality* (accessed August 2017).

Warning: The US Gini use a different definition of income than the other countries, see Table 5.1.

the opposite attributes.[1] In Figure 5.8 we present a comparison of four countries which span this divide. Note the warning that the US data uses a different definition of income than the other three so is not directly comparable but it is the series for which there appears to be the longest time span.

What is striking about the four countries shown in Figure 5.8—the US and UK being the Anglo-Saxon representatives and Sweden and Norway representing the Nordic model—is how very different they all are from each other. In fact, at the beginning of the period shown, and at the end, the measure of the Gini is the same for the UK and Sweden, while Norway wins the prize for keeping inequality low. As we will see in the next chapter, by 2014 Norway had the highest per capita income in the world, so it is clearly—on the criteria of high income and low inequality—a spectacular success.

[1] See, for example, Atkinson and Piketty (2007).

Rich and Equal, Poor and Unequal?

When we looked at the evidence across countries it seemed that it was true that rich countries were much more equal than poor ones. However, as Figure 5.8 shows, such averages hide large differences among rich countries over time, even between ones that are often classed together as are the US and the UK. What can account for these differences? The answer is rather obvious for those countries basing their Gini measure on household equivalized disposable income. Inequality is a choice of the government in terms of how it taxes and spends the money raised through taxation. Just as absolute poverty in poor countries is overwhelmingly due to governments choosing policies that impoverish their people, so in rich countries, with the ability to raise substantial amounts in taxes, the extent of relative poverty, and thus inequality, is chosen by those governments.

Appendix Data for Figure 5.4 The Gini and GDP per Capita US$ (PPP 2011 prices) 1981–2014

World Bank Code	Country	GDP per Capita	Gini	World Bank Code	Country	GDP per Capita	Gini
AGO	Angola	5,086	47.3	KHM	Cambodia	1,405	35.1
ALB	Albania	5,441	29.7	LBR	Liberia	799	36.5
ARG	Argentina	15,354	47.4	LKA	Sri Lanka	5,481	36.7
ARM	Armenia	5,593	33.5	LSO	Lesotho	1,570	56.3
AUS	Australia	36,301	33.7	LTU	Lithuania	14,778	33.2
AUT	Austria	32,648	30.2	LVA	Latvia	14,171	33.9
AZE	Azerbaijan	9,135	24.6	MAR	Morocco	5,113	39.8
BDI	Burundi	555	36.3	MDA	Moldova	3,753	33.9
BEL	Belgium	30,996	29.0	MDG	Madagascar	1,464	41.8
BEN	Benin	1,679	41.0	MEX	Mexico	13,216	49.7
BFA	Burkina Faso	1,003	43.3	MKD	Macedonia	8,712	38.0
BGD	Bangladesh	1,775	30.1	MLI	Mali	1,232	40.6
BGR	Bulgaria	10,939	31.4	MNG	Mongolia	8,024	33.1
BIH	Bosnia	7,820	32.7	MOZ	Mozambique	537	45.7
BLR	Belarus	11,167	28.1	MRT	Mauritania	2,615	39.9
BOL	Bolivia	4,326	53.3	MUS	Mauritius	10,415	35.7
BRA	Brazil	11,733	57.4	MWI	Malawi	959	50.6
BWA	Botswana	9,827	60.0	MYS	Malaysia	13,618	47.3
CAF	CAR	957	53.7	NAM	Namibia	6,625	62.1
CAN	Canada	35,093	32.7	NER	Niger	847	37.5
CHE	Switzerland	51,178	32.9	NGA	Nigeria	3,515	43.7

CHL	Chile	13,065	54.2	NIC	Nicaragua	3,949	47.8
CHN	China	4,844	42.5	NLD	Netherlands	36,144	29.4
CIV	Côte d'Ivoire	2,951	40.5	NOR	Norway	66,021	27.8
CMR	Cameroon	2,541	44.0	NPL	Nepal	1,683	35.5
COG	Congo	5,715	48.1	PAK	Pakistan	3,332	31.6
COL	Colombia	8,698	55.1	PAN	Panama	11,319	55.0
COM	Comoro Islands	1,704	55.9	PER	Peru	7,017	49.7
CPV	Cape Verde	4,007	49.8	PHL	Philippines	4,696	43.5
CRI	Costa Rica	9,024	47.4	POL	Poland	14,228	32.1
DEU	Germany	36,261	31.5	PRT	Portugal	21,450	36.9
DJI	Djibouti	2,552	43.1	PRY	Paraguay	6,613	52.2
DNK	Denmark	38,443	27.9	ROU	Romania	13,985	30.6
DOM	Dominican Republic	7,586	49.4	RWA	Rwanda	1,164	46.3
ECU	Ecuador	7,865	51.4	SDN	Sudan	1,736	35.4
ESP	Spain	26,617	34.5	SEN	Senegal	1,896	43.3
EST	Estonia	15,730	33.3	SLE	Sierra Leone	1,548	37.1
FIN	Finland	30,087	27.7	SLV	El Salvador	6,556	48.0
FRA	France	32,025	32.1	STP	Sao Tome	2,799	31.5
GAB	Gabon	19,436	42.2	SVN	Slovenia	20,069	26.0
GBR	United Kingdom	27,787	34.6	SWE	Sweden	32,730	26.9
GEO	Georgia	6,281	40.4	SWZ	Swaziland	6,575	55.0
GHA	Ghana	2,106	38.5	SYC	Seychelles	17,662	44.1
GIN	Guinea	1,264	41.8	TCD	Chad	1,059	41.6
GMB	Gambia	1,548	47.9	TGO	Togo	1,394	44.1
GNB	Guinea Bissau	1,495	43.3	THA	Thailand	8,916	41.9
GRC	Greece	21,255	34.9	TJK	Tajikistan	2,692	31.3
GTM	Guatemala	5,614	54.8	TKM	Turkmenistan	11,021	33.6
HND	Honduras	3,982	55.5	TTO	Trinidad	20,430	41.4
HRV	Croatia	15,860	30.0	TUN	Tunisia	7,488	39.9
HTI	Haiti	2,049	60.1	TUR	Turkey	13,086	40.5
HUN	Hungary	17,727	28.0	TZA	Tanzania	1,621	37.7
IDN	Indonesia	5,960	39.5	UGA	Uganda	1,239	42.6
IND	India	2,688	35.2	UKR	Ukraine	8,636	28.0
IRL	Ireland	37,903	32.6	URY	Uruguay	11,535	44.3
IRN	Iran	13,055	42.3	USA	United States	42,204	40.2
ISR	Israel	22,670	39.3	UZB	Uzbekistan	5,141	34.8
ITA	Italy	31,852	34.2	VEN	Venezuela	15,904	49.3
JAM	Jamaica	7,001	42.6	VNM	Vietnam	2,634	37.8
JPN	Japan	31,279	32.1	ZAF	South Africa	9,670	61.5
KAZ	Kazakhstan	14,536	30.2	ZMB	Zambia	2,940	52.1
KEN	Kenya	2,463	49.0	ZWE	Zimbabwe	2,155	43.2

6

Inequality and Poverty across the World

The Sources of Poverty and the Two Waves of Globalization

We began this book with a discussion of the extraordinary range of incomes that can be seen across the contemporary global economy and, more specifically, contrasting the incomes of the very poor with the incomes of the plutocrats. As the report from Oxfam we cited indicated, these differences seem grotesque and manifestly unfair and what can be done about them is clearly at the forefront of political debate in both rich and poor countries. In the last chapter we focused on one measure of inequality, the Gini, across countries. In this chapter we are going to take a step closer to the concerns of the Oxfam report by looking at the incomes of those at the bottom, and those at the top, of the income distribution. It is, however, only a step, as our data will not include the incomes of the real plutocrats; they will not appear until Chapter 8, as almost all data sources that enable a comparison of the poor and the rich exclude them for a simple reason— there are too few of them for the survey data we will be using in this chapter to capture. As the Oxfam report indicates, the smallness in number may not imply smallness in importance.

As we have shown in earlier chapters these differences have a long history and, as we noted at the end of Chapter 4, their source is a controversial issue. One interpretation of the differences sees the success of the 'West' in the combination of its technology and its institutions. Another, less impressed by the technology of the 'West', sees the rise in incomes of the 'West' as a result of the colonial exploitation of both the Americas and Asia. 'Poverty was created' is the argument advanced by Jason Hickel (2017) is his book *The Divide*, which is a recent re-statement of a view which has a long history of tracing the transformation of the UK economy in the late eighteenth century to its trade and colonial history.

The problem with any view that poverty is, in some sense, created is that poverty has been the natural state for most people for most of human history. We need to be clear that by poverty we mean a lack of access to material resources. As Angus Deaton (2013) points out in *The Great Escape*, the life of the individual in a hunter-gatherer society, before the advent of agriculture, may have been more conducive to human happiness than life in a modern society—albeit a much shorter one. Happiness, or well-being, are very different from an escape from poverty, although Deaton does argue that richer societies are ones with higher levels of well-being; a conclusion which, possibly surprisingly, is very controversial.

While in 1500 the gap in incomes between countries was very small compared with what was to occur over the next five centuries, a significant gap had emerged between some countries. In Chapter 3 we documented that gap for five countries—the US, the UK, Brazil, India, and China. On a per capita basis the UK was much richer than the others, although all were poor by the standards of later centuries. The argument advanced by Ian Morris (2011), which we outlined in Chapter 4, is that the gap between 'East' and 'West' was, on average, closed between 1500 and 1700. That may be so, but such averages hide the importance of the individual countries. As we saw in Figure 3.1 the gap that grew up between the UK and China from 1500 to 1700 was a result of modestly increasing per capita incomes in the UK and falls in China. To understand the reasons for such differences in growth rates is to understand the first element in understanding the sources of poverty.

The second element is how that growth impacts the incomes of the poor. There is no automatic, or mechanical, link between growth and such an impact. In some periods, and for some countries, there was a direct link. The one we have already stressed is the first three-quarters of the twentieth century when the price of unskilled labour rose rapidly. While it is not simply the rate of growth that matters for reducing poverty, without growth poverty, in its absolute sense, is inevitable for most. So how, in terms of growth, have countries fared during the fist wave of globalization from 1700 to 1913? Table 6.1 tells us.

In 1700 the Netherlands was by far the richest country in the world on a per capita basis, nearly twice as rich as the United Kingdom. Some of the countries that would rank very high by 1913—the United States, Canada, Australia, and New Zealand—were among those with the lowest incomes in 1700. Italy, third in 1700, had sunk to 17 by 1913. Spain and Portugal, the imperial powers over much of South America in 1700, were among those falling fastest in rank over the period. The only country that saw actual falls in the level of their income over this period was China, although India came

Table 6.1. Changing Places: 1700 to 1913

Rank	Countries ranked from richest to poorest in 1700	GDP per capita in 1700 in (2011 PPP) US$	Population in 1700 (in thousands)	Average Growth Rate (% pa) 1700–1913	Countries ranked from richest to poorest in 1913	GDP per capita in 1913 in (2011 PPP) US$	Population in 1913 (in thousands)
1	Netherlands	4,352	1,900	0.24	Switzerland	9,943	3,864
2	Iraq	3,675	1,000	0.28	Australia	9,118	4,821
3	Italy	2,500	13,300	0.30	New Zealand	8,625	1,122
4	UK	2,324	8,565	0.53	United States	8,569	97,606
5	Norway	2,086	500	0.57	Canada	7,388	7,852
6	Switzerland	2,074	1,200	0.74	Germany	7,355	65,058
7	Denmark	1,912	700	0.62	Netherlands	7,333	6,164
8	Germany	1,835	15,000	0.65	Denmark	7,201	2,983
9	Belgium	1,832	2,000	0.61	UK	7,149	45,649
10	Spain	1,676	8,770	0.40	Norway	7,071	2,447
11	Austria	1,668	2,500	0.59	Belgium	6,756	7,666
12	Iran	1,635	5,000	0.24	Iraq	6,681	2,613
13	Sweden	1,596	1,260	0.54	Ireland	5,980	4,346
14	Ireland	1,563	1,925	0.63	France	5,862	41,463
15	France	1,531	21,471	0.63	Austria	5,819	6,767
16	Portugal	1,465	2,000	0.20	Sweden	5,057	5,621
17	F. USSR	1,324	26,550	0.42	Italy	4,748	37,248
18	Turkey	1,252	8,400	0.33	Spain	3,916	20,263
19	Egypt	1,197	4,500	0.30	Finland	3,414	3,027
20	Mexico	1,093	4,500	0.52	Mexico	3,334	14,970
21	Finland	1,032	400	0.56	F. USSR	3,230	156,192
22	China	998	138,000	−0.20	Greece	2,897	5,425
23	Greece	965	1,500	0.52	Iran	2,725	10,994

24	Brazil	962	1,250	0.27	Turkey	2,532	15,000
25	Japan	913	27,000	0.42	Egypt	2,274	12,144
26	United States	852	1,000	1.08	Portugal	2,236	5,972
27	India	836	165,000	0.04	Japan	2,221	51,672
28	Morocco	743	1,750	0.24	Brazil	1,699	23,660
29	Canada	714	200	1.10	Morocco	1,227	5,111
30	Australia	707	450	1.20	India	904	303,700
31	New Zealand	670	100	1.20	China	655	437,140

Source: The Maddison-Project, http://www.ggdc.net/maddison/maddison-project/home.htm,2013 and PENN World Tables 9.0. Updated from Angus Maddison, Historical Statistics of the World Economy, 1-2001AD.

close with a growth rate so low it implied stagnating income over the two centuries.

Now if we wish to summarize trends, then identifying a 'West' and an 'East' is essential for clarity but, if we want to understand the reasons for the changing geography of incomes over this period, such aggregates make little sense and the reason for that was implicit in our analysis in Chapter 4. Growth rates are enormously variable, both across countries and over time within countries. What we are doing in Table 6.1 is providing an average growth rate over a period of 213 years. Across these countries the growth rates varied from -0.2 per cent per annum to 1.2 per cent per annum. Those differences may seem small but over a period of more than two centuries a growth rate of 1 per cent per annum can increase income nearly nine-fold. Within countries the differences in growth rates over time can be much greater. In the United States, one of the best performers on average over this period, annual growth rates varied from -11 per cent per annum to 18 per cent per annum. In Australia, on average an even better performer than the US, the range was from falls of 16 per cent per annum to increases of 26 per cent annum.

The rise of the 'West' shown in Table 6.1 occurred through two routes. The first, taken by Europe, was modest growth rates combined with being relatively rich in 1700. The second route, taken by North America and Australasia, was relatively high growth rates from much lower income levels. In Figure 6.1 we compare the rates of growth in the first wave of globalization, from 1700 to 1914, with the second wave from 1950 to 2014. In the first wave growth rates across countries average 0.5 per cent per annum, in the second wave they were four times higher at 2.0 per cent per annum. Not only much higher, but much more variable, with growth rates ranging from −1.5 to 4.5 per cent per annum. Not only were countries getting richer far faster in the second wave of globalization but the differences across countries were exploding.

As we showed in Chapter 4 rich countries are no more likely than poor ones to have high growth rates. So, growth is not related to income. The sources of poverty are to be found in countries that failed to grow and why they failed is both a very large, and very difficult, question.

Broadly speaking, countries can grow either in an extensive way, using more and more capital relative to labour to produce more output per unit of labour; or in an intensive manner, where the same inputs are used to produce more output—a process of increasing the mysterious factor TFP, which we introduced in Chapter 1. The evidence points strongly to the

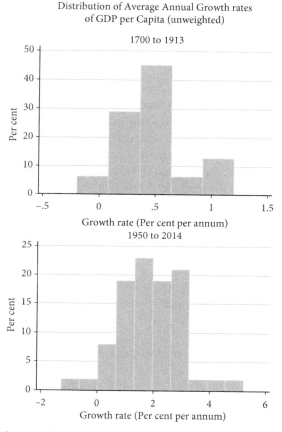

Distribution of Average Annual Growth rates
of GDP per Capita (unweighted)

Figure 6.1. The Two Waves of Globalization: 1700 to 1913 and 1950 to 2014
Source: As for Table 6.1.

second process being the more important in understanding how countries grow. The implication is that countries with high growth rates, on average over a long period, are ones which have successfully marshalled the options available from the technological and organizational innovations which came onstream from the eighteenth century. These countries have seen a sustained increase in both their inputs—capital (broadly defined to include both physical capital in equipment and human capital in the form of skills) and labour—and in TFP the process that enables these inputs to be used more productively. So, to understand which countries grew we need to know how they came to increase their investment in capital and, more importantly, how they learnt to use that capital more productively. While economists have devoted a lot of effort to both those questions there is no agreement as to the answers. Indeed, William Easterly (2002) describes the answers as 'elusive'—*The Elusive Quest for Growth Economists' Adventures and Misadventures in the Tropics.*

While we may not understand how it is done, we do know that if it is not done then absolute poverty for those living in those countries is inevitable. The source of such poverty is to be found in that failure. Such a perspective is very different to the one which sees 'globalization' as the problem. The reason that a focus on globalization is misleading is to miss the role of agency by countries. The increase in trade and flows of capital that have characterized the world economy in its two great waves of globalization, from 1700 to 1913 and from 1950 to 2014, have created both opportunities and potential costs. How countries have sought to exploit those opportunities and to diminish those costs is the story of those who have grown—and seen dramatic reductions in their levels of absolute poverty—and those who have not. In summary, the problem for poverty is not globalization, it is the policies of governments which have failed to use the opportunities from globalization well for their citizens.

Are the Levels of Absolute Poverty Falling?

In the light of the concerns of the Oxfam report it will seem puzzling that, as reported in the opening section of Chapter 4, the World Bank's claim is that the total numbers of the absolutely poor are falling faster than they ever have before. No doubt the origin of the claim in the World Bank, an institution second only to the IMF as a perceived advocate of neo-liberal policies which impoverish the poor, will reduce the puzzlement. The view that the World Bank numbers are simply wrong can by found in Hickel (2017).

What are the sources of the disagreements? Let us begin with the use of the World Bank poverty line, which is currently US\$ (PPP) 1.9 per day. That is indeed dire poverty. In his writings Hickel (2017) advocates US\$5 per day in the context of the earlier US\$1.25 poverty line. If we update that to the 2011 PPP prices being used in this book it comes to about US\$ (PPP) 7 per day which does produce the roughly 4 billion poor people that Hickel cites in his book. So, the question posed is this: does the World Bank poverty line tell us only about the desperately poor, not those who would, on any

Numbers of Poor in the World 1988 to 2008 (in billions)

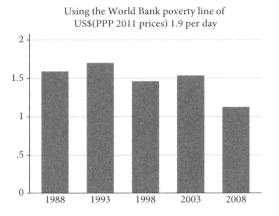

Using the World Bank poverty line of
US$(PPP 2011 prices) 1.9 per day

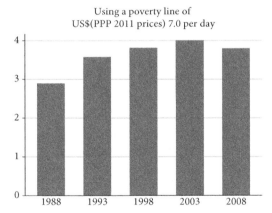

Using a poverty line of
US$(PPP 2011 prices) 7.0 per day

Figure 6.2. Comparing the Numbers Poor with Different Poverty Lines
Source: Lakner-Milanovic (2013) World Panel Income Distribution (LM-WPID) database.

reasonable grounds, be considered poor? In Figure 6.2 the numbers of the absolutely poor are presented using the two poverty lines. If we use the US$7 per day poverty line it is indeed true that the number of the poor increased substantially between 1988 and 2008 from just under 3 billion to nearly 4 billion. In contrast, using the World Bank poverty line shows a substantial fall in the number of the poor. Under either poverty line the absolute numbers of the poor fell between 2003 and 2008.

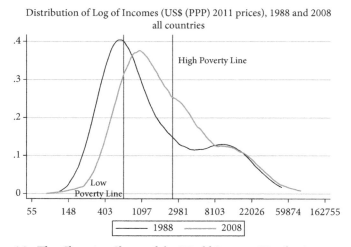

Figure 6.3. The Changing Shape of the World Income Distribution

Note: The distribution is of the log of per capita annual incomes. The logs have been converted to actual incomes on the horizontal axis. The high poverty line uses US$(PPP) 7 per day, the low one is the World Bank Poverty line of US$(PPP) 1.9 per day. These poverty lines have been converted to annual amounts.

Source: Lakner-Milanovic (2013) World Panel Income Distribution (LM-WPID) database.

Why do we get a quite different pattern of changes in poverty depending on which poverty line we use? The answer can be seen in Figure 6.3. The low poverty line of US$1.9 per day converts to US$735 annually and the high poverty line of US$7 per day converts to US$1,980 annually. What has happened to the world income distribution between 1988 and 2008 is that there has been a large increase in the numbers between these two poverty lines. So, with the low poverty line we see large falls in the number and with the high poverty line we don't. That does not mean that people have not been getting richer, it just means that many haven't got richer enough to cross the higher poverty line.

It is clearly true that whether or not the numbers in poverty have been falling will depend on where we draw the poverty line if, as is the case, the distribution is not symmetric. However, it is also true that the distribution of incomes for the poorer part of the world have been shifting to the right much faster than the distribution of incomes for the richer, the implications of which we come to below.

Inequality across the Rich and the Poor over the Last Two Decades

That rising inequality is what explains the rise of the plutocrats in a world of great poverty might seem too obvious to be worth stating. However, such a statement merges the two definitions of poverty that we have stressed need to be kept distinct. The data in Figure 6.2 are for absolute, not relative, poverty. The Gini coefficient tells us about relative poverty, it does not tell us about absolute poverty. In his book—*Inequality: What can be done?*—the late Tony Atkinson focuses on this relative issue. In a detailed breakdown of possible tax and benefit programs for the UK in 2014/15, he argues that inequality as measured by the Gini can be reduced by some 3–5 percentage points and that this is a salient decrease in inequality—one that a social democratic government could pursue with popular support.

The underlying source of the economic problem that underlies such redistributive policies is that they imply, by definition, making some of the rich poorer and the poor richer. Indeed, an old objection to democracy was that, in a democracy, such policies would inevitably be imposed on the rich and that such immiseration of the rich would damage growth and thus impoverish all. This view, unsurprisingly, was much supported by the rich. It is one of the rather striking aspects of some very rich countries, of which the United States is probably the most conspicuous example, that politicians can get elected promising to do the opposite, namely changing taxes to make the relatively rich richer and the relatively poor poorer—although they may not quite frame their policies in those terms.

Such arguments, as that last sentence stresses, focus on *relative* poverty. It is the *absolute* notion of poverty that underlies a concern with the co-existence of the poor in much of sub-Saharan Africa and parts of Asia and the plutocrats of the US and China. In China plutocrats have emerged as the number of the poor have fallen dramatically and inequality has (almost certainly) risen. Far from rising inequality implying greater absolute poverty it has been associated with much less. Keeping relative and absolute poverty separate is crucial for understanding what is happening in a world producing many fewer poor people (absolutely) and many more super-rich—while (sometimes) creating more relative poverty and (sometimes) not. We now want to show how a pattern of rising inequality and falling absolute poverty has proved possible.

To see what has been going on, at least up to the financial crisis of 2008, we return to the measure of the Gini for the world reported in the bottom panel of Figure 1.1. When we compare the value of the Gini across the world, reported there, with the values of the Gini reported in the last chapter we see that the only country with levels of inequality directly comparable with the world level is South Africa. That is not a coincidence. In South Africa there are two quite disjointed economies—one for white, and one for black, South Africans. The historical origin of these differences is well known, as are their current political implications. For our purposes there are parallels between the inequality within South Africa and the inequality across the world, with one crucial exception. Since the end of apartheid all South Africans can move within South Africa but inequality has not fallen; indeed it has risen slightly over the post-apartheid period. The same is clearly not true of people who live in poor countries, they cannot move to rich ones. But South Africa alerts us to a possible paradox. It suggests that even if they could, inequality might not fall. We turn now to seeing differences in incomes across the rich and the poor world and how that has changed over time.

The data of which we drew for Figure 1.1 is from work by Christoph Lakner and Branko Milanoviv reported on in Lakner and Milanovic (2013, 2016).[1] These authors have compiled a panel of data for five years—1988, 1993, 1998, 2003, and 2008—for nearly 160 countries and provide a break-down of incomes by ventiles (that is from the poorest 5 per cent to the richest) for all these countries in a common price measure. In their paper they use 2005 PPP US$ but to maintain comparability with our data we use 2011 PPP US$. We also report the data in terms of deciles again to maintain comparability with earlier charts. For China, India, and Indonesia we include both rural and urban surveys.

While the Lakner and Milanovic data uses the same definition of income for all the years for individual countries, it does not use the same definition across the countries. The reason for this, which we have discussed before, is that in poor countries consumption is a much better measure of the living standard of the household than any income measure as many, in poor countries, do not work for wages and their 'income' results from own production and a range of self-employment activities. In contrast, in rich countries income is much easier to measure. It turns out that if we divide their sample between surveys that use the consumption measure, and those that use the income measure, that coincides very closely with a divide

---

[1] I am indebted to Christoph Lakner for an update that has enabled me to use 2011 prices to ensure comparability with the data in other chapters.

between poor and rich countries as can be seen in Table 6.2 which shows their data for 1988 and 2008.

The median per capita income of poor countries, which in Table 6.2 are those using the consumption measure, is less than a tenth of rich countries, which are those using the income measure. The average income shown in the first two columns is, just like the average income in South Africa, not a good indicator of the income of any country. However, the data does provide us with by far the most comprehensive view of the range of incomes across countries with the important proviso, which we have already noted, that the richest among the rich will not be there. It is also probably true that in poor countries the poorest of the poor are not there either but the range is sufficiently large to capture the vast majority of the range of incomes across the world.

Looking at the measures of inequality in Table 6.2 we note an apparently puzzling finding. Looking at the average incomes across the world income inequality falls, both the standard deviation of the log of income and the Gini go down. However, when we look at rich and poor countries separately in columns (3)-(6) in the table inequality goes up and indeed it goes up much more in the poor than in the rich countries. Further, median incomes double in the poor countries as against a rise of only 25 per cent in rich countries. In Figure 6.4 we look behind these averages to see what is going on.

In the top part of Figure 6.4 we show the incomes for 1988 and 2008 for poor countries in the left-hand panel and for rich countries in the

Table 6.2. World Income per Capita: 1988 and 2008

| | Measured in 2011 Purchasing Power Parity (PPP) dollars | | | | | |
| | All Countries | | Countries Using Income Measure | | Countries Using Consumption Measure | |
	1988	2008	1988	2008	1988	2008
Mean	4,063	5,173	10,507	13,866	954	2,055
Median	907	1,715	7,512	9,401	652	1,209
SD of Log	1.33	1.22	1.12	1.14	0.68	0.85
Gini	69.7	66.5	47.3	50.4	41.3	49.1

Note: All averages are weighted by the population in the country.

Source: Lakner-Milanovic (2013) World Panel Income Distribution (LM-WPID) database.

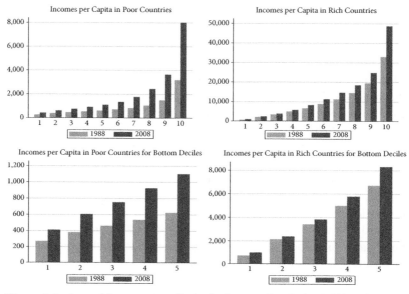

Figure 6.4. Annual Incomes per Capita by Income Decile (in US$(PPP) 2011 prices) for Poor and Rich Countries

Source: Lakner-Milanovic (2013) World Panel Income Distribution (LM-WPID) database.

right-hand panel. As the poor are hard to see, in the bottom part of the figure we confine attention to those below the median.

As can be seen from the bottom right part of Figure 6.4 the increase in incomes for the relatively poor among the rich has been very modest. It is important to stress the relative in that last sentence. The poorest of the poor in rich countries have higher incomes than the majority of those living in poor countries. The top left-hand panel of Figure 6.4 shows that the relatively rich among the poor countries have done much better, in percentage terms, than the relatively rich in rich countries. Again, it is necessary to stress the word relative. The richest of the rich in poor countries have average incomes substantially below the median of rich countries.

In Figure 6.4 we cannot see easily how the distribution of income across rich and poor countries has changed over this twenty-year period. In Figure 6.5 we provide such a picture where we now use logs to show the distribution of incomes in the two periods for rich countries in the right-hand panel and for poor countries in the left-hand panel. Among both poor and rich countries there has been a shift of the distribution to the right and

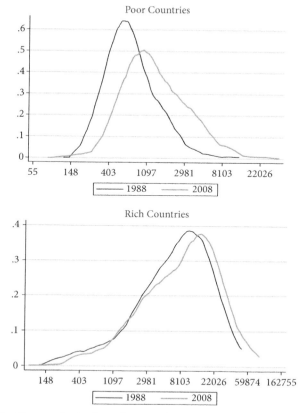

Figure 6.5. Changes in the Distribution of Incomes (in US$(PPP) 2011 prices): in Poor and Rich Countries from 1988 to 2008

Source: Lakner-Milanovic (2013) World Panel Income Distribution (LM-WPID) database.

for both there has been an increase in the spread of incomes across countries. In Figure 6.6 we translate these distributions into the Lorenz curve which show clearly that income inequality has risen more in poor than in rich countries.

The 'Elephant' Chart

Finally, in Figure 6.7 we show in the top panel the growth rates by deciles for both poor and rich countries on the same chart. This shows, what is implicit

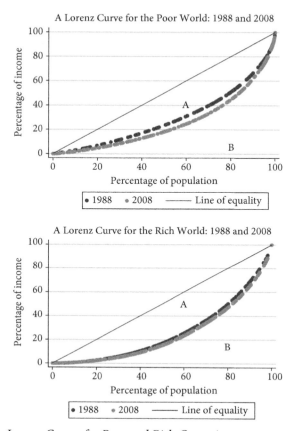

Figure 6.6. Lorenz Curves for Poor and Rich Countries
Source: Lakner-Milanovic (2013) World Panel Income Distribution (LM-WPID) database.

in the above figures, that across the whole range of incomes those living in poor countries have seen, in percentage terms, much higher growth in their incomes than those living in rich countries. Those who have done least well are the relatively poor in rich countries who are absolutely well off by world income standards.

In the bottom panel of Figure 6.7 we show a version of the 'elephant' chart made famous in the Lakner and Milanovic (2016) paper which arises from combining the data from poor and rich countries. In the version shown here the trunk is shorter than in their version as no attempt has been made to separate out the relatively rich in the data, which is done in Lakner and

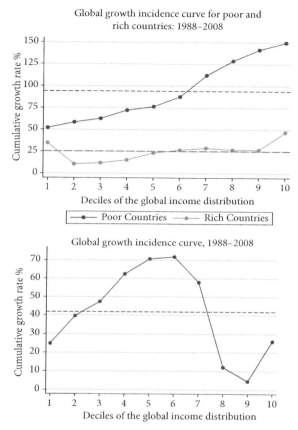

Figure 6.7. The 'Elephant' Chart

Notes: Y-axis displays the growth rate of the decile average income (in US$ PPP 2011 prices). Weighted by population. Growth incidence evaluated at decile groups (e.g. bottom 10% to top 10%). The horizontal line in the top chart shows the average annual growth rate for poor and for rich countries, in the bottom chart for the world economy.

Source: Lakner-Milanovic (2013) World Panel Income Distribution (LM-WPID) database updated.

Milanovic's presentation of the data. The data in the 'elephant' chart is based on houshold survey data and, as we have stressed, such a source will exclude the super-rich as they are too small a proportion of the population to make it into even the largest surveys. The super-rich will appear in later chapters.

In the next chapter we are going to see how these patterns in the data are consistent with the fall and rise of the 1 per cent in now-rich countries.

Rich and Poor Countries in 1950 and 2014

Before turning to the very rich within countries we conclude this chapter by considering how the ranking of countries has changed from 1950 to 2014. Table 6.3 compares the ranking of countries in 1950 with their rank in 2014, a similar chart for the second wave of globalization as we presented in Table 6.1 for the first wave. That table was entitled changing places and covered a period of more than two centuries. For the much shorter period of 1950 to 2014 the changes, which are shown in Table 6.3, have been less dramatic although one clear pattern emerges, which indeed we should expect from our regional decomposition of growth, namely the dominance of sub-Saharan Africa amongst the poorest countries.

As we have far more countries in our data for the period 1950 to 2014 than we had covering the two centuries from 1700 to 1913 we only present in Table 6.3 for the top and bottom eighteen countries. The most striking additions to the top eighteen in 2014 are Singapore, ranked second and Hong Kong, ranked tenth, whose grow rate, by historical standards were spectacular. Both are very small countries in terms of population, but both demonstrate the potential for income grains if policies harness the opportunities from globalization. At the other end of the spectrum are the countries of sub-Saharan Africa. While in 1950 twelve of the bottom eighteen countries were located there, by 2014 all the bottom spots were taken by countries from that region. The poorest of which are as poor as some of the poorest of countries in 1700.

Such poverty at the country level implies a very large rise in the dispersion of country level incomes. In 1950 the income gap between the richest country, the United States, and the poorest, Burundi, was forty-six times. By 2014 the gap between the richest country, now Norway, and the poorest, now the Central African Republic, was 130 times, a three-fold rise over this sixty-four-year period. As we will see in the following chapters the rises in the dispersion of incomes at the household and individual level are even greater than these across countries. However, we have answered our question of what explains the rise of the global divide at least at the country level—differential rates of success.

Table 6.3. Rankings for the Second Wave of Globalization 1950 to 2014

Rank	Countries ranked from richest to poorest in 1950	GDP per capita in 1950 in (2011 PPP) US$	Population in 1950 (in thousands)	Average Growth Rate (% pa) 1950–2014	Countries ranked from richest to poorest in 2014	GDP per capita in 2014 in (2011 PPP) US$	Population in 2014 (in thousands)
1	United States	14,619	152,271	1.98	Norway	78,293	5,148
2	Switzerland	13,758	4,694	2.37	Singapore	66,482	5,507
3	Australia	12,060	8,267	2.03	Switzerland	62,637	8,211
4	Canada	11,227	14,011	2.11	United States	51,959	319,449
5	New Zealand	10,934	1,908	1.78	Ireland	51,927	4,675
6	Saudi Arabia	9,880	3,860	2.48	Netherlands	48,179	16,868
7	UK	9,454	50,127	2.20	Saudi Arabia	48,175	30,887
8	Sweden	9,281	7,014	2.38	Germany	46,507	80,646
9	Denmark	9,280	4,271	2.45	Austria	45,705	8,517
10	Iraq	9,113	5,163	0.45	Hong Kong	45,134	7,227
11	Norway	9,107	3,265	3.36	Denmark	44,423	5,647
12	Lebanon	8,127	1,364	0.88	Australia	44,241	23,622
13	Netherlands	7,756	10,114	2.85	Canada	43,368	35,588
14	Belgium	7,107	8,639	2.70	Sweden	42,605	9,703
15	France	6,867	42,518	2.70	Belgium	39,951	11,226
16	F. USSR	6,168	179,571	1.71	UK	38,757	64,331
17	Hungary	6,078	9,338	2.06	France	38,584	66,100
18	Uruguay	5,909	2,194	1.89	Finland	38,343	5,480
	Bottom 18						
82	Sudan (Former)	1,003	8,051	2.05	Tanzania	2,334	50,444
83	Niger	966	3,271	−0.15	Benin	2,126	10,598

Continued

Table 6.3. Continued

Rank	Countries ranked from richest to poorest in 1950	GDP per capita in 1950 in (2011 PPP) US$	Population in 1950 (in thousands)	Average Growth Rate (% pa) 1950–2014	Countries ranked from richest to poorest in 2014	GDP per capita in 2014 in (2011 PPP) US$	Population in 2014 (in thousands)
84	Viet Nam	932	25,348	2.77	Chad	1,994	13,587
85	Chad	873	2,608	1.29	Zimbabwe	1,912	15,246
86	Nepal	870	8,990	1.71	Uganda	1,869	37,783
87	India	844	359,000	2.92	Rwanda	1,637	11,342
88	Uganda	817	5,522	1.29	Guinea	1,582	12,276
89	Rwanda	706	2,439	1.31	Burkina Faso	1,554	17,589
90	Guinea	671	2,586	1.34	Mali	1,515	17,086
91	Mali	650	3,688	1.32	Ethiopia	1,504	96,959
92	Egypt	603	21,198	4.51	Togo	1,454	7,115
93	El Salvador	589	1,940	4.08	Sierra Leone	1,365	6,316
94	China	532	546,815	4.94	Madagascar	1,250	23,572
95	Malawi	509	2,817	1.01	Mozambique	1,237	27,216
96	Burkina Faso	499	4,376	1.77	D.R. of the Congo	1,206	74,877
97	Cambodia	466	4,471	2.92	Malawi	972	16,695
98	Mozambique	385	6,250	1.82	Niger	878	19,114
99	Ethiopia	337	20,175	2.34	Burundi	842	10,817
100	Burundi	318	2,363	1.52	CAR	600	4,804

Source: As in Table 6.1.

Stellar Growth Performers

That may sound like a statement of the obvious, but it directs our attention to the scale of success over the period after 1950 and the source of the gaps that have merged. It is the stellar growth performers in the second wave of globalization that have generated a gap bigger in the 40-year period since 1950 than emerged after more than 200 years of the first wave of globalization. In Figure 6.8 we highlight these stellar growth performers and contrast them with those who have gone backwards.

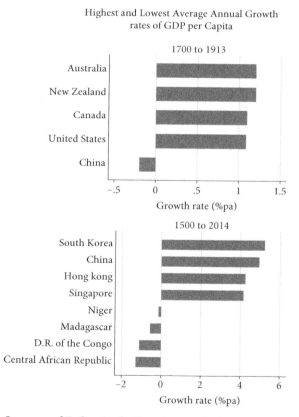

Figure 6.8. Success and Failure in the Two Waves of Globalization: 1700 to 1913 and 1950 to 2014

Source: As in Table 6.1.

Only four countries saw actual falls in their incomes—Niger, Madagascar, the Democratic Republic of the Congo, and the Central African Republic, all beset by wars and conflicts, some of very long duration. With those exceptions all countries saw rises in their incomes so, by differential success, we mean that almost all grew but at radically different rates.

But what of the richest within those countries, who have not appeared in household surveys? To that question we now turn.

7

The Fall and Rise of the 1 Per Cent

From the Gini to the Share of the 1 Per Cent

No doubt the news in the last chapter that the poorest have been getting richer as fast as the richest will have struck many readers as a little puzzling, not to say absurd. Is not the rise of the 1 per cent at the expense of the 99 per cent a well-established fact? Indeed, did not the data presented in the very first chapter shown the remorseless rise of the share of the 1 per cent in the UK and the US since the 1970s? How can that be squared with the results of the last chapter? The answer to that question frames this chapter. The 1 per cent number refers to individual tax incomes which includes the richest people. The basis for the comparisons summarized in the 'Elephant' Chart of the last chapter use either consumption or income per capita and are based on survey data. The plutocrats are missing from the survey data; they are present in the tax data. The reason is simple—there are so very few very rich people, if by that we mean incomes in the tens of millions of US dollars, or higher, as we will see in the next chapter. The sample size of even large household surveys means they are unlikely to capture the super-rich, given their scarcity. A recognition of this concern has led some authors to seek to adjust the Gini, derived entirely from surveys, to reflect the possible omission of the super-rich. There is a parallel concern, at the other end of the distribution of incomes, that surveys may miss the very poor who are destitute and possibly homeless.

There is another reason why the incomes of the 1 per cent may be of particular interest, quite separate from any problem they pose for the Gini measure of inequality. In earlier chapters we have given two, equivalent, interpretations of the Gini. In Chapter 1 we introduced the Lorenz curve which shows how much income goes to how many people. So, for our World Lorenz Curve, which is based on the Lakner-Milanovic data, we could read that the top 20 per cent of people in the world get some 85 per cent of its income. In Chapter 5 we presented another interpretation of the Gini in terms of the differences we will observe, on average, between two households chosen at random in the country. Now the implication of these interpretations is that the Gini is a relative measure of inequality. It does not tell you how far apart are incomes. To emphasize this point we illustrate this aspect of the Gini in Table 7.1 with a 'toy' world of three people where the richest person gets 90 per cent of income, the second richest 9 per cent, and the poorest person has 1 per cent but all incomes grows by 10 per cent per year.

In our 'toy' world shown in Table 7.1 the richest person gets 90 per cent of income in time period 1, that person still gets 90 per cent of income in time period 3, but the gap between the richest and poorest person has increased from 9,900 to 11,979. The Gini, reflecting proportions, has not changed at 59.5. An economist will explain to the poor of this world that inequality has not changed when the poorest person observes the richest getting further and further away from them. Thus confirming in their minds the low esteem in which they have always held economists.

So, to understand the full extent of income differences within rich countries such as the UK and the US, we need to move on from a focus on the Gini. In any case, the Gini does not have quite the impact on political debates as the shares of the rich, so in this chapter we will investigate those shares and ask what changes have occurred in the share of the top 1 per cent for the UK and the US. To put these two countries in context in Figure 7.1 we use data from *The Chartbook of Economic Inequality* to present their data for how the share of the top 1 per cent has changed across the countries for which this data has been collated.

The general pattern from Figure 7.1 is clear. For nearly all countries there is a decline until the 1970s and then in most, but not all, a rise. Japan stands out as having a precipitous fall in the 1950s and then a constant share of some 10 per cent. By far the most visible changes are for the UK and the US, where large falls from the early part of the twentieth century until the 1970s were succeeded by (nearly) equally large increases, although the lows in the UK were not matched by the US and the rise in the UK underperformed that of the US. It is this rise in the income share of the top 1 per cent, in both the UK and the US, that has made the headlines.

How Have the Top 10 Per Cent Fared?

It is a matter of very simple logic that if the share of income going to the top 1 per cent is increasing then the share going to the bottom 99 per cent is falling. But who, among the 99 per cent, have been missing out most on their

Table 7.1. Unchanging Gini and Rising Dispersion of Incomes

	Time period 1	Percentage of income	Time period 2	Percentage of income	Time period 3	Percentage of income
	(1)	(2)	(3)	(4)	(5)	(6)
Person 1	100	1.0	110	1.0	121	1.0
Person 2	1,000	9.0	1,100	9.0	1,210	9.0
Person 3	10,000	90.0	11,000	90.0	12,100	90.0
Total income	11,100		12,210		13,431	
Gap between richest and poorest	9,900		10,890		11,979	
Gini	59.5		59.5		59.5	

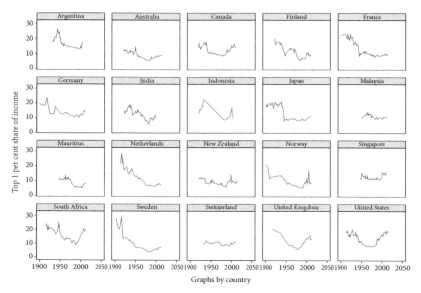

Figure 7.1. Changes in the Shares of the Top 1 Per Cent
Source: The Chartbook of Economic Inequality (Accessed August 2017).

share? In Figure 7.2 below we show the shares of both the top 1 per cent and the top 10 per cent for the UK and the US since the 1910s. On the right-hand axis of both figures we show the share of the top 1 per cent in the share of the top 10 per cent and, as you will see, this has the same pattern as the shares. What this means is that in the period when the shares of both the top 1 and 10 per cent were declining, from the 1910s to the 1970s, the proportion of income within the top 10 per cent going to the top 1 per cent was declining. Then, once both shares started rising from the middle 1970s, the share of the 1 per cent in the top 10 per cent also rose.

Now, you might well object as to why you should care how well the very richest are doing within the class of rich people. Well the answer is that is where the plutocrats are going to come from and why there are far more in the US than in any other country. Another way of saying what Figure 7.2 shows is that up until 1970 the top 1 per cent were doing much less well than the 90–99 per cent; after the 1970s they did better, in the case of the US very much better. If the share of the top 1 per cent within the top 10 per cent is rising in an economy, which is growing, then you will see the emergence of the super-rich within the rich. There will be a stretching out of incomes among the rich and, as we will see, that turns into a well-known distribution

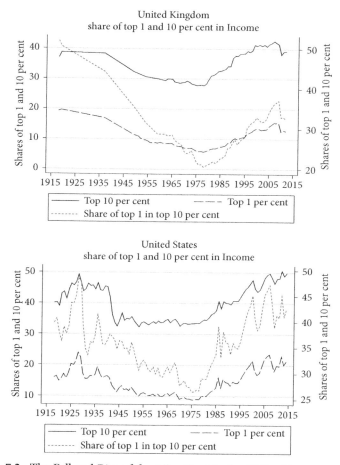

Figure 7.2. The Fall and Rise of the 1 Per Cent in the 10 Per Cent

Source: Facundo Alvaredo, Anthony B. Atkinson, Thomas Piketty, Emmanuel Saez, and Gabriel Zucman, The World Wealth and Income Database, http://www.wid.world, 08/08/16.

for top incomes called the Paretian distribution which we will meet in detail in the next chapter.

While shares make good headlines, they do not actually tell you what is going on in terms of how incomes are changing. The share of the top ten per cent may be rising because its income is rising and the bottom 90 per cent falling. Or, it may be that its income is simply growing faster than the bottom 90 per cent. It matters which it is. We want greater equality with the poor seeing faster growth in their incomes than the rich. And, equally important, which measure of incomes do we care about? In the last chapter the preferred measure of inequality was based on equivalized disposable income, but that measure is based on household income from surveys, far removed from the individual based tax data that underlies Figure 7.1 and the rhetoric of rising share for the 1 per cent. In rich countries these incomes depend importantly on the wages of the individual but they also depend on income from capital. So, if we want to link wages with inequality, which we do, there are many steps to take. In the data that follow we will show how market incomes, called original income by the Office for National Statistics (ONS) in the UK, which is the income for individuals either from wages, rents or capital translate into incomes after taxes and transfers. In other words, we make the crucial distinction between market and disposable incomes. Inequality in market incomes depends on how markets reward labour and capital; inequality in disposable income is a choice of governments.

In discussing how well an economy is doing, by far the most frequently cited measure is its GDP. That is for excellent reasons. Data on GDP is available far quicker than data on its distribution. In Chapters 2 and 3 we noted the de-linking of the GDP data from wages for the unskilled dating from the 1980s in the US and from the financial crash in the UK. We now want to investigate if this de-linking of wages from GDP is also reflected in a de-linking of household market incomes from GDP. We will then turn to how these market incomes have translated into disposable incomes.

Household Market Income and GDP Growth in the UK and the US

In Figure 7.3 we show the changes in median and average household market incomes together with the level of GDP per capita for both the US and the UK. Table 7.2 summarizes trend growth rates.

In the figure we show the years in which the prime ministers or presidents changed. As the data is in logs we can interpret the slope of the curves as growth rates. In Table 7.2 below the figure we report the trend growth rates for both household market incomes and GDP per capita, all are in real terms, that is adjusted for changes in prices within the countries. These are long-term trends, missing out all the bumps along the way. The table shows that for all measures of growth over the period since the 1970s the UK has performed better than the US, in terms of increases in median per capita household market incomes twice as well. One of the prominent arguments of those arguing for the UK to leave the EU was that, freed from Brussels red

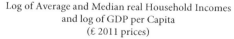

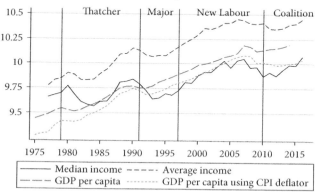

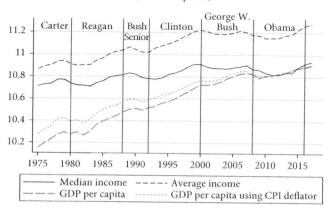

Figure 7.3. Household Market Incomes and GDP per Capita in the UK and the US

Table 7.2. Trend Growth Rates for the UK and the US in Per Cent Per Annum

United Kingdom: 1977–2016

Household Market Incomes		Household Per Capita Market Incomes		GDP per Capita		GDP per Employee	Employment to Population
Average	Median	Average	Median	Using GDP deflator	Using CPI Deflator	Using GDP deflator	
1.8	1.0	2.2t	1.5	2.1	2.0	1.8	0.3

United States: 1975–2017

Household Market Incomes		Household Per Capita Market Incomes		GDP per Capita		GDP per Employee	Employment to Population
Average	Median	Average	Median	Using GDP deflator	Using CPI deflator	Using GDP deflator	
0.9	0.4	1.1	0.7	1.8	1.4	1.6	0.2

Sources Table 7.2 and Figure 7.3: UK Earnings data from Clark (2016), http://www.measuringworth.com. Updated from ONS data. US Earnings from Lawrence H. Officer and Samuel H. Williamson Annual Wages in the United States, 1774–Present, URL: http://www.measuringworth.com/uswages/. UK GDP data from Williamson (2020).

tape, the UK economy could emulate the US. It is probable that they do not mean that growth of median household incomes should half, but that is indeed the implication of their argument.

It is clear that while the growth of GDP per capita for the UK is a good guide to the growth of income, the same is certainly not true for the US where the growth of GDP per capita is far faster than the growth of either median or average incomes. There are several reasons for this divergence for the US but one is that the prices that are used to deflate incomes differ from the prices used to deflate GDP.[1] That sounds rather technical but it has a straightforward economic interpretation. Prices for GDP can be thought of as producer prices, they are what you can sell your goods for. Prices used to deflate incomes are those that consumers pay. If those prices are higher than producer prices then incomes will grow less fast than GDP per capita. In Figure 7.3 we allow for this and see then that the growth of GDP per capita, when using consumer prices, is lower than if consumer prices are used but still higher than the growth of average incomes, and much higher than the growth for median incomes.

As Figure 7.3 shows, the pattern of growth of household incomes in the UK and the US has been very different. The financial crisis of 2008–09 is frequently cited as a turning point for both economies. While this is clearly true for the UK, it is equally clear it was not for the US. The problems of growth in household incomes in the US long pre-dated the financial crisis. In fact, for the US, rather than the financial crisis being the cause of falls in income it was the failure of incomes to grow that caused the financial crisis as underlying that crisis were mortgages the home owners could not afford to pay.[2] The break in the growth of average household incomes in the US can be seen clearly in Figure 7.3 to date from 2000 the advent of George W. Bush to the US presidency. It is clear too from the figure that from the 1980s onwards median household income growth failed to match that of average household incomes.

In contrast for the UK growth in both average and median household incomes continued from the advent of the New Labour government in 1997 until the financial crisis of 2008–09. Even with that crisis the UK economy has, in terms of both GDP per capita and in terms of the growth of median and average household incomes, outperformed the US economy. For the UK

---

[1] A full discussion as to why GDP per capita may not measure median household incomes can be found in Nolan et al. (2016).
[2] See the account of the crisis, its causes and aftermath in Mian and Sufi (2014).

the financial crisis represented a turning point; for the US it was a blip in a long-term pattern of virtual stagnation in median household incomes.

We have here a direct link with the wages for the unskilled which we documented in Chapters 2 and 3. Household incomes grew far faster in the UK than in the US over this period because wages grew much faster. In seeking to understand this pattern of low household income growth we need to understand the reasons for the failure of unskilled wages to rise in the US since the 1980s and for the UK, since the financial crash.

Who Gained and Who Lost: From Thatcher and Regan to Major and Clinton

We now look at how the poor and the rich fared in the UK and the US from the 1970s until the elections of New Labour and George W. Bush. These were years of radical political innovation in both countries with the Reagan Presidency in the US and the Thatcher premiership in the UK. The data is presented as far as possible on a comparable basis across the two countries, although there is not an exact match in terms of how incomes are measured. Also, comparability is only possible for both countries using quintiles, that is dividing up the population into five parts, so within the bottom quintile we will not see the poorest and in the top quintile we will not see the richest. However, the US data enables us to look within the top quintile and we will come to that after comparing how the rich and poor fared across the quintiles in the two countries.

In Figure 7.4 in the first row we compare the Thatcher years (1979–91) with those of Reagan (1979–89), in the second row we compare the Major years (1991–97) with those of Bush Senior and Clinton (1989–2000). The charts in Figure 7.4 show two definitions of income, one seeking to measure the incomes delivered by the market, the second the incomes available to the household after transfers to them and taxes subtracted, which is termed disposable income.

There are two differences between the UK measurement of market income and that which is used for the US. For the US equivalized market income is presented which means that an adjustment has been made for household size, while no such allowance is made in the UK data for market income (which the ONS terms original income). The second difference is in how the underlying data have been used to present household outcomes. For the US the basis is for individuals within the household, while for the UK it is

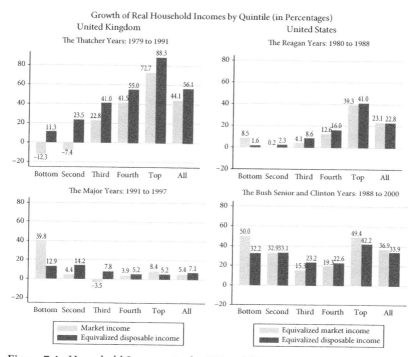

Figure 7.4. Household Incomes in the UK and US: 1979–2000

Note: The growth shown in the figure are based on the trend growth rate over the period covered. These are then aggregated up to the numbers shown in the figure based on the time period covered.

Sources and Definitions: See Appendix at the end of this chapter.

simply household based. (This difference is explained more fully in the Appendix.) The implication of these different bases for income is that if we wish to scale up the incomes to an overall level for the UK we need to scale up by the number of households, while for the US we need to scale up by the number of individuals.

For the measure of disposable income for both the UK and the US it is equivalized in that an adjustment is made for household size. However, the methods used for making incomes equivalent differ between the two countries. Thus, while not defined and measured in exactly the same way they are consistently measured within the country and the comparison is as close as seems possible with currently available public data. So, we are now able to answer our question as to who gained and who lost for the long period of conservative government in the UK from 1979 to 1997 and compare this with a similar period for the US. Figure 7.4 has been drawn so you can compare how successful the governments were in increasing incomes both on average (the final column in the figure) and across the distribution by having a common vertical axis for each chart within the figure. The use of such a common scale shows the relative success of the Thatcher period in raising both average and medium incomes which can be read off from the third quintile.

Indeed, it is not widely appreciated just how much more successful Thatcher was compared with Reagan, even allowing for the longer term of the Thatcher premiership. Median household disposable incomes grew more than three times faster during her period in office than they did in the US under Reagan. In terms of average disposable income Thatcher was twice as successful as Reagan. Those in the poorer part of the distribution also did much better under Thatcher than under Reagan in terms of disposable income. All of which may suggest that the Thatcher period was one of great success. However, a closer look at the chart shows the nature of the problem which the Thatcher period posed. Unlike during the Reagan presidency market incomes for the bottom 40 per cent of the population actually fell, on average, by about 10 per cent. That is truly remarkable and underlying this fall was the rise in levels of unemployment which, prior to the Thatcher premiership, had been regarded as politically unacceptable.

The aspect of both the Thatcher premiership and the Reagan presidency, which we have already covered in Chapter 5, is the rise in inequality. Just how much, in both countries, the top outperformed the bottom is very clearly visible in the chart. In the UK disposable income for the top quintile at 75 per cent compared with 8 per cent for the bottom, a gap of more than nine times, for the US the gap was even wider at 25 times, although the rich did far less well! In one of her last House of Commons appearances as prime minister, Margaret Thatcher acknowledged the rise in inequality but argued that it was not a problem as, if all gained, what did it matter if some gained more than others. Her defenders would no doubt agree, but what if the poorest could gain as much as the rest. Implicit in her defence was a view that that was not possible; yet as we will see, that is exactly what New Labour achieved under Tony Blair and Gordon Brown.

Before turning to that period it needs to be noted that in the bottom panel of Figure 7.4 both the Major government in the UK and the two administrations in the US, of Bush Senior and Bill Clinton, reversed the pattern of growth of the Thatcher/Reagan years and reversed too the ranking of the performance across the two countries as the US income growth very substantially outperformed that of the UK. Dramatic rises in inequality during the Thatcher/Reagan periods were not sustained, indeed under Major they were reversed as the poorest quintile disposable income rose three times as fast as the top.

Who Gained and Who Lost: From New Labour and Bush Junior to the Coalition and Obama

One reprise for disenchanted voters in both the UK and the US has been that 'all politicians are the same' so there is no point in voting. Whether or not they are similar in style and discourse, the results of their policies could scarcely be more radically different as is apparent when we view the very different outcomes shown across Figure 7.5 where we present a similar comparison to that shown in Figure 7.4 but now taking the story of relative performance from the late 1990s to 2016, the most recent year for which comparable data is available.

The New Labour years and those of George W. Bush saw very similar rises in average incomes. However, while the Bush years continued the pattern seen under the Reagan Presidency of by far the largest rises in income being concentrated in the top quintile for the UK, under New Labour exactly the opposite was true. Disposable income in the bottom quintile rose by 47 per cent as compared with 29 per cent for the top quintile. Even more remarkable, and the most dramatic possible difference with the Thatcher years, market incomes for the bottom quintile nearly doubled while for the top quintile the increase was only 30 per cent.

In the UK it has been a commonplace of political rhetoric in the Labour Party, under its leader Jeremy Corbyn, that the New Labour governments failed to address inequality and the rich benefited relative to the poor. As Figure 7.5 shows nothing could be further from the truth. This figure shows that the New Labour years saw sustained rises in both market and disposable incomes of the bottom 20 per cent in marked contrast to the Thatcher years. During the Thatcher years there is a steady march upwards in growth of income across quintiles while under New Labour the highest growth in incomes is in the bottom 40 per cent. There is no evidence here for the, possibly implicit, assumption of those defending the Thatcher years that increased inequality is necessary for gains to the poorer parts of the population.

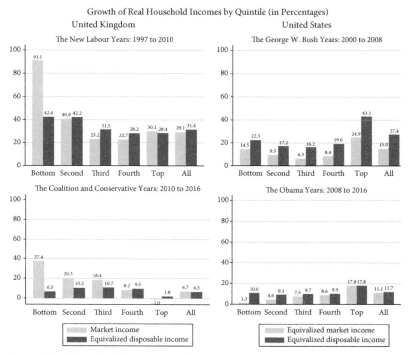

Figure 7.5. Household Incomes in the UK and US: 2000–2016
Sources and Definitions: See Figure 7.4.

One source of strong political disagreement across Conservative and Labour/Democratic supporters is the role of transfers. A 'right-wing' view is that they reward the undeserving for not working. A 'left-wing' view is that they are the necessary part of a civilized society where incomes are so unequally distributed. Common to both should be a wish to see higher market incomes for the poorest. Figures 7.4 and 7.5 are instructive in showing the quite extraordinary failure of Republican administrations in the US to pursue policies which increased the market incomes of those in the bottom two quintiles. Again, the New Labour years are ones of, by far, the greatest success in this respect.

Of course, the New Labour years ended with the financial crash causing the most serious recession in the UK since the 1930s. The fate of the rich and the poor in the decade from the eve of the recession to 2016 is shown in the bottom part of Figure 7.5. The contrast with the period from 1997 to 2010 is clear from the figure. In the period from 2010 to 2016 average incomes in the UK grew by 7 per cent and in the US by 12 per cent. In the UK incomes in the top quintile scarcely grew at all while in the US the pattern of the top quintile outperforming those poorer continued, although the gap between their growth rates and those of the poorest quintile was much more modest than in earlier Republican administrations.

Winners across the Distribution of Income for the UK and US: 1979–2016

In Figure 7.6 we show the long-term trend over the whole period we have covered in the previous sections. As explained in the notes to Figure 7.4 the

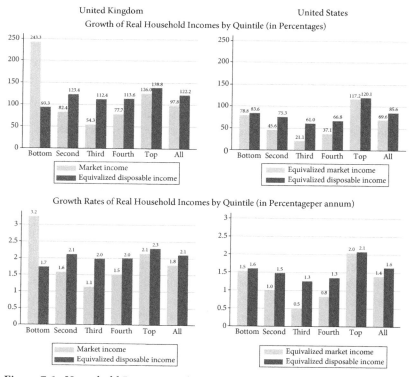

Figure 7.6. Household Incomes in the UK and US: 1979–2016
Sources and Definitions: Sources and Definitions: See Figure 7.4.

data in the figures is based on the trend growth rate over the period covered by each prime minister or president. Thus, what Figure 7.6 tells you is that this trend growth rate was substantially higher in the UK than the US over the period from 1979 to 2016.

The period is averaging very different outcomes across the different political administrations. In both countries there has been a rhetoric of the squeezed middle. Looking at the equivalized disposable income measure there is some evidence for this in the US, but none in the UK. While it is true in both countries that the top 20 per cent saw higher rates of growth than the bottom eighty per cent the differences are much greater in the US than in the UK. Possibly the most striking difference across the two countries is the success of the UK in raising market incomes for the bottom quintile, a policy success which underlies the success of New Labour's policies for the poor, which we further document in the next section.

The Unsung Success of New Labour

In the last sections, for reasons of data availability, we need to compare quintiles of the population. Now that may hide a lot of changes and the rise of the 1 per cent may get hidden in the average of the top 20 per cent. Indeed, it clearly has. So, as a first step to finding the 1 per cent in this section we examine incomes for the UK and the US by decile (that is each 10 per cent) as a prelude to our pursuit of the 1 per cent in the next section—Figure 7.7.

In the top panel of Figure 7.7 we show household disposable equivalized incomes for the bottom and top 10 per cent of the distribution for both the UK from the 1970s to the most recent period for which we have data. As a common currency is used for both countries, US$ PPP in 2011 prices, it is now possible to compare how well the poorest and richest parts of the distribution have done in the UK relative to the US. The results show the dramatic differences between the UK and the US and the magnitude of the achievement under New Labour.

Not only under New Labour was there virtually no change in the ratio of the top to bottom decile (top right in the figure) in contrast to its continued rise under George W. Bush, but the incomes of the bottom decile in the UK grew so much quicker than those in the US that UK incomes at the bottom actually exceeded those of the US during the New Labour period (bottom left of the figure). Further, as the middle panels of the figure show,

New Labour was the only administration that saw a sustained rise in median incomes.

The scale of this success remains unsung as the 'left' within the UK, under Jeremy Corbyn, wishes to distance itself from this successful period of Labour government and the 'right' wish to hide the scale of its failure to maintain the growth of income achieved under New Labour. Indeed, the Coalition and Conservative governments, since 2010, have overseen a

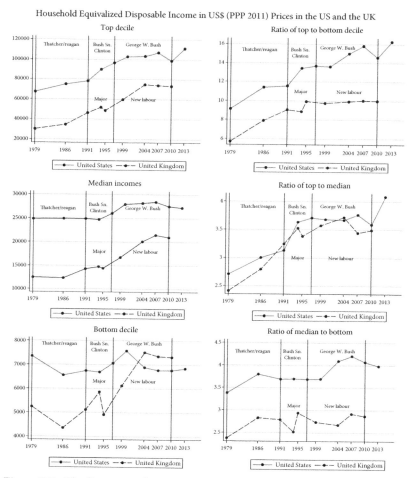

Figure 7.7. The Bottom and Top Deciles in the UK and the US from 1979
Source: Thewissen et al. (2016). Incomes across the distribution database. https://ourworldindata.org/incomes-across-the-distribution.

sustained fall in both median and average earnings and a decade of no growth in productivity, which we document in Chapter 9. 'Achievements' without precedence in any government for more than 100 years.

The Pay of 'Fat Cat' Managers and the 1 Per Cent

How can these findings be squared with the (highly publicized) increases in the take-home pay of bankers and the heads of large companies whose salaries—often combined with poor performance of the companies they manage—excite much public outrage? To find the 'fat cat' managers we need to look at individual income data for the very rich and how that income has changed. For that we need tax data and that is presented in Figure 7.8.

Three aspects of the data can explain the divergence between our results so far and public perceptions. The first is that, for reasons of data availability, we needed to compare quintiles, or deciles, of the population. Now that may hide a lot of changes and the rise of the 1 per cent may get hidden in the

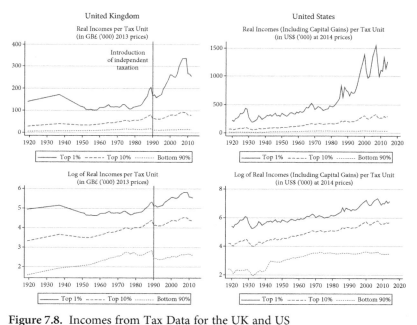

Figure 7.8. Incomes from Tax Data for the UK and US

Source: Alvaredo et al. (2018), The World Wealth and Income Database, http://www.wid.world, 08/08/16.

Table 7.3. Trend Rates of Growth of Tax Income

United Kingdom

	Top 1 per cent	Top 10 per cent	Bottom 90 per cent	Average
Before 1990	0.6	1.5	1.7	1.6
After 1990	3.1	1.8	1.3	1.5

United States

	Top 1 per cent	Top 10 per cent	Bottom 90 per cent	Average
Before 1990	1.2	1.7	2.4	2.1
After 1990	2.5	1.6	0.0	0.7

United States

	Top 1 per cent	Top 10 per cent	Bottom 90 per cent	Average
Before 1970	0.9	1.7	2.8	2.3
After 1970	3.1	1.8	0.0	0.7

average of the top 10 per cent, the importance of this we have already shown in Figure 7.2. The second is that this is data for household, not individual, incomes and we would expect the gaps between households to be less than the gaps across individual's earnings. In Figure 7.2 we showed shares but, as already noted, such shares tell us nothing about what has happened to incomes, shares can change for radically different reasons.

The data is in terms of tax units which for the UK changed in 1990 from a family-based classification to one based on individuals. So below Figure 7.8 we report, in Table 7.3, the trend growth rate of taxable income before, and after, 1990, for both the UK and the US. As the US tax base has been individual based over the whole period we also report for the US trend growth before and after 1970.

So, a direct comparison between the fate of the 'fat cats' in the US and the UK can only be made comparing the period before 1990 with the period after. For the US there was very little difference in the trend rate of growth for the incomes of the top 10 per cent before, and after, 1990. The rise in the share of the 1 per cent in the US was due to an acceleration of their growth rate, it roughly doubled, combined with the collapse in the growth of incomes for the bottom 90 per cent. For the US what we need to explain (and it's the same question as to where the plutocrats came from), is why there was this stretching out of incomes within the top 10 per cent combined with zero trend growth for the bottom 90 per cent. Recall this is tax income, actual household income is very different as we know from earlier figures.

For the UK the rise of the incomes of the 1 per cent had very different origins. Before 1990 at 0.6 per cent per annum the growth rate of the 1 per cent was half the rate of the US. After 1990 it was higher at 3.2 per cent, a staggering fivefold increase in a trend growth rate. But, and it's a big but, the trend growth rate for the bottom 90 per cent was 1.3 per cent a year; true, less than what it was before 1990, but way better than that of the US. So, in the UK the origins of the rising share of the 1 per cent was a rapid acceleration of growth within the 1 per cent and a marginal slowing down of growth in the incomes of the bottom 90 per cent.

The common factor across the US and the UK, based on the tax data, is the acceleration in the growth of income of the 1 per cent. For the US all of this occurred within the top 10 per cent, while in the UK most of it did. The big difference between the countries was that growth in incomes for the bottom 90 per cent ceased in the US—in fact as the bottom row of Table 7.2 shows it ceased after 1970—while for the UK it simply slowed down.

What Happened to Incomes within the Top 20 Per Cent in the US: From Reagan to Obama

The last section was based on tax data which cannot cover adequately the poorer parts of the population. In earlier sections we were confined to looking at quintiles or deciles, that is the top 20 and the top 10 per cent. It is clear from the last section that may miss much of the action.

It is possible for the US data to extend our earlier analysis of market and disposable incomes by looking at changes within the top 20 per cent and this we do in Figures 7.9 and 7.10 (a similar analysis is not possible for the UK from the ONS published data). Figure 7.9 shows the growth within the top 10 per cent for each of the presidencies we identified in earlier charts and compares the growth with that of the top quintile. While for each chart the growth in income of the top 1 per cent is higher than in lower ranges the gap is particularly large for the Reagan and George W. Bush presidencies. The gap is much smaller for the Obama years but they were years of much lower growth for all within the top 20 per cent.

In Figure 7.10 we present the data covering the whole period from 1979 to 2016. The massive gain for the top 1 per cent stands out in marked relief to the growth in incomes among the rich. We can now ask if this data, which has a quite different basis to the tax data used in Figure 7.8 and Table 7.2, confirms the patterns found there. There is a remarkable concordance for the top 1 per cent. Both figures show a trend growth in income for the top 1 per cent of just over 3 per cent per annum. Thus, the tax data on earning seems wholly consistent with the data for market and disposable incomes for the top 1 per cent. Figure 7.10 also confirms that this growth largely occurred within the top 10 per cent. Where the tax earnings data diverges from the income data is for the bottom 90 per cent. While the tax data for the US shows zero growth this is clearly misleading.

Indeed, the most striking aspect of Figure 7.6 is that the bottom 40 per cent of the population, in both the UK and the US, saw more rapid increases in their incomes than those in the third and fourth quintiles. It was only the top 20 per cent who saw more rapid rises than the bottom 20 per cent.

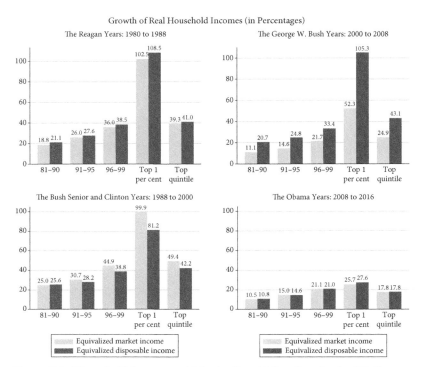

Growth of Real Household Incomes (in Percentages)

Figure 7.9. Household Incomes within the Top 10 Per Cent in the US: From Ragan to Obama

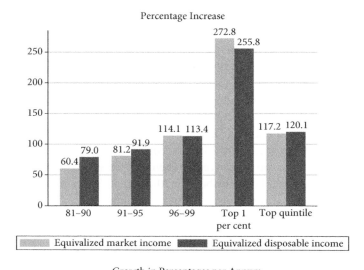

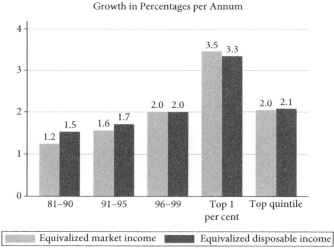

Figure 7.10. Household Incomes within the Top 20 Per Cent in the US: 1979–2016

Sources and Definitions for Figure 7.9 and 7.10: See Figure 7.4.

Changes in the Gini in the US and UK with a Comparable Income Definition

We began this chapter with a move from the Gini to the 1 per cent. We conclude it by returning to the Gini for the UK and the US but using a common definition of income across the two countries—Figure 7.11. In this figure the Gini is defined using household equivalized disposable income where now the method of making households equivalent is the same across

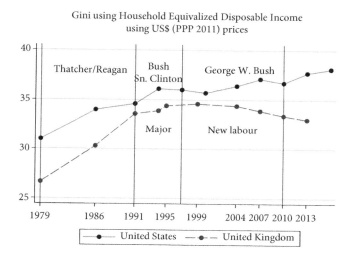

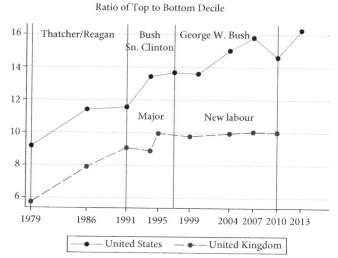

Figure 7.11. US failure and New Labour Success in Reducing Inequality

Source: Thewissen et al. (2016). Incomes across the distribution database. https://ourworldindata.org/incomes-across-the-distribution.

the two countries. In a race to close the gap in inequality between the US and the UK the Thatcher period is clearly the winner with a far more rapid rise in inequality in the UK than the US, ensuring that by 1991 there was little difference in the extent of inequality in the two countries. After that the paths diverge. For the US the inexorable rise in inequality is starkly apparent while the Major years halted the steep rise and New Labour, and the Coalition, reversed it.

Such a decline in inequality is very much the opposite of public perceptions. The 'toy' model which we introduced at the beginning of the chapter explains how inequality can have declined under New Labour when the gap between the richest and the poorest increased. If we look at the top right chart in Figure 7.7, we see that under New Labour the gaps in household incomes between the top and bottom decile did not change so, by that measure, there was no increase in inequality. However, a 40 per cent increase in income for the richest, about US$ (2011 PPP) 45,000 is some 18,000, while for the poorest decile a rise of 40 per cent for an income of US$ (2011 PPP) 5,000 is 2,000—an enormous increase in the dispersion of incomes with no change in this measure of inequality. It is this dispersion of incomes that people have in mind when they think about the extent of inequality in their society, and that has certainly increased.

Appendix: Notes on Data for Figures 7.4 to 7.6 and Figures 7.9 and 7.10

The UK data used in these figures can be found on the ONS web site as:

Average Incomes, Taxes and Benefits by Quintile Groups of Non-Retired Households.

It is available from 1977 and is updated annually. The data is deflated by the CPI to give real incomes in 2011 prices. The background to the sources used by the ONS is as follows:

The Living Costs and Food Survey (LCF) began in 2008, replacing the Expenditure and Food Survey (EFS). The LCF, conducted by the Office for National Statistics, collects information on spending patterns and the cost of living that reflects household budgets across the country. A household expenditure survey has been conducted each year in the United Kingdom since 1957; from 1957 to 2001, the Family Expenditure Survey (FES) and National Food Survey (NFS) provided information on household expenditure patterns and food consumption. In April 2001 these surveys were combined to form the Expenditure and Food Survey (EFS), which completely replaced both series. From January 2008, the EFS became known as the Living Costs and Food (LCF) module of the Integrated Household Survey (IHS).

In this data a distinction is made between original income, which is termed market income in the figures above, and disposable income. The following table shows what is included in these two measures.

The annual data is deflated by the Consumer price Index.

Original income
Wages and salaries
Imputed income from benefits in kind
Self-employment income
Private pensions, annuities
Investment income
Other income
Total

Direct benefits in cash
Job seeker's allowance (Contribution based)
Job seeker's allowance (Income based)
Employment and support allowance
Incapacity Benefit
Income Support
Statutory Maternity Pay/Allowance
Child benefit
Tax credits
Housing benefit
State pension
Pension Credit
Widows' benefits
War pensions/War widows' pensions
Carer's allowance
Attendance allowance
Disability living allowance
Personal independence payment
Severe disablement allowance
Industrial injury disablement benefit
Student support
Other benefits

Total cash benefits
Gross income

Direct taxes and Employees' NIC
Income Tax
Employees' NI contributions
Council Tax and Northern Ireland rates
less: Council Tax benefit/Rates rebates
Total

Disposable income

Equivalized disposable income

The US data is taken from the data supplement to the Report:

Congressional Budget Office (July 2019) *The Distribution of Household Incomes*, 2016. Washington DC.

Before-tax income is market income plus government transfers. Market income consists of labour income, business income, capital gains (profits realized from the sale of assets), capital income excluding capital gains, income received in retirement for past services, and other sources of income. Government transfers are cash payments and in-kind benefits from social insurance and other government assistance programs. Those transfers include payments and benefits from federal, state, and local governments.

Income is converted to constant price dollars using the personal consumption expenditures price index. Income groups are created by ranking households by before-tax income, adjusted for household size. Quintiles (fifths) contain equal numbers of people; percentiles (hundredths) contain equal numbers of people as well.

8

The Incomes of the Plutocrats in a Comparative Perspective

Was Mr Darcy a Plutocrat?

Sources of income have changed completely over the last 200 years. As Thomas Piketty observes in his study of long-run capital accumulation, there was a shift from income from rents on land to incomes from capital during the nineteenth century, at least in Europe. He notes that the Dashwood family's wealth in Jane Austen's *Sense and Sensibility* depended on the size of their estate in Sussex. Indeed, land remained by far the most important source of wealth in Britain well into the nineteenth century.

> During the first half of the nineteenth century—one or two full generations after the beginning of the Industrial Revolution—the non-landed wealthholders were a virtually insignificant percentage of the entire wealthy class. An observer entering a room full of Britain's 200 wealthiest men in 1825 might be forgiven for thinking that the Industrial Revolution had not occurred.   (Rubinstein, 2006, p. 79)

In possibly the best known of Jane Austen's novels, *Pride and Prejudice*, Mr Bingley has an income of £5,000 a year and his friend, Mr Darcy, twice that at £10,000. Both are single and the plot hinges on their being very acceptable husbands for the daughters of Mr Bennet whose income is never explicitly revealed but he would seem to have an estate worth about £5,000. Mr Darcy has a home in Derbyshire which is compared with Blenheim Palace in Oxfordshire. If these incomes were converted into 2011 prices, so as to be comparable with our earlier numbers, the income of Mr Bingley would be some £300,000 a year; that of his friend Mr Darcy, who the heroine of the novel eventually captures, some £600,000. Would these be such desirable husbands today? Surely your average ambitious woman out to live off a man would be looking for at least £1 million. Indeed, to be sure of capturing someone in the top 0.05 per cent she would have to aim for £2 million. Not, of course, that any self-respecting woman would, but the question still arises—would a contemporary Mr Darcy be thought such a good catch; indeed, would he be regarded as a plutocrat?

Assuming the novel is set in about 1810 the average annual income of a labourer would be £1,800 in 2011 prices, a wage difference of over 300 times between their income and that of Mr Darcy. Current average earnings are some £25,000, so a contemporary Mr Darcy would need to earn £8 million to be as rich as his nineteenth-century predecessor relative to the average wage. So, does earning £8 million make one a plutocrat? The term 'plutocrat' carries a pejorative element suggesting not simply someone who is very rich, but one who uses their wealth for political ends. The dictionary definition of a plutocrat is, indeed, one who is powerful because of the wealth, rather than for more acceptable reasons. The fictional Mr Darcy did not have political ambitions or, if he did, they are not reported, but we can ask whether an income of £8 million today would be the basis for exercising powerful political influence if one wished. This question, of the malign role of the super-rich in politics, has been much more prominent in US political debate than in the UK and, as we are going to see below, in US terms a contemporary Mr Darcy would be, among the super-rich, not very rich at all.

Our problem in seeking to define members of a plutocratic club, which we will come to below, is that it appears not to matter how rich you are, there is always someone very much richer, until you get to the top. That is only the richest person does not have to worry about their (relative) poverty. While it might seem rather prosaic to say so, the problem arises from the shape of the income distribution which we noted first in the opening chapters, in that its long right tail is such that the richest disappear from view unless we confine the sample to the comparatively very rich. The paradox is that while those with spectacular incomes are very visible to the public—due mainly to their large incomes being associated with great wealth—through their lifestyles, they are largely hidden in the data given their scarcity. We are going to show what the distribution of incomes looks like among the super-rich. In doing so we will show that there is an extraordinary range of incomes among these very rich people. Just as being poor is a relative concept within a country, so it will be shown, is being rich.

We need to ask if there is some economic reason why the right tail stretches out so far and whether the length of that right tail can be linked to the changes in inequality in societies that we noted in the last chapter have, over the long term, been so large. It is not only differences in income within societies that have been our concern, it is also in differences across countries. At the beginning of Chapter 3 we quoted from the Oxfam report directing attention to the differences between the very richest and the very poorest who are virtually all in very poor countries. We are going to begin by comparing incomes across Ghana, whose Lorenz curve we introduced in Chapter 1, and the United Kingdom. In Chapter 6 we provided evidence as to how incomes on average across poor countries had changed, which included Ghana. We now want to look at the spread both within and across countries at a point in time. Ghana can be regarded as a middle-income country among the poor—its per capita income in 2014 was US$3,700 (PPP 2011)—and the UK as a middle-income country among the rich—its income per capita was US$36,500 (PPP 2011)—a differential of nearly 10 times.

Once we have examined this spread of incomes, we will turn to the problem posed by seeking out these nearly invisible plutocrats and show how we can, at last, get them onto our Figures. We will then be in a position to show the full range of incomes across the globe from the richest of the rich to (very nearly) the poorest of the poor.

The Poor and the Rich in Ghana and the United Kingdom (2012–14)

We now want to bring the data for Ghana and the United Kingdom, that we have already presented, together to ask how incomes compare across the two countries. If comparing incomes within a country is a challenge comparing it across countries is more so. However, Figure 8.1 bravely makes the attempt.

Several steps are required to make the comparison presented in the Figure. The first is that the data need to be presented in a common currency. As we have stressed, using actual exchange rates won't do because a pound buys far more in Ghana than it would in the UK. So, in the comparison we have converted Ghana cedi income to Great British pounds (GBP) using a purchasing power parity exchange rate. This gives roughly triple the income that would be obtained using actual exchange rates. The second step in the comparison is to use consumption per capita. The reason for this is one we have already given. Consumption is not only a better measure of long-run incomes than a direct measure of income but, in the case of a poor country, the poorest often have no incomes apart from those implicit from their own production. We need to standardize across households as the composition of households matters and, in general, households are larger in poorer countries.

With all those adjustments, Figure 8.1 presents the household expenditure per capita for the period 2012–14 in levels in the top and in logs in the bottom panel. Seeking to put the levels for both countries on the same chart accentuates the problem we have already encountered of the long right tail.

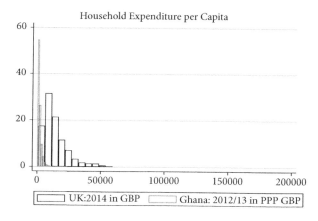

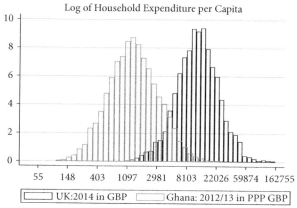

Figure 8.1. The Distribution (in percentages) of Household Expenditure per Capita in the UK and Ghana

Note: In the bottom Figure on the horizontal axis the logs have been converted to actual incomes.

Sources: Ghana data is from the GLSS6 survey for 2012/13, the UK data is from the ONS Living Costs and Food Survey for 2014.

Given the size of this tail for the United Kingdom, where the highest income is some £250,000, the Ghana data is hard to see and crunched up in the left of the Figure. As we know the problem is that the data is close to log normally distributed and using the log transformation produces the bottom chart of Figure 8.1. Indeed, the distribution appears strikingly log normal in both countries.

The use of the log scale enables a clear comparison of the Ghana and UK data. The range of incomes shown in the Figure is very large indeed but, with a log scale, is easily shown. As we have already noted a unit change in a log scale is an equal proportional changed in the value of expenditure. So, we see in the bottom panel that for Ghana expenditure increases from £148 to £403, a 2.7-fold rise and then a similar increase from £403 to £1,097. Using this scale enables us to see more clearly that there is some overlap in expenditure between Ghana and the UK. Between £3,000 and £8,000 some in Ghana are richer than the poorest in the UK. We also see that across these two countries we span those who would be in the top 1 per cent in the UK and the bottom 1 per cent in Ghana. Indeed, those at the bottom of the Ghana distribution are probably among the poorest in the world. The gap between the very bottom of the Ghana distribution and the very top of the UK distribution is a gap of about 300 times, which is similar to the gap between Mr Darcy and average incomes in the early nineteenth century in England. However, being at the top of the income distribution for the UK is a long way from being the richest. As we already know, a contemporary Mr Darcy, who retained his relative position, would not be in the Figure.

Now the absence of Mr Darcy is partly due to the range of the data as the survey is insufficiently large to capture the very richest. However, it is also partly due to the shape of the distribution as the log normal distribution ensures that there are very few people in the tails of the distribution. In order to see the very rich, and by that we mean those even richer than the richest shown for the UK data, we need to present the data in another way that enables us to see if the data is, across its whole range, log normal.

To do that we need to show how we can use our data to show the probability of observing people with different incomes. We will want a way of describing the probability of observing the very rich. Before that though let us re-present our histogram of the log of incomes in a manner that enables us to read off it such probabilities. This we do in Figure 8.2.

Now the shape of these density functions looks very like those of the histogram in Figure 8.1. That is no accident, they are both presenting the same information. It is quite clear from Figure 8.2 that our data fits very well

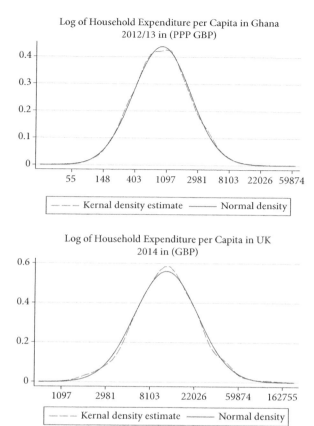

Figure 8.2. The Distribution of the Log of Household Expenditures per Capita in Ghana and the UK as a Density Function

Note: In the Figure on the horizontal axis the logs have been converted to actual incomes.
Sources: See Figure 8.1.

to the log normal density function. Now we need to understand what a density function is telling us as, in our search for plutocrats, we know they will be on the extreme right of the curve and hard to see. The area under any density function between two points tells us the probability of observing values between those two points. In fact, we already know for the normal density function that approximately 95 per cent of observations lie within two standard deviations of the mean.

For the incomes shown in Figure 8.2 we can use its shape to tell us that some 2.5 per cent of Ghana households have incomes greater than £ (PPP) 7,000 in 2012/13 while for the UK some 2.5 per cent have incomes greater than £51,000 in 2014. (These numbers come from the mean and standard deviation of the distributions.) Remember these numbers are for household expenditure per capita so not individual incomes where we will find our plutocrats. But our density functions will enable us to find the plutocrats as they enable us to answer a question that will prove very useful:

What Is the Probability of Observing Someone Richer Than You?

It will turn out that answering that question provides us with a way of charting the richest of the rich and the path to finding the incomes of plutocrats on our charts. Let us begin with the density functions shown in Figure 8.2 and ask for the UK one what is the probability of observing someone richer than you. Say you are right at the centre of the distribution which we know is £14,472. The probability of observing someone richer than you is 50 per cent, which is the area to the right of where you are in the middle. Now as you move to the right the probability of observing someone richer than you declines, until you reach the richest person in the data when it becomes zero, nobody is richer than you. Now we can plot out this probability of observing someone richer than you if we can plot out the changing area under the density function, this we do in the top panel of Figure 8.3.

So, what the top panel of Figure 8.3 is telling us is that the probability of someone having an income of more than £403 is one (i.e. it is certain as that household is the poorest in the data). We can then follow down the curve and read off that there is an 80 per cent change of observing someone with an income greater than £8,103, a 20 per cent chance of observing someone with an income of £22,026 and no chance at all of observing someone with an income of over £170,000, there is no one that rich in the data. The bottom panel of Figure 8.3 plots the log of that probability against the log of expenditure per capita.

Now it's a bit hard to think what changing the log of income and changing the log of the probability of seeing someone richer than you means. There is in fact another way of presenting the same information which gives us a very clear way of understanding the implications of the

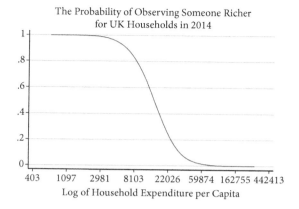

The Probability of Observing Someone Richer for UK Households in 2014

Log of Household Expenditure per Capita

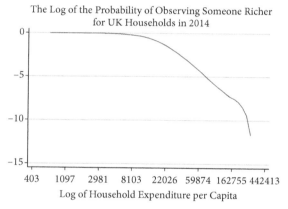

The Log of the Probability of Observing Someone Richer for UK Households in 2014

Log of Household Expenditure per Capita

Figure 8.3. The Probability of Observing Someone Richer than You
Note: On the horizontal axis the logs have been converted to actual incomes.
Source: ONS Living Costs and Food Survey for 2014.

shape of the curves in Figure 8.3. To do that we are going to rank everyone from the richest first (S_1) to the poorest at the bottom (S_n):

$$S_1, S_2 \ldots \quad \ldots \, , \quad \ldots S_n$$

If we have n people on our list then the probability of observing someone with a higher income if you are the ith person on the list is i/n where i is the rank of the person, which shows how far down they are on the list, and n is the number of people being ranked. Figure 8.4 shows such a plot.

The key aspect of Figure 8.4 is that it looks very like Figure 8.3 and that is because it is presenting the same information. If we look at the rank relative

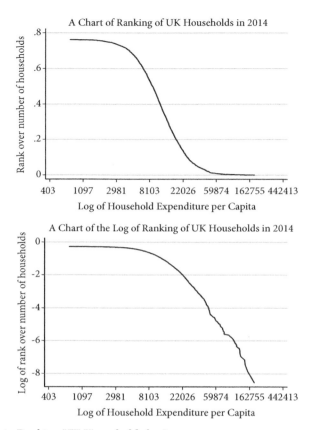

Figure 8.4. Ranking UK Households by Income

Note: On the horizontal axis the logs have been converted to actual incomes.

Source: ONS Living Costs and Food Survey for 2014.

to the numbers in our data, providing we have ranked everyone from the richest to the poorest, then, to a good approximation, we are looking at the probability of observing someone richer than you, wherever you stand in the ranking.

Mr Darcy on a Chart at Last

You may well feel, quite reasonably, that Figure 8.4 is no more intuitive than Figure 8.3. However, it is, if we recognize that the use of logs enables us to interpret a straight line, and in the bottom panel of Figure 8.4 the line is fairly straight after about income levels of £10,000, as telling us about percentage changes. What that straight line tells us is that for any given percentage change in income the percentage change in the ranking of the individual on the list is the same, whatever the level of income. Now that straight line is very useful for finding Mr Darcy as the shallower the line, that is the closer it is to being flat, the more likely you are to find Mr Darcy at the far end of the scale. We have already noted we cannot find him in the survey data as the range of incomes is too small but let us return to our tax data from Chapter 2 and see if we can show the Mr Darcys of the current UK economy with our new chart.

We see we can now find the contemporary Mr Darcy as 16 in logs converts to nearly £9 million as an annual income. In comparing Figures 8.4 and 8.5 notice that the plot shown in Figure 8.5 is much closer to being linear over its whole length than the plot in 8.4 which has a very distinct curve to it. In fact, the shape of this plot is the difference between a log normal distribution and a Paretian one. Pareto thought he had found a 'law' of what governed incomes, or wealth, at the top-end of the distribution in that the slope as in Figure 8.5 is linear. It is, rather amazingly, the factors that determine the slope of that line that governs how many plutocrats we are going to find in an economy. We are going to find them now and, in doing so, it should be clearer what the slope does and how we need to

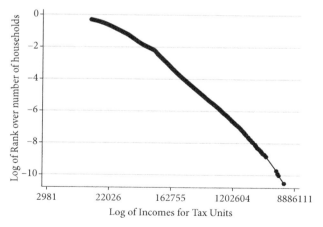

Figure 8.5. The Log of Rank and Log of UK Incomes in 2014–15
Note: On the horizontal axis the logs have been converted to actual incomes.
Source: HMRC Tax Data for 2014–15.

understand what changes that slope if we wish to understand how to reduce the number of plutocrats in an economy. We begin with the UK.

The Super-Rich in the UK

In Figure 8.6 we show the threshold, and average, levels of income for those in the top 1 per cent and those in the top 0.1 per cent.

The threshold is the level of income you need to enter these exclusive clubs. For the rich among the rich, that is the top 0.1 per cent, the average income in that category is far above the level needed to enter the club. The implication is that among this group incomes are enormously spread out and, if we are willing to assume they are spread out in the manner suggested by Pareto, we are in a position to identify both the numbers of the very rich and their incomes.

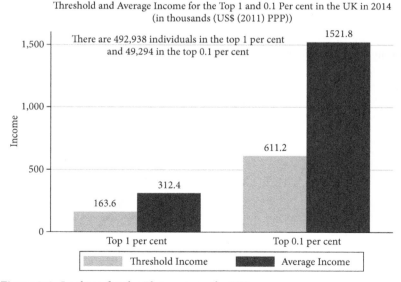

Figure 8.6. Looking for the Plutocrats in the UK

Source: World Wealth and Income Data (accessed 2019). Now on the web as World Inequality Database (wid.world). A report on this data can be found in Facundo Alvaredo et al. (editors) (2018) *World Inequality Report*, Harvard University Press.

To do that we need two pieces of information. One is the income of the richest person in the country and the second is the slope of the Paretian curve, that is how shallow, or steep, is the line we showed in Figure 8.5 (and the bottom panel of Figure 8.4). Clearly, we cannot get the income of the richest person from the tax data as it would violate the confidentiality of that source. However, we do know the wealth of the richest person in the UK in 2014 from the Forbes richest list which was some US$13 billion in 2014 which converts to US$ (2011 PPP) 11.4 billion. This is a number for their wealth, not their income. To translate that into income we need an assumption as to the return on their capital. A return of 5 per cent per annum, while high, is not impossible, so to try and be nice to those who will undoubtedly be viewed as plutocrats let us assume a 5 per cent return on their capital. That translates into an annual income for the richest UK person of US$ (2011 PPP) 570 million—unbelievable you will say, but we show next the actual income numbers are consistent with such extraordinarily high incomes.

In Table 8.1 we show what a Paretian distribution implies as to the incomes of the richest people in an economy where the richest person has an income of US$ (2011 PPP) 570 million. For the UK we know from Figure 8.6 that there are some 50,000 individuals in the top 0.1 per cent so we can look at Table 8.1 and see which value of the slope parameter from the Paretian distribution implies that at 50,000 their income will be some US$ (2011 PPP) 644,000. The closest value of the Paretian slope is 1.6 where the 50,000th person has an income of US$ (2011 PPP) 659,202 and the average income of those above this level is US$ (2011 PPP) 1.7 million.

If we look at the top 1 per cent where, again in round numbers, we have 500,000 people we see from Table 8.1 that the threshold income for entering the top 1 per cent is, with a Paretian slope parameter of 1.6, US$ (2011 PPP) 137,322 and an average income for the top 1 per cent of US$ (20111 PPP) 363,547. These numbers accord very closely with the threshold and average numbers shown in Figure 8.6 which were obtained from the World Wealth and Income Data. The advantage of the procedure shown in Table 8.1 is that we can look in detail at the incomes of the super-rich which are hidden in any of our usual data sources, either because the surveys are too small to cover this small number of people or, in the case of tax data, where confidentiality requirements prevent the degree of detail we have given in the Table.

Table 8.1. The Incomes of the Super-Rich in the UK in 2014 in (2011 PPP US$)

Rank	Slope unity	Slope 1.5	Slope 1.6	Slope 1.7
1	500 million	500 million	500 million	500 million
2	250 million	315 million	324 million	333 million
3	167 million	240 million	252 million	262 million
4	125 million	198 million	210 million	221 million
60	8.3 million	33 million	39 million	45 million
100	5.0 million	23 million	28 million	33 million
600	833,333	7.0 million	9.2 million	12 million
2,000	250,000	3.1 million	4.3 million	5.7 million
15,000	33,333	822,000	1.2 million	1.7 million
50,000	10,000	368,400	578,248	860,736
500,000	1,000	79,400	137,000	222,000
Average income of the top 0.1 per cent	114,000	1.1 million	1.5 million	2.1 million
Average income of the top 1 per cent	13,700	235,663	363,547	537,611

$$rank = (y^{max})^{\lambda/y^\lambda}$$

$$rank = ((y^{max})^{\lambda/rank})^{1/\lambda}$$

Table 8.1 is a big step towards our goal of linking the richest of the rich to the poorest of the poor. We still have some way to go as the UK is by no means the country with the richest billionaires. The data presented in Table 8.1 is intended to illustrate the importance of this Paretian slope as it shows the implication for the distribution of income among the super-rich as that slope increases. The higher the slope the less the extent of inequality among the super-rich. As we move across the Table we see that incomes fall at a slower rate and once we reach a slope of 1.6 we can square the income of the richest person, inferred from their wealth, with average and threshold incomes obtained from the actual tax data and reported in the World Wealth and Income Data.

While the top 1 per cent are referred to as the super-rich, what Table 8.1 shows is that entering even the top 0.1 per cent with an income of US$

(2011 PPP) 659,202 is a very modest income compared to those at the very top of the distribution. That is, strange to say, the consequence of the Paretian distribution so both where that distribution comes from and what affects its slope are crucial questions for understanding how we reduce a level of inequality which, as shown in Table 8.1, will appear to most as grotesque.

As we have already noted, the UK is not the country with the richest people by any means so if we want to know the extent of these pluto-cratic levels of income we need to look across the world and, in the next section, we present the data for the US and China, the two countries with the most billionaires in the world with, in 2014, 528 and 193, respectively.

The Super-Rich in the US and China

We proceed as we did with the UK and show the distribution of income where we impute the income of the richest person in each country. For China the richest billionaire has a larger fortune than the richest person in the UK if we use market US$ to compare them, at US$15.1 billion as compared with US$13.0 billion for the UK (both for 2014). However, such comparisons are misleading due to the very different price levels between the UK and China. So, once we use PPP US dollars the value of the wealth of the richest Chinese person is US$ (2011 PPP) 26.8 billion which, assuming the 5 per cent return on capital, gives an imputed income of US$ (2011 PPP) 1,340 million. For the US the richest billionaire has a fortune of US$ (2011 PPP) 76 billion which, again on our assumption of a 5 per cent return on their wealth, translates into an income of some US$ (2011 PPP) 3.8 billion. For both China and the US this is clearly another yet higher level of income than we observed in our UK data. In Figure 8.7 we show threshold and average incomes for both the top 1 per cent and the top 0.1 per cent for these two countries.

In Table 8.2 we proceed, as we did in Table 8.1, to show the distribution of incomes among these super-rich individuals. We have experimented with different values of the Paretian slope and for both countries a value of 1.55 produces results which provide a close fit for the top 0.1 per cent for both countries. To see this note that for the US there are 235,000 individuals in the top 0.1 per cent so we see from the first columns of Table 8.2 that the entry level is imputed to be US$ (2011 PPP) 1.3 million and the average level of income 3.6 million. For China there are just over one million individuals in the top 0.1 per cent and we see from Column (2) of Table 8.2 that the threshold level of income is US$ (2011 PPP) 173,704 and the average level of income US$ (2011 PPP) 486,664. These numbers match very closely the threshold and average for these two countries from the World Wealth and Income Data shown in Figure 8.7.

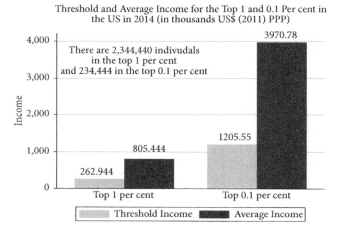

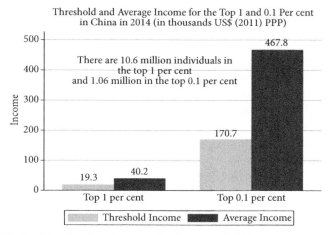

Figure 8.7. Looking for the Plutocrats in the US and China
Source: See Figure 8.6.

Table 8.2. The Incomes of the Super-Rich in the US and China using a Paretian slope parameter of 1.55

	United States	China
1	3,800 million	1,340 million
2	2,430 million	857 million
3	1,871 million	660 million
4	1,554 million	548 million
100	195 million	69 million
600	61 million	22 million
2,000	28 million	10 million
15,000	7.7 million	2.7 million
50,000	3.5 million	1.3 million
235,000	1.3 million	459,092
1,060,000	511,465	173,704
2,350,000	294,725	
10,600,000		39,323
Average income of the top 0.1 per cent	3.6 million	486,664
Average income of the top 1 per cent	826,923	110,533

Relatively Poor Billionaires: The Range of the Paretian Slope

In the last section we have shown for three countries how an assumption about the slope of the Paretian distribution allows us to impute the income of the richest people in those countries. It is an assumption, but when we look at what we know from the World Wealth and Income Data source, we see that the averages and threshold numbers given there match closely to values of the Paretian slope of between 1.5 and 1.6. In Chapter 10 we will return to these billionaires to consider their total wealth and where it comes from. However, here our purpose is to highlight the implications of the slope and the factors that drive market inequality.

We bring together the log normal distribution of incomes for the whole sample and for the top 1 per cent for the ONS household data in Figure 8.8. The difference in the slope of the Paretian function is readily apparent. For the top 1 per cent it is close to linear while for the whole sample it has a distinct curve. Recall that by using logs we can interpret the Paretian slope as telling as how fast for any given percentage change in income the percentage change in rank occurs. The change in rank being the probability of observing someone richer than you. So, the steeper that line the faster the probability

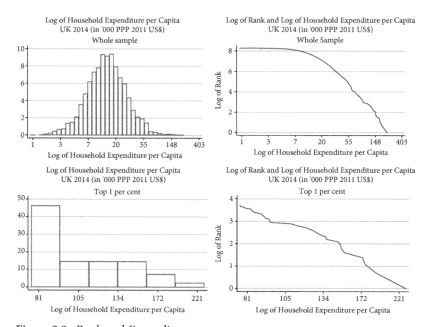

Figure 8.8. Rank and Expenditure

Note: On the horizontal axis the logs have been converted to actual expenditures per capita.

Source: As for Figure 8.1.

of observing someone richer than you falls. In other words, the less inequality there will be in the data.

If the value of the slope is about 1.6 then, as our Tables have shown, there will be a lot of relatively poor billionaires. It is this spreading out of income at the top which generates the sensational income differences that are such a vivid part of the popular perception of inequality.

Growth and the Paretian Distribution

While the income of almost everybody in an economy can be shown to fit into the log normal distribution which 'random' growth will produce, we have shown that at the top end this pattern breaks down and is replaced by a Paretian distribution and it is this distribution which shows the extremes of incomes in now-rich countries. So, two obvious questions that arise from the patterns shown above—what can be creating the Paretian distribution and what can change the slope?

One answer is that it comes from the log normal distribution where something stops the pattern of income from that distribution continuing indefinitely. Given that the data point to the Paretian distribution being a good description of incomes for very high incomes then death would solve our problem, albeit it might seem a little callously. The idea is simply that the top end growth of income is driven by those who combine ability and luck in well-above-average quantities. Once their luck changes their incomes fall and they 'die', possibly simply in the sense they exit from the high end of the data. This idea is developed formally in a paper by Charles Jones and Jihee Kim, 'A Schumpeterian Model of Top Income Inequality'.[1] The reference is to Schumpeter's idea of 'creative destruction' by which more successful firms and enterprises drive out less successful ones. It is an idea popular in business schools, although less popular in businesses as few like being destroyed, however 'creative' the destruction. In their model 'heterogeneous entrepreneurs', broadly interpreted, exert effort to generate exponential growth in their incomes, which tends to raise inequality. Creative destruction by outside innovators restrains this expansion and induces top incomes to obey a Pareto distribution. In their model, the two factors that are going to matter for the shape of this Paretian distribution are the 'death' rate, that is how many entrepreneurs fail, and the growth rate of income.

Mr Darcy and the Super-Rich

We began this chapter with a question as to whether a contemporary Mr Darcy would count as a plutocrat. Our investigation suggests not, with a contemporary income of under £1 million. If we up this income to about £8 million (say US$ (2011 PPP) of 10 million), thus retaining his relative position in society, then probably yes. From Table 8.1 only a few hundred people in the UK would earn more. If we wished to confine our definition of plutocrats to persons with wealth of US$1 billion or more, then again with our 5 per cent return on capital, their incomes would exceed US$50 million. So even a Mr Darcy, who retained his relative position in society, would not make it into that exclusive club of plutocrats.

---

[1] Jones and Kim (2018).

Appendix: A More Formal Presentation
of the Paretian Distribution

To see how the distributions are derived we need to state Pareto's law slightly more formally.

Vilfredo Pareto found that the upper-tail distribution of the number of people with an income or wealth S greater than a large x is proportional to $1/x^\lambda$ for some positive number λ; that is, it can be written:

$$P(S > x) = kx^{-\lambda}$$

In Figure 8.4 we have approximated that probability as i/n where i is the rank of the person and n is the number of people being ranked. We can then use our Paretian distribution to tell us what these probabilities will be:

$$\frac{i}{n} = kS_i^{-\lambda}$$

As already noted the last person has $i = n$ so probability is 1 and the highest ranked person is $1/n$ which provided n is large enough can be approximated as zero. Let's take a special, but very important, case of the Pareto distribution where $\lambda = 1$. Then what the distribution says is that an individual's rank in the listing we have made will be proportional to $1/S_i$ where S_i is the level of income. We can write this as:

$$i = \frac{nk}{S_i}$$

If we take US$80 billion as being the wealth of the richest person in the world and still assuming our 5 per cent return that gives them an income of US$4 billion. What would the income of those below them look like if we had a distribution like in Figure 8.4? First, we have to set it up so that the person with an income of US$4 billion has rank 1 so we have:

$$Rank = \frac{4}{Income}$$

That just says that as US$4 billion is the income of the richest person they will be first as:

$$Rank = \frac{4}{Income} = 1 \; if \; Income = 4$$

Now with this Paretian distribution and our unity slope we can work out what the income of the richest people in the world will be from the rule that

$$Income = \frac{4}{Rank}$$

That gives us the first column in Table 8.2. The other columns come from noting that

$$i = \frac{nk}{S_i^{\lambda}}$$

What this will mean is that the higher is λ, which is the slope of the line shown in Figure 8.4, the less inequality there is as incomes will decline more slowly with rank as will be seen in Tables 8.1 and 8.2.

9

Sources of Increasing Inequality

Earnings of the Relatively Unskilled

Where Does Inequality Come From?

In political rhetoric it is often argued that the rich are rich because the poor are poor. Such arguments can be found when analysing inequality within countries and inequality between countries. An example of an argument along these lines for inequality between countries can be found in Jason Hickel's *The divide—A brief guide to global inequality and its solutions* which sees poverty as being created by the trading relationships between rich and poor countries. That countries become rich by making others poor is indeed a major theme in discussions of the impact of colonialism on now-poor countries. Inequality within countries is often interpreted as either an inevitable consequence of capitalism or, of current political relevance, the result of a perversion of rules by the elite within rich countries to benefit the elite. This is in essence the argument advanced by Joseph Stiglitz in his book *The Great Divide* where the divide to which he is referring is within America, as distinct from the divide between countries.

There are two points to be kept in mind on these issues. The first is that while trade may increase income its effects are one-off, you don't get sustained rises in income from trade by itself. For that you need investment in new capital and infrastructure. The second point is that in a growing economy—and the option of economies growing in a sustained way has been available since the industrial revolution of the late eighteenth century—all *can* gain, there is no need for the rich to get richer at the expense of the poor. The stress on the word *can* in that last sentence is important. How growth impacts on the poor can differ greatly over time and across countries. Joseph Stiglitz's argument is that there is nothing inevitable about the rise of inequality in the US; it is due to a set of policy choices made, he argues, by the 1 per cent to benefit the 1 per cent.

Changes in inequality come about as a result of differential rates of growth of income for the rich and for the poor. The key fact we have sought to highlight is the role of the price of relatively unskilled labour in effecting how growth impacts on both the absolutely, and relatively, poor and thus on inequality. This important mechanism can be seen most clearly in the case of the UK and the US where sustained growth started first and has continued for longest. The rise in this price since the nineteenth century, and its acceleration in the first half of the twentieth century, is a key part of the mechanism by which inequality fell rapidly in those two countries until the 1970s.

The rather remarkable fact is that in now-rich countries in the first three quarters of the twentieth century the poor saw faster rates of growth of their incomes than the rich. Where this pattern has gone into reverse, particularly in the US, the rich have raced away. We want to understand why. So, the answer to our question as to where inequality comes from is twofold. Growth of unskilled wages has slowed, growth of incomes among the rich have accelerated. In this chapter we want to investigate the reason for the first of these sources of increased inequality.

Earnings for the Unskilled and Labour Productivity in the US and the UK

We have argued that the key to success in reducing inequality by so much in the period up to the 1970s was the rise in the earnings of relatively unskilled labour. The underlying factor that drove earnings growth in the past was labour productivity—the amount of output in the economy produced by labour. The link is, or ought to be, very direct. The more productive is labour the more it can be paid and the more it can consume. In Figure 9.1 we show the patterns of growth for labour productivity and earnings for both the UK and the US.

The top part of Figure 9.1 shows the data in level while the bottom part uses logs. The use of logs enables us to see, from the slope of the curve, how growth rates of earnings and labour productivity compare. In the bottom part of the figure we also show a quadratic fitted line, that is a line which allows for a curve so we can see if the growth rate is declining over this time period. As the bottom right-hand chart shows this is dramatically so for the US. Equally striking is that a similar pattern is not apparent in the UK although it is true there is some decline in the growth rate it is very modest compared to what has happened in the US. Once again, any notion that the US and UK are similarly performing economies is dispelled by this figure.

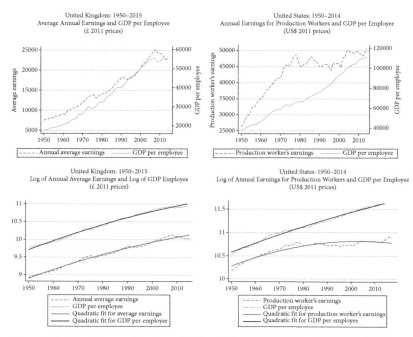

Figure 9.1. Earnings and Labour Productivity in the UK and the US: 1950 to 2014/15

Sources: UK Earnings data from Gregory Clark, What Were the British Earnings and Prices Then? (New Series), MeasuringWorth, 2016, URL: http://www.measuringworth.com. Updated from ONS data. US Earnings from Lawrence H. Officer and Samuel H. Williamson Annual Wages in the United States, 1774-Present, URL: http://www.measuringworth.com/uswages/. The productivity data is from PENN World Tables 9.0.

America is exceptional, in this case in divorcing productivity growth from earnings growth. The evidence points to the UK being far more successful than the US in translating its productivity growth into low-skill earnings rises, at least up to the financial crash.

However, has the UK caught the US disease in that are there signs this relative success of the UK is failing? In Figure 9.2 we look in more detail at the earnings and productivity numbers for the period after 2000. In the period following the financial crash of 2008–09 the UK looks even more extreme than the US with a period of rising labour productivity coinciding with falling average wages. As Figure 9.2 brings out rather dramatically, the financial crash is invisible in the US productivity data and very apparent in the UK data.

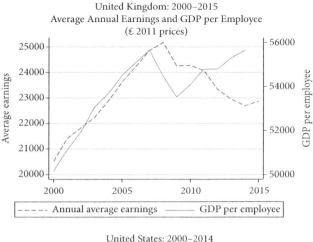

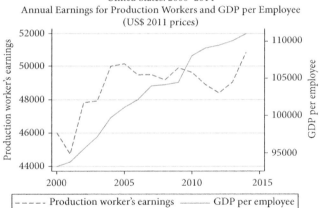

Figure 9.2. Earnings and Labour Productivity in the UK and the US after the Financial Crash

Source: As for Figure 9.1.

In the US the financial crisis was produced by a housing crisis and in turn caused one, but the fall in the growth rate of unskilled earnings and its divorce from the underlying growth rate of productivity long preceded the financial crisis. That was not the case in the UK, the labour market which seemed to be working well up to 2008–09 changed radically. After a very brief rise in unemployment the previous rise in employment continued but now de-linked from rising wages.

The patterns of GDP and employment growth which underlie the changes in productivity also are quite different across the two countries as is shown in Figure 9.3. The fall in GDP was very similar in both countries, about 5 per cent, but in the UK falls in employment were more modest while in the US they were much greater. The result was falling labour productivity in the UK and rises in the US.

So the answer to our question seems to be no: the UK has not caught the US disease, but it does seem to have caught one possibly worse. Not stagnating wage levels but falling ones.

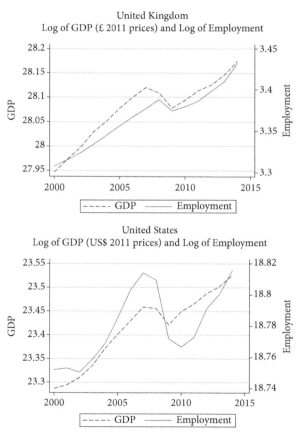

Figure 9.3. GDP and Employment in the UK and the US: 2000–14
Source: As for Figure 9.1.

The falling wages are the background to the decision to leave the EU in the Brexit Referendum held in June 2016. While explicit discussions of the causes were largely absent, one issue dominated the campaign and arguably was a key element that swung the final vote—immigration. That the relatively high level of low-skill immigration from the EU threatened British workers' living standards was one of the most powerful arguments underlying the leave campaign. Indeed, Alan Milburn has argued that the politics of Britain has come to be dominated by three "Is"—identity, immigration, and inequality.

At the time of the Brexit Referendum median wages were lower than they were more than a decade earlier. Figure 9.4 links these median wages to EU immigration.

The period of this fall in median wages saw increasing EU immigration. The decision to hold a referendum, knowing the political toxicity of the migration question, with this background of falling wages was an act of political suicide on the part of the then- prime minister David Cameron.

Figure 9.4 alerts us to the problem posed by thinking that migrants are the source of the problem. Migration was rising in a sustained way during the period when both average and median wages were rising rapidly. In

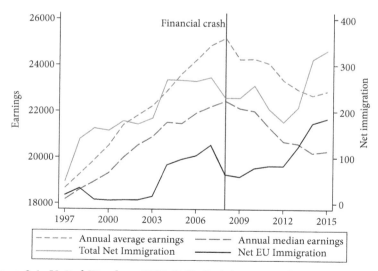

Figure 9.4. United Kingdom, 1997–2015: Real Average and Median Annual Earnings (both in £ (2011) prices) and Net Immigration (in Thousands)
Source: ONS data for immigration and earning.

fact, the fall in wages from 2008 to 2012 coincides with a fall in migration. Such facts matter little in the heat of political debate, but such correlations are uninformative as to how migration and wages are linked. Low-skill immigration is seen as a threat to the wages of the unskilled. It is quite possible unskilled wages would have risen more without the migration. We need some way of isolating the effect of migration on wages.

Falling UK Wages: Did the Immigrants Do It?

There are few subjects more toxic in public debate than immigration and it is an area where the gap between what is popularly believed and what the evidence shows is as great as it is possible to imagine. In political discourse it seems to the average elector that an inflow of low-skill immigrants must lower wages, put pressure on schools and housing, and generally make life more difficult for the natives. In fact, none of those outcomes are necessary and the evidence shows that the effect on wages at least is, on average, positive. We will examine that evidence below but why may the apparently obvious belief that more immigrants means more pressure on housing and schools and lower wages be wrong? There are two missing elements. The first is that insofar as the incoming labour works it produces more output and income. So, more output makes possible more houses and schools if the government wants them. The second is that more labour may make profitable more investment so, with rising investment, wages can rise.

Now, of course, it is possible the immigrants do not work and it is possible that the new labour is not matched by increased investment so wages do fall. Even if they do not fall on average, they may not rise for all. It is this relative wage effect, how big have been the rises for the well-off relative to the unskilled, which has motivated a language of the left-behinds. Yes, unskilled labour helps the skilled but hurts the unskilled. If it does by how much is the crucial question and how easily can other policies compensate? These are empirical issues we need to investigate. We are going to look at the evidence for the period in the UK from 1997 to 2005 when, as Figure 9.4 shows, total immigration rose rapidly. In fact, the level of 2005 was not to be reached again until a decade later.

The most comprehensive evidence for the UK we have is in a paper by Dustmann et al. (2013). This paper documents a very important fact about the immigration which occurred in the UK from 1997 to 2005. On average the skill mix of immigrants was *higher* than that of natives. In fact, substantially higher. The authors identify three levels of education. Those with 'High' education left full-time education at age 21 or later; those with 'Intermediate' education left full-time education between age 17 and 20 (included); and finally, those with 'Low' education left full-time education not after age 16 or never had full-time education. In 2005 45.4 per cent of recent immigrants had a 'High' level of education as compared with less than half of natives of whom only 16 per cent had this level. At the other end of the scale migrants with 'Low' education were only 14 per cent of migrants while for natives the share was 58 per cent. So, the data present a puzzle. The belief that the migrants had low skills in terms of education levels is quite without empirical basis. How come then they were regarded as a threat to low-skilled natives? The answer supplied by the authors is that while their educational qualifications were higher than the natives, the migrants worked much lower down the occupational ladder than those natives with similar levels of education.

The wage gap between the highest occupation identified by the authors (higher managerial and professional) and the lowest (routine operations) was nearly three times—£18.92 per hour as compared with £6.74 (those are 2005 prices). However, while only 1.2 per cent of natives with 'High' education worked in routine occupations just over 12 per cent of recent migrants with 'High' education did. Among migrants with 'Low' education—although they were a much smaller percentage than natives—they were far more concentrated in routine occupations than natives. So, the 'picture' the critics of migration painted of low-skilled migrants posing a threat to native workers was correct—not because they had low educational levels but because, for all educational levels, the migrants were much more likely to be in lower-paid occupational work. Anecdotal examples would be the graduate being an Amazon delivery driver or a cleaner, and strawberry pickers all being migrants.

Given this pattern asking how low-educated migrants compete with native low-educated workers would clearly be misleading as those in routine occupations are actually competing with much higher-educated migrants. Allowing for this the authors ask how migrants within these occupational groups impact on wages across the wage distribution. They find the impact is very different. They find a pattern of effects whereby immigration depresses wages below the 20th percentile of the wage distribution but leads to slight wage increases in the upper part of the wage distribution. This pattern mirrors the evidence on the location of immigrants in the wage distribution.

The real hourly wage increased over this period, from 1997 to 2005, by 18p (4.28 per cent) per year at the 1st decile, by 25p (3.25 per cent) per year at the median, and by 53p (3.18 per cent) per year at the 9th decile (in 2005 terms). Notice that this data for hourly earnings is consistent with two pieces of evidence we have already presented. This is the period of the Blair New Labour government and we showed in Figure 2.3 the decrease in the dispersion of wages after the introduction of the minimum wage. This is reflected in the numbers here, which have a different source, showing that, in percentage terms, wages rose fastest for the lowest paid. We also showed in Figure 7.5, that over the period of the New Labour government both original (that is incomes from the market before taxes and transfers), and disposable, incomes grew faster for the bottom quintile than for the top quintile. So, by how much did immigration change these numbers?

To answer that question we need to know how much a change in the immigrant–native working-age population ratio changed in wages. The finding in the Dustmann et al. (2013) paper is that each 1 per cent increase in the immigrant–native working-age population ratio led over the period studied to a 0.5 per cent decrease in wages at the 1st decile, a 0.6 per cent increase in wages at the median, and a 0.4% increase in wages at the 9th decile. The average increase in the immigrant–native working-age population ratio over the period considered was about 0.35 per cent per year. So, the 1st decile would have lost 0.75 pence per hour, the median would have gained 1.64 pence per hour and the 9th decile would have gained 2.9 pence per hour.[1]

So, it is true, unskilled immigration did hurt the unskilled, not because most immigrants were unskilled but because they worked further down the occupational ladder. The effects though were very small, less than 1 pence per hour or, for a worker on 35 hours a week, less than £14 per year. Indeed, even at the top the gains are extremely modest at £53 per year. If these numbers are even roughly right, they pose a big question. Why are the effects so small and how does immigration benefit the economy? The answer is that the economy is bigger as a result of the immigration and the determinants of wages are related, not to immigration, but to how far the increased income made available by the immigration is used to enhance the productivity of labour generally. In the next section we will show that it

---

[1] The 1st decile would have had, using those numbers, $0.35 \times 0.5 \times 4.34 = 0.75$ pence per hour lower incomes. The median $0.35 \times 0.6 \times 7.78 = 1.64$ pence per hour more. The 9th decile would have been $0.35 \times 0.4 \times 21.12 = 2.9$ pence per hour more.

is the collapse of that productivity in the aftermath of the financial crash that underlies the collapse in wages shown in Figure 9.4.

So Why Did Earnings Fall in the UK after the Financial Crash?

In the UK, unlike in the US, there is a very close link between labour productivity—that is the amount of output per employee produced in the economy—and wages. While the fall in labour productivity is well known, and well documented, its causes remain an open question. Broadly there are two possible ways we will see a decline in labour productivity. The first is that the amount of capital, or other inputs, with which the worker is employed declines. The second is that TFP declines, that is back to our mysterious X factor introduced in Chapter 1 by which the output produced by all inputs declines. Both TFP and higher amounts of capital per worker have, in the past, been key mechanisms for raising labour productivity.

In fact, we have evidence that at the time of the financial crisis the level of TFP in the UK economy fell substantially in the service sector which is by far the largest part of the UK economy—this is documented in a paper by Richard Harris and John Moffat *The UK Productivity Puzzle, 2008–2012*. Now a fall in TFP does not necessarily translate into a fall in labour productivity, which is what is relevant for wages, and that study shows that, for both manufacturing and services, there were substantial falls in labour productivity—of the order of 20 per cent. For manufacturing it is the fall in inputs, for services the fall in TFP, which accounts for the decline. This timing of this fall in labour productivity coincides exactly with the timing of the fall in both average and median wages.

Given the relative size of the service sector in the UK it is the fall in both TFP and labour productivity in this sector that seems the most promising explanation for the falls in wages. That, of course, simply pushes our question one step back as to what can explain those changes. There are two broad classes of explanation that have been advanced. One is that there was, following the financial crash, an increase in low-quality labour in the service sector. The second possible source of the problem is the macro policies pursued after the crash, which reduced both public expenditure and raised taxes. Such policies are usually summarized as 'austerity' but that is very misleading as public sector finances can be balanced by growth and cutting expenditure, particularly capital ones, can be self-defeating.

The second is a demand-side explanation, the first points to supply side problems in the economy.

These two classes of explanation for this outcome reflect views on the left and right of the political spectrum. The left-wing view is that the fall in demand which occurred with the crisis ensured productivity would fall as—essentially—the ability of firms to produce is constrained by the level of demand they face. The right-wing view is the mirror image of the left, that there are fundamental problems on the supply side and if they are not addressed productivity cannot rise. Such a view would point to the collapse in productivity in the low knowledge-intensive part of the service sector and see the problem there as the result of increasing employment of low-quality labour. Jobs were to be had but the skills of those employed made product-ivity lower and lower wages inevitable followed.

Political battles along these lines have been, and no doubt will continue to be, fought across almost all countries. Recent examples include the refusal of the Republican-controlled congress to allow further fiscal expansion at the time of the 2008–09 crisis. Their demands for fiscal rectitude were forgotten with the advent of the Trump presidency which can be seen as an experi-ment in carrying out a left-wing economic prospectus—at least as far as it implicitly endorses the view that fiscal stimulus can raise growth rates. A counter view from Europe is the insistence of Germany within the Eurozone of fiscal balance where moves in late 2018 by the Italian govern-ment to run increased deficits are meeting objections—Germany is essen-tially asserting the view that such fiscal stimulus will be futile. In the UK what 'austerity' has come to mean is reducing the budget deficit by a combination of increased taxation and reduced public expenditure when growth is low. The scale of the collapse in growth in the UK since the financial crisis was highlighted in Figure 3.4 and Table 3.1.

As has often been pointed out, the most striking example which supports the 'left' view is the experience of the US during the Second World War when, again as Figure 3.4 and Table 3.1 showed, the US grew faster than it was to grow after 1950. Generalizing from this experience though might mislead. When the US entered the Second World War it was preceded by a decade when output was arguably far below potential. Further, technology was intensive in the use of relatively unskilled and Robert Gordon (2016) argues that the 1930s had seen a series of innovations in technology just waiting to be fully exploited. Wages also grew strongly over the period and this was helped, Gordon argues, by the strong unions in place at the end of the 1930s. Take away those factors and would expansionary fiscal policy work? Those on the left are sure it would, those on the right are sure it would not. The implication of the Gordon study is that such faith in either view is misplaced. Sometimes it will and sometimes it will not.

While how the productivity problem in the UK can be addressed remains an open question, there is little doubt it is by far the most important factor underlying the collapse in real wages after the financial crisis. As we showed in Figure 9.1, the problem in the US is quite different. The stagnation in real wages preceded the financial crash by decades. Indeed, it would be more accurate to say that the stagnation in wages was a cause of the financial crash rather than caused by it.

US Manufacturing Employment and Wages: Enter the Chinese

Can the wage rates of relatively unskilled workers be increased substantially is the key unanswered question facing both the UK and the US. While we have focused on those two countries, as very long runs of comparative data are available, it is one being asked across most of the now-rich countries. We need though to beware of assuming patterns are similar across countries—in fact, as we have shown for the UK and the US, the patterns of real wage growth have been very different. We need to be able to explain when unskilled wages stagnate, as was the case in the US, and when they rise, and fall, with rising, and falling, labour productivity.

Further, a fact, which understandably does not feature in domestic political debates, is that wages for the relatively unskilled in now-rich countries are very high relative to those in now-poor countries. This is particularly true for the US. Just how high these wages are compared with those in now-poor countries should be a puzzle. Insofar as it is the openness to trade that is driving the wages of the unskilled, we should expect that gap to be falling and quite possibly falling rapidly. Work on the US has enabled us to see how far this perceived threat to the wages of the unskilled is an accurate one.

In Figure 9.5 we show the trends for Chinese imports into the US and manufacturing employment. The left-hand axis shows the import penetration ratio, that is the share of Chinese imports in total US spending. This ratio increased from 0.6 per cent in 1991 to 4.6 per cent in 2007. The right-hand axis shows the ratio of manufacturing to total population and this fell from 12.6 per cent to 8.4 per cent.

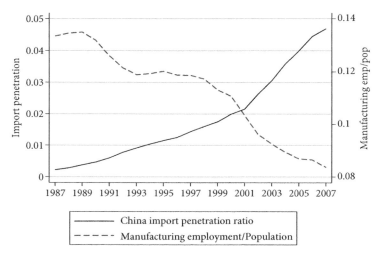

Figure 9.5. Chinese Exports and Manufacturing Employment in the US
Source: Data from the paper by Autor et al. (2013).

When you see the kind of trends shown in the figure it is very easy to conclude that the two are related. On the face of it the figures seem to speak for themselves. The spectacular growth of the Chinese economy has been associated with a large rise in Chinese imports into the US and a large trade imbalance for the US relative to China, implying that the growth of Chinese imports into the US has not been matched by an expansion of US exports to China. However, before we agree with President Trump that the Chinese are responsible for the decline in manufacturing jobs in the US, we need to consider other possible reasons for what we observe. After all, manufacturing jobs disappeared in the UK economy long before the rise of the Chinese economy. A shift out of manufacturing into services may reflect changing demand, it may reflect changes in technology that have reduced the demand for labour in manufacturing. In short, that Chinese exports rose and manufacturing jobs declined in the US over the period from the 1990s, and that this process may well have accelerated after 2000, does not show in any convincing way that the two phenomena are related. How can we get some convincing evidence that the two are in fact related?

In fact, exactly this question—namely how to establish if Chinese exports did lead to a decline in jobs and wages in the US—was asked in a paper by Autor et al. (2013) and we are going to present their evidence to show how it is possible to check if what might at first appear obvious is in fact so.

The underlying reason why one cannot impute any relationship between the two variables of interest is that other factors may explain the correlation. So, the task of the researcher is to find a way of comparing two sectors, one of which was subject to competition from Chinese exports and one which was not—or to a lesser degree—and ask if the two sectors saw differences in the decline in their employment. What the researchers do is to compare different labour markets in the US which have been subject to very different levels of competition. They argue that these local labour markets defined by 'commuting zones' (CZ) can be treated like mini-countries within a country so that impacts that spread out across the whole country are limited. They then ask if the local labour markets that have seen a lot of competition saw declines in employment and wages relative to those that did not.

The researchers take two sub-periods, one from 1990 to 2000 and the second from 2000 to 2007. Over these two sub-periods they calculate the change in Chinese import penetration and ask how it affects a range of outcomes in the different regional labour markets. These outcomes include both manufacturing and non-manufacturing wages, employment effects and increases in unemployment and transfer payments. Over the whole period they consider from 1990 to 2007 their measures of import competition, which is imports from China to the US per worker, increased from US$290 to US$3,580, an increase of more than 12 times. This increase in imports from a low wage economy was without precedent in US history so the interest, and concern, it raised was not in any way surprising. In Figure 9.6 below we show how the measure of import penetration links to the change in manufacturing employment. In the top panel we show all the data, while in the bottom panel we show the data confined to labour markets where import penetration was less than US$15,000 which we can see from the top panel is where most of our observations lie. We have also drawn a line in the figure which shows how the change in import is related to the change in the manufacturing employment.

While the figure shows only that there is a correlation, the researchers go further and argue convincingly that there is a causal relationship between Chinese imports and manufacturing employment in the US over this period. Their calculations

> conservatively estimate that Chinese import competition explains 16 per cent of the US manufacturing employment decline between 1990 and 2000, 26 per cent of the decline between 2000 and 2007, and 21 per cent of the decline over the full period. For the mainland US working-age population,

these estimates imply a supply-shock driven net reduction in US manufacturing employment of 548,000 workers between 1990 and 2000 and a further reduction of 982,000 workers between 2000 and 2007.

Autor et al. (2013, p. 2140)

They also find that local labour markets that are exposed to rising low-income-country imports due to China's rising competitiveness experience

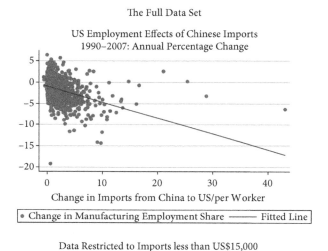

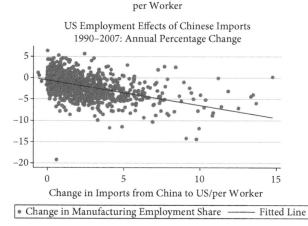

Figure 9.6. How much did Imports from China reduce US Employment?
Source: Data from the paper by Autor et al. (2013).

increased unemployment, decreased labour-force participation, increased use of disability and other transfer benefits and lowered wages.

By contrast, Chinese import exposure significantly reduces earnings in sectors outside manufacturing. Nonmanufacturing wages fall by 0.76 per cent for a $1,000 increase in Chinese import exposure per worker, an effect that is comparable for college and noncollege workers. This result suggests that a negative shock to local manufacturing reduces the demand for local non-traded services while increasing the available supply of workers, creating downward pressure on wages in the sector. The results of this section demonstrate that an increase in the exposure of local US labour markets to Chinese imports stemming from rising Chinese comparative advantage leads to a significant decline in employment and wages in local markets.

While the rapid rise of Chinese imports has been a highly visible aspect of changes in world trade of the last thirty years, equally contentious has been the issue of offshoring by which 'American jobs' are transported to low-income countries, of which China is one but there are others too. A paper which addresses the effects of this offshoring is by Ebenstein et al. (2014). They tackle the question as to how far offshoring affected American workers by looking at the wages of workers in industries most affected by offshoring. They find that there is a crucial difference between the effect on the sector in which you work, that is manufacturing or services, and the occupation you work in. Similar to the work already discussed on the effects of Chinese imports, these authors find no effect from offshoring, or imports, on wages in manufacturing. However, when they look at the occupation in which the worker is employed across all sectors they do find an adverse effect from both offshoring and imports.

In the first row of column 5, the coefficient on low-income affiliate employment suggests that a 10% increase in employment offshored within an occupation is associated with a 0.4% wage reduction for US workers. For workers in the most routine occupations, we find that a 10% increase in low-income affiliate employment abroad is associated with a 0.7% decline in domestic wages, whereas workers in less routine occupations were largely unaffected by offshoring. Although the magnitude of the effect is small, the results are consistent with an interpretation that workers in low-income locations perform the same tasks that low-skilled workers perform in the United States and are therefore substitutes for workers in the United States.   Ebenstein et al. (2014, p. 589)

One explanation for this pattern is that the most productive workers retain their jobs in manufacturing, thus biasing the estimates against finding a reduction in manufacturing wages. An alternative possibility, suggested in a paper by Bloom et al. (2016) is that manufacturing plants react to import competition by accelerating technological and organizational innovations that increase productivity and may raise wages.

Stagnant Earnings in the US and Immigration

The evidence from trade suggests that the most important impact is not on manufacturing wages but on wages outside the manufacturing sector and in particular is concentrated in areas where work is of routine tasks. While workers in foreign countries compete in this area through trade, the other equally contentious political issue is that this is exactly the area where it is believed immigrants compete too. In the US immigration has been an even more contentious issue than in the UK, both currently and historically. While for the UK there is some consensus, at least among economists, that the effects on wages are small, this is not the case for the US.

In one of the possibly few areas where popular sentiment coincides with basic economics, it seems obvious to most electors that an increase in the supply of unskilled labour will reduce the price of native labour. Indeed, this is the economically elementary proposition that the demand curve (that is how labour demand is affected by price) slopes down—the title of a paper by the economist George Borjas (2003) who has consistently argued that the evidence does point to an adverse effect of immigration on the wages of natives. In seeking to establish the impact of immigrants in his paper, to show demand curves do slope down Borjas examines the relative wages of workers and immigrants, in particular skill groups where skills are defined by education and work experience. He then uses data drawn from the population census and population surveys to create a data set for these relative wages by skill for the period from 1960 to 2000. He argues that the data shows a significant and large adverse effect of immigrants on native wages. A 10 per cent supply shock, namely an immigrant flow that increases the number of migrants in the skill group by 10 per cent, reduced weekly earnings by about 4 per cent. Over the period he is considering—from 1960 to 2000—in some skill categories the increase in the migrant share was as much as 40 per cent, so the numbers imply a large reduction in the wages of natives competing with migrants.

The Borjas study was a pioneering one in that it showed the need to think which types of workers the migrants would be competing with. That is also a theme of the study of UK immigration we considered above. It is not, however, the only problem that arises in seeking to establish the effects of immigration. Borjas seeks to isolate the effect of immigration by holding everything else constant. But what if immigrants do reduce wages initially that may well lead to increased investment. The period of the Borjas study—1960 to 2000—is a period when wages for the relatively unskilled rose very rapidly. It may of course be the case that wages would have risen even faster with lower immigration but it does suggest that other factors affecting wages may be as, or more, important than migration or indeed trade.

It is not always understood that the US grew to be such a rich country not because its GDP per capita grew particularly rapidly but because its population did. If we look back to Figure 3.2, we see that population growth was far faster than in the UK, in fact more than three times as fast. Trend growth rates of population in the US after 1700 were 1.7 per cent a year while in the UK the growth rate was 0.5 per cent per year. It is true too that GDP per capita growth was higher in the US at 1.6 per cent as against 1.2 per cent in the UK. Over the 300 years plus since 1700 a difference in per capita growth rates of 0.4 per cent per annum matters, but not nearly as much as a difference of 1.2 per cent per annum in population growth. As we have seen this rapid growth of population, fuelled in substantial part by immigration, saw rapid rises in the wages of unskilled labour. To understand the effects of immigration we need to understand what else changes as well. In the historical case of the US it was the expansion across a continent and rapid growth in capital and TFP.

Sectoral Shifts, Earnings, Productivity Collapses, and Inequality

The evidence for the US points to lower earnings not being due to falling manufacturing wages as a result of either imports or offshoring but to the shifts out of manufacturing jobs. As the data also show, factors other than trade were more important in effecting this shift. The factors that have moved both the UK and the US from ones where manufacturing is a relatively important source of employment to ones here it is relatively unimportant operate both on the supply and demand side. Changes in technology are the most important factor on the supply side as income grow there is a shift in demand to service based industries. For earnings, and the implications for inequality, it is the labour market consequences of this shift that matters.

Given the differences in labour market outcomes, the implication is that the UK was, until the financial crash, much more successful than the US in enabling incomes to grow in the service sector. One conspicuous difference between the two countries was in policy towards the minimum wage whose introduction in the UK in 1998 we have shown to have had a major impact on raising earnings at the bottom. It is also the case that productivity and income growth over the period from 1977 to 2016 was higher in the UK than the US—see Table 7.2. After 1990 inequality in the UK stopped rising while it rose continuously in the US. One argument advanced by Joseph Stiglitz (2013) is that inequality can reduce growth through its effect on demand. If UK growth was more equally spread, and that impacted on earnings opportunities among the lower skilled, that could be part of the explanation for the relative success of the UK economy prior to the financial crash.

For the UK the financial crash was for all workers a watershed, for the relatively unskilled in the US a blip in long-running stagnation. For the UK, we have argued that this collapse in earnings was caused by the collapse in productivity. A collapse that led to a decline in inequality as measured by differential growth rates of incomes in the bottom and top quintiles. It was these top incomes that grew slowest—see Figure 7.5 over the period 2010 to 2016. For the US the pattern was very different with top incomes growing faster than bottom ones since 2000, albeit much slower in the period from 2008 to 2016 than in the decade before. In the next chapter we are going to look into the sources of those top incomes.

10

Sources of Income for the Plutocrats

Plutocrats as Capitalists, Workers, or Rentiers

While one engine for the decline in inequality, namely increased wages for the unskilled, seems to have stalled or gone into reverse, a motor for increased inequality seems to have revved up in the rapid increase in the number of billionaires shown in Figure 10.1.

In earlier chapters we considered if a contemporary Mr Darcy would count as a plutocrat. The answer depended on how exclusive we wished to make the club of plutocrats. However, it is clear from the novel that he did not work which is in marked contrast to some current billionaires and this shift in the sources of income for the very rich is an important part of the story of the changing sources of income shown in Thomas Piketty's (2014) work on the evolution of capital over the last 200 years. Plutocrats do not all have the same source of income and what that source is will influence how we assess the social value of their incomes. We come to that below.

So far we have focused on income, not wealth. The reason for this is that the question we have set ourselves is why those incomes can differ so much across countries and within countries. Wealth differences flow from those income differences, often for individuals from incomes earned long in the past by their ancestors. However, if we wish to consider the income of the currently super-rich, those who would undoubtedly be regarded as plutocrats, we need to turn to their current wealth. The reason is that there are so few of them as Figure 10.1 shows, only a few thousand, and we would have no chance of seeing them, albeit anonymously, in any survey. We are going to make use of the data collated by Caroline Freund and Sarah Oliver in *The Billionaire Characteristics Database* to look at the sources of the wealth of these billionaires to throw light on the sources of their incomes. As we will see those sources are diverse and that diversity matters if we wish to understand the mechanisms that create such great wealth.

In the world of early nineteenth-century Britain the income of the rich depended on their ownership of land and to a rather surprising extent access to political power (see Rubinstein, 1983). By the latter part of the century

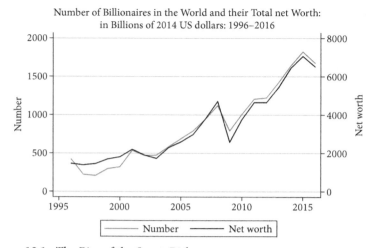

Figure 10.1. The Rise of the Super-Rich

Source: Freund and Oliver (2016), https://www.piie.com/publications/working-papers/origins-superrich-billionaire-characteristics-database.

fortunes from sources other than land were becoming important. In the US this period saw the rise of fortunes in steel, oil, and finance controlled by the plutocrats of their time—J.P. Morgan, Andrew Carnegie, Andrew W. Mellon, and John D. Rockefeller. These very rich men were termed 'robber barons' or 'captains of industry' depending on the political perspective of the commentator, but the issues raised by their extreme wealth were strikingly similar to the concerns raised by the wealth of the current members of the plutocrats club. This shift from land to industrial, commercial, and financial sources of income represented a fundamental shift for the very rich from their principal source of income being as rentiers to both the capital they created—or inherited—and their labour input into their enterprises.

We are used to thinking of capitalists as people who own capital and do not work, but employ labour which does. Indeed, such a distinction goes back to the earliest socialist thinking after the first industrial revolution. However, such a distinction is far more appropriate for those whose capital is in the form of land than for those who came to be owners of the great industrial empires at the end of the nineteenth century. Men such as J.P. Morgan, Andrew Carnegie, Andrew W. Mellon, and John D. Rockefeller clearly worked. The objection to them was not that they simply owned capital, it was to how the capital was acquired. In the case of Rockefeller by creating an effective monopoly in the ownership of oil. In the case of bankers such as J. P. Morgan in the excess profits available from their control of mammoth financial assets. These objections—made by their critics at the end of the nineteenth century—echo down to the current critics of current plutocrats.

If we ask how rich were the rich in the US at the turn of the twentieth century, compared with now, then some make it into our plutocrats club. The *New York Times* obituary referred to John D. Rockefeller as America's first billionaire. If we take 1918 as the peak of his wealth then a billion in 1918 converts to about US$17 billion in 2014 prices, well below the wealth of the richest of current billionaires, but still comfortably into the most exclusive of the club of plutocrats. Andrew Carnegie reportedly sold his company, US Steel, to J.P. Morgan for $480 million in 1901 which converts into some US$14.6 billion in 2014 prices, again comfortably into the exclusive billionaire club. Both Rockefeller and Carnegie were entirely self-made men, while J.P. Morgan and Andrew W. Mellon had more money and educational advantages.

While Mr Darcy is a fictional character, the work of W.D. Rubinstein *Men of Property: The very wealthy in Britain since the industrial revolution* shows, as we noted in the introduction to Chapter 8, that Britain's industrial revolution did not create the wealthy of that time. This contrast between the lack of wealth creation in the first industrial revolution in Britain, and the dramatic wealth creation in the second in the US, matters for understanding where plutocrats come from and highlights the parallels between the second industrial revolution, at the end of the nineteen and early twentieth century, and the third industrial revolution of the digital age which began in the 1980s and reached its apotheosis in the financial crash of 2008–09. One of the most striking aspects of the rise of current plutocrats has been the importance of labour incomes in their total incomes, as we see in Figure 10.2.

The work of Thomas Piketty and his collaborators has enabled us to see how capital and labour incomes for the very rich have changed and what Figure 10.2 shows is that, for both the top 1 per cent and the top 0.1 per cent in the US, their labour income grew far faster than their income from capital in the period from 1962 to 2000. Indeed, by 2000 the income from labour for the top 1 per cent was higher than the incomes from capital. After 2000 capital incomes continued to rise while labour incomes stagnated, albeit at the more than adequate level of nearly US$2 million for the top 0.1 per cent. Between 2000 and 2014 capital income took off reaching over US$4 million a year. While understanding the sources of the incomes of plutocrats' labour incomes matter, understanding why their capital pays so well is crucial too.

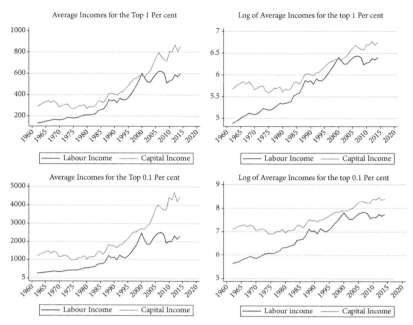

Figure 10.2. Average Incomes from Labour and Capital in the US: 1962–2014 (in Thousands of 2014 US Dollars)

Source: World Wealth and Income Data (accessed 2019). Now on the web as World Inequality Database (wid.world). A report on this data can be found in Facundo Alvaredo et al. (editors) (2018) *World Inequality Report*, Harvard University Press.

Where Do Plutocrats Come from in the UK and the US?

So, where do the extraordinarily high incomes shown in Figure 10.2 come from? There are fundamentally two different views as to the answer to that question. There is a view that it has to do with merit (a view unsurprisingly endorsed by the members of the plutocrats club), and there is a view that it has nothing to do with merit and everything to do with how society is organized (a more popular view than the former). The merit view has several rationales and the contrary view also takes different forms.

Possibly the two most obvious groups in which merit cannot be argued to be relevant are those who inherited their wealth and those dependent on oil wealth. Economists refer to the incomes from such assets as oil as containing a substantial element of 'rent'. The reason is that the cost of extracting the oil is, in many cases, only a fraction of its price; the difference is what is termed the rent from oil. But this concept of rents has a much wider connotation and, as we will see, much of plutocratic incomes comes from rents which reflect scarcity of various forms of which talent may be one, as distinct from the rents from oil ownership which reflect the luck of owning the land where oil is located.

How far merit or talent, broadly defined, can generate the rents that form the basis of plutocratic incomes is a subject of much disagreement. An example of rent through talent, which would seem relatively uncontentious, would be Premier League footballers whose income, if they were not to play football, would be a small fraction of what they earn as footballers—we come to those incomes below. This argument that 'rent' in this form is the basis for the income of the super-rich is a double-edged one. True, it might be related to talent but, if it is a 'rent' in this economic sense of the term, it can be safely taxed away—safely in the sense that the footballer cannot stop playing football and do something else.

Taxing such extreme wealth has become a very live political issue in both the UK and the US and is a prominent feature of Thomas Piketty's book (2014). As has often been pointed out, even if the incomes are rent, and thus taxable without altering incentives they need to be international ones. A 99 per cent tax on Premier League football players would not be good news for the league itself. The players would all move to Europe.

It is this mobility of capital more generally which has been used as an argument as to why national tax policies are, in a world of globalization, necessarily circumscribed. Indeed, Joseph Stiglitz has argued that it is the mobility of capital and the immobility of labour that lies at the heart of the problems that globalization creates. We will return to these issues, but first we need to address the central question of this chapter: where do plutocrats come from and what are the alternative interpretations of the source of their very high incomes?

The Merit View of Plutocrats

Can merit or talent explain entry into the plutocracy? One possible rational comes from the theory of 'Superstars'. In a paper which dates from 1981— long before the super-rich became the focus of attention they are today— Sherwin Rosen put forward a theory to explain what he describes as the 'phenomenon of Superstars, wherein relatively small numbers of people earn enormous amounts of money and dominate the activities in which they engage' (Rosen, 1981, p. 845). While a model rather than empirical evidence it is highly suggestive of what we observe. Two ideas motivate the analysis. The first is that the returns to talent rise far faster than any increase in talent. An example that Rosen gives is a surgeon who is 10 per cent more successful than others in saving lives will command a premium on their services much greater than 10 per cent. In other words, reward grows far faster than talent and the more outstanding the talent the greater the reward. The second element of the model is the technology of production. The example given by Rosen is the production of books. The costs of production do not rise in proportion to the size of the seller's market. A contemporary example of the pay of Superstars, to which we have already referred, would be Premier League footballers.

On average footballers playing in the Premier League have an average weekly pay, as of 2018, of just over £50,000 per week, so only making it into the less exclusive club of plutocrats. However, the five best-paid footballers earned in excess of £250,000 per week so they would qualify for the more exclusive club requiring annual incomes in the tens of millions. Notice, once again, the irrelevance of averages, even within a category as narrow as footballers good enough to play in the Premier League, as the lowest paid earn some £13,000 a week, less than 5 per cent of the top earners. These numbers clearly are in line with the Rosen model.

A model which develops similar ideas is due to Xavier Gabaix and Augustin Landier who are concerned to explain the rising gap between the pay of chief executives and their employees.[1] As with the Rosen model once again the focus is on 'talent', clearly a more contentious notion than that Premier League footballers have talent. Their analysis is focused on the US and is designed to explain the six-fold increase of CEO pay between 1980 and 2003. As they note this increase has proved a source of contentious political debate and that is as true in the UK as in the US.

What has happened since 2003 is even more striking. It is reported that in 2016, the CEOs of the top 350 US firms earned on average $15.6 million. Further, according to a report from the Economic Policy Institute, the average CEO pay is 271 times the nearly $58,000 annual average pay of the typical American worker. That may appear high but it's still not as high as in previous years. In 2015, CEOs made 286 times the salary of a typical

---

[1] X. Gabaix and A. Landier (2008).

worker and 299 times more in 2014. Compare that to 1978, when CEO earnings were roughly 30 times the typical worker's salary.[2]

In August 2018 the *Guardian* reported that pay for chief executives at Britain's biggest listed companies rose more than six times faster than wages in the wider workforce last year as the median boss's pay packet hit £3.9m. Chief executive pay at businesses on the FTSE 100 index surged 11 per cent on a median basis in 2017 while worker earnings failed to keep pace with inflation, rising just 1.7 per cent, according to the High Pay Centre's annual review of top pay. A worker on a median salary of £23,474 would have to work 167 years to earn the median annual pay of a FTSE 100 boss—up from 153 years in 2016, the report showed. The gap between bosses and workers widened despite government efforts to hold companies accountable for runaway pay.

While clearly readers of the *Guardian* are not being invited to feel sorry for CEOs in the UK, the gap between their pay and that in the US is large—US$15.6 million as compared with £3.9 million (US$5.3 at 2017 exchange rates). As we would expect, if the underlying distribution is Paretian, these numbers hide enormous differences within CEO pay. In the US the source cited above reports that some CEOs earn in the hundreds of millions—note the plausibility that some will reach our highest incomes used in Tables 8.1 and 8.2. For the UK Persimmon's CEO, Jeff Fairburn, had the highest pay in 2017, which was largely due to a long-term incentive plan—it came to over £47m, over ten times higher than the median of £3.9million.

These numbers are widely cited and more or less universally regarded as evidence as to how unfair society has become. Now while almost everyone objects to the pay of CEOs, almost no one objects to the pay of professional footballers—the best of whom are paid more than CEOs. The reason is rather obvious. While all recognize the 'talent' of the footballers, all are equally sceptical of the 'talent' of the average CEO—especially when some have been found to have engaged in criminal, or highly unethical, behaviour.

This makes the question asked by Xavier Gabaix and Augustin Landier all the more pertinent—can 'a talent to manage' explain this rising differential for CEO pay relative to that of the average worker? Two key features of their model are that the distribution of firm size is Paretian and there is assortative matching which, in this context, means that the most 'talented' managers are matched with the largest firms. They argue that the six-fold

---

[2] https://www.cnbc.com/2018/01/22/heres-how-much-ceo-pay-has-increased-compared-to-yours-over-the-years.html (accessed 11 August 2020).

increase of CEO pay between 1980 and 2003 can be fully attributed to the six-fold increase in market capitalization of large US companies during that period. They find a very small dispersion in CEO talent, which nonetheless justifies large pay differences. The intuition of their result is that if pay is related to firm size and firms bid for the best 'talent', then quite small differences in talent will result in larger firms getting the best managers and, given how spread out firm size is, thanks to the Paretian distribution, pay will be equally spread out.

Their rationale for this assumption about firm size, which has a long history in the analysis of the firm, is one with which we are already very familiar; it is related to the process by which growth is unrelated to the size of the firm.

Plutocrats as Rent Seekers

As already noted not all are convinced that the wealth of plutocrats reflects merit—however broadly defined. While the most vocal, and often strident, critics of their wealth come from the left of the political spectrum, which is always suspicious of market-based outcomes, that is not always the case. A book entitled *The Captured Economy* by Brink Lindsey and Steven Teles (2017) has as its subtitle *How the Powerful Enrich Themselves, Slow Down Growth and Increase Inequality*. Whereas those on the left see competition as the source of inequality, these authors argue that the root of the problem is actually a lack of competition. If an economy were actually competitive large profits would attract competitors and result in the reduction of those profits. That they argue is exactly what is not occurring—'the machinery of creative destruction is slowing down, the evidence of which is increasing corporate profits, declining new firm formation, and disturbingly increasing stability of the top firms over time' (p. 13). Their argument is, in some respects, the mirror image of the argument of Charles Jones and Jihee Kim (2018) whose paper is entitled 'A Schumperterian Model of Top Income Inequality'. Whereas Jones and Kim see creative destruction as restraining the growth of inequality, the argument in *The Captured Economy* is that these top incomes are the result of the failure of the process of creative destruction that underlies a successful capitalist, and competitive, economy.

A related argument to that of *The Captured Economy* is the work of Joseph Stiglitz (2013) who argues in his book *The Price of Inequality* that the growing extent of inequality is due to a combination of rent seeking and the manipulation of the rules of the 1 per cent to benefit themselves at the expense of the 99 per cent. These rules include the lack of controls on the mobility of capital, the restrictions on the role of unions and the manipulation of the tax system so the rich end up having lower, not higher, tax rates than those further down the income scale.

The Wealth of the Plutocrats

So, we have two very different interpretations of what we observe in terms of why certain individuals have such vary large incomes. As we have stressed, it is the richest among the rich which has seen a rapid acceleration in their incomes. We can observe, thanks to the work of Caroline Freund and Sarah Oliver, what are the sources of incomes for these super-rich individuals. A central theme of the book by Caroline Freund (2016), *Rich People Poor Countries: The Rise of Emerging-Market Tycoons and Their Mega Firms*, is that the number of billionaires in countries outside the 'West' is increasing rapidly. However, we are going to consider those from the UK and the US as that enables us to link the wealth of theses billionaires with the incomes of the super-rich in those countries. In Figure 10.3 we show the number of billionaires in the two countries and the wealth of the richest one. Over this period, from 1996 to 2016, the number of billionaires in the UK increased from very few to about 50, while in the US the number rose from just over 100 to nearly 500. Rather strikingly the richest billionaire in the US—always Bill Gates over this period except for 2008 when Warren Buffett beat him to the top spot—did not see a continuous rise in his wealth, reflecting the fortunes of the IT industry. In contrast the richest billionaire in the UK over this period did see a tripling of their wealth. For most of the period that was the Duke of Westminster and a major source of his wealth was land. The landed interest as the source of great wealth in the UK clearly is not past.

Figure 10.4 shows how other billionaires have fared. Here the gap between the UK and the US, at least after 2000, is smaller with an average US$3 billion in the UK and US$5 billion in the US as can be seen in the top panel of Figure 10.4. Thus, the large rises in total wealth of billionaires shown in the bottom panel of Figure 10.4 is a rise in the total number of billionaires, not to their becoming much richer. The totals for the US remain impressive at US$2.5 trillion.

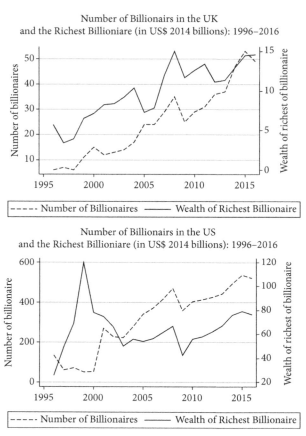

Figure 10.3. Numbers of Billionaires and the Richest One in the UK and US
Source: See Figure 10.1.

Where Does the Wealth Come From?

Above we have outlined what we have termed the merit and the rent-seeking interpretations of the sources of billionaire's wealth. We can now put some numbers on how important these two sources are in the case of UK and US billionaires. In Figure 10.5 we present the data collated by Freund and Oliver (2016) for the sources of their wealth. In this data two of these sources can, relatively uncontentiously, be regarded as based on a 'merit' view and these are 'Executives' and the 'Founders of non-finance enterprises'—the example

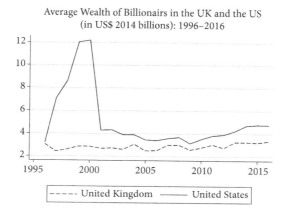

Average Wealth of Billionaires in the UK and the US
(in US$ 2014 billions): 1996–2016

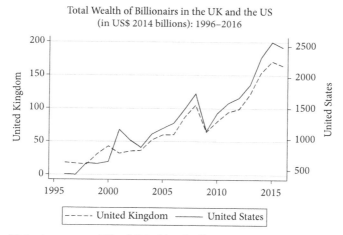

Total Wealth of Billionaires in the UK and the US
(in US$ 2014 billions): 1996–2016

Figure 10.4. Average and Total Wealth of Billionaires in the UK and the US
Source: see Figure 10.1.

par excellence of the latter being Bill Gates. Two sources are clearly open to a 'non-merit' view. These are wealth from inheritance and from what are termed 'Privatized and resources' which is intended to capture both those whose wealth depends on resources like oil and those who have benefited from the kind of corrupt privatization which characterized the rise of the Russian oligarchs. A final category 'Self-made finance' is deeply contentious as, with echoes of the populist objections to the bankers more than a century before, it is the behaviour of these billionaires which has made financial fortunes the focus of populist outrage.

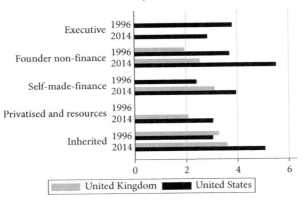

Figure 10.5. The Growth of Average and Total Wealth of Billionaires 1996 to 2014
Source: see Figure 10.1.

The top panel of Figure 10.5 shows the average net worth while the bottom panel shows the total. For the UK there are no billionaires in 1996 for three of the categories—'Executive', 'Self-made finance' and 'Privatized and resources', although they are an important source of UK fortunes by 2014. Two findings stand out from this attempt to trace the sources of the fortunes of current billionaires. The first is that the US far outstrips the UK in the size of these fortunes which, as we have already noted, flows from the much higher number of billionaires there than in the UK. The second is that three categories dominate total wealth—'Founder non-finance', 'Self-made finance' and 'Inherited' of which only one 'Founder non-finance' uncontentiously fits into a 'merit' view of wealth creation. Admittedly this is the largest at US$800 billion for the US but inherited wealth, by far the least defensible on 'merit' grounds, was not far behind.

It is probably true to say that the rage at the 1 per cent has not been directed mainly at those with wealth from rents or inheritance but from those with incomes from finance. It is the perceived venality of the financiers who benefited most from the pre-financial crash boom and did not, in the main, face the consequences of the bank failures which has generated the anger. As the data presented in Figure 10.5 shows, while not the most important source of wealth for the plutocrats, at over $US500 billion in 2014 it was a lot of wealth shared between very few people.

The case that most, if not all, of that wealth was created by activities which were not socially useful is the theme of *The Captured Economy*. It is also an argument advanced by John Kay (2016) in *Other People's Money: Masters of the Universe or Servants of the People?* As John Kay points out, banking used to be thought of as a rather dull occupation. Captain Mainwaring in *Dad's Army* is in civilian life a bank manager and no one would imagine him as a master of the universe through his banking activities—or, indeed, any other. While there is much dispute as to how far private greed and venality, or government regulatory failure, was to blame for the extent of the 2008–09 financial crisis, the authors of both books agree that the fundamental underlying problem was the role of debt in leveraging investment.

Leveraging is what most people who bought houses in both the UK and the US were doing big time before the financial crisis struck. Leverage simply means you incur debt for the bulk of the investment. You use US$100,000 of your money to borrow US$900,000 to buy a US$1 million flat, the flat doubles in value and your US$100,000 has turned into US$1.1 million (US$2 million–US$900,000), a return on your investment of over 1000 per cent. Pure financial magic it appears. But what if prices half, then you face a loss of US$400,000 (US$500,000–US$900,000). Less magical. Fortunes it seems can be made (and lost) simply by financial manipulation which, in turn, appears wholly divorced from the process of actually producing goods people value, which leads to the view that, in American terms, the interests of 'Wall Street' are wholly divorced from the interests of 'Main Street'.

It is though not the case that nothing of interest to 'Main Street' is being produced. What the finance is facilitating is home ownership and in both the

UK and the US home ownership as a goal has been heavily promoted by all of the main political parties. The problem arose from the convergence of two separate forces. On the one hand banks had a strong incentive to lend more than they should, partly because of the implicit, and sometimes explicit, subsidies to ensure they did not face the full risk they were undertaking. On the other hand incomes were not growing fast enough, or at all, to finance the interest rates when the initially subsidized levels rose.

As viewers of the film *The Big Short* will recall, the bankers there thought anyone who did not expect housing prices to keep rising was a fool. It turned out they were wrong, but why did that precipitate disaster? As Lindsey and Teles (2017) point out, the dot com bubble of 2000 was much less destructive of the real economy than the housing crash of 2008. The reason, they argue, is that, in the main, the dot com bubble was financed by equity while the housing boom was fuelled by bank lending. Once it was clear the banks were insolvent letting them go bust would have precipitated a credit contraction similar to that which set off the Great Depression of 1929–31.

It is in this context that people see the creation of plutocratic wealth as being wholly harmful. However, as Figure 10.5 shows, this is not the only source of such wealth. Can the 'merit' view we outlined above defend other plutocrats?

So, Which View Is Right?

The continuing rise in the incomes of plutocrats from both labour and capital in the US, shown in Figure 10.2, stands in stark contrast to the stagnation in most wages for the relatively unskilled, since the 1980s in the case of the US, and since the financial crash of 2008–09, in the case of the UK. This contrast motivates the question sometimes explicit, and always implicit, at the rage directed at the 1 per cent. Is their good fortune due to the bad fortune of the 99 per cent?

The critics of the plutocrats see their very high incomes as harmful for the 99 per cent for two, rather different, reasons. The first is that their incomes come from rents in the economic sense of the term, in that it reflects high profits which are protected from competition. The implication is that if these rents could be reduced the incomes of the plutocrats would fall and the real incomes of the rest would rise through falls in the prices of the products created by the plutocrats. That would simply redistribute the income of the plutocrats to the 99 per cent in the form of lower prices.

The second argument advanced by the critics is that these high incomes reduce the growth of the economy, partly by limiting innovation and partly by the patterns of demand created by the inequality that results from so much of any increase in income going to the plutocrats. This is a very different argument from the one focusing on plutocrats as earners of rents. If they reduce growth, and their removal could increase growth, then not only are the incomes of the 99 per cent lower as a result of the plutocrats' access to rents, but the growth in their incomes is lower too.

That takes us back to one of our central themes, which is that understanding the efficiency with which an economy operates, and how the technology used links to the demand for relatively unskilled labour, is key to understanding the problems, not possibly of the 99 per cent, but of those at the bottom of the scale. At first it might seem obvious that higher profits imply lower wages but that is not so with growth. It is here too that the differences between the UK and the US since the financial crash are so great. The collapse in productivity in the UK economy since the crash means, as Figure 7.5 showed, that incomes of the top quintile actually grew slower than any other quintile. In contrast in the US they grew faster. This reflects, in part, that since the financial crisis the US economy has outperformed the UK economy and, in part, its underlying pattern of growth by which wage growth of most is limited relative to the income growth of the plutocrats. So, the question here is whether limits to that plutocratic income growth would increase the overall efficiency of the economy *and* its growth rate. It is certainly possible and we have shown in previous chapters that over the period from 1980 to the financial crash in terms of growth rates the UK economy greatly outperformed the US and was particularly successful in raising the incomes of the poorer part of society. The rhetoric that the increased inequality is a price to pay for increased incomes for all is just that—rhetoric.

In summary, the data of the previous section do suggest that most plutocratic wealth does not come from finance, an industry where rents and restrictions on entry seem rather clear. A combination of talent and technology clearly explains the incomes of 'superstar' footballers. That pay is related to firm size and that managing is more challenging the larger is the firm certainly seems likely. Equally, as the critics of the plutocrats point out, much of their incomes does come from the 'rents' that flow, not from any limitations on the supply of talent, but from regulatory capture which boosts market incomes way over the social value of the activities. As we have stressed, the example most prominent in the public mind is finance and the anger that arose from the banking and financial crisis of 2008–09 has been influential in the rise of populism across the now-rich countries documented by Roger Eatwell and Matthew Goodwin (2018) in their book *National Populism: The Revolt Against Liberal Democracy*.

That revolt has taken aim not simply at the super-rich in finance but at globalization, which is seen as having created the super-rich, and at migrants who are seen as threatening the living standards of the unskilled in now-rich countries. In the next chapter we conclude our search for the poor and the plutocrats by examining how far the current populist revolt is aimed at the right targets.

11

From the Poor to the Plutocrats

Poverty and Inequality

Our objective in this book has been to understand the sources of both relative and absolute poverty, and the rising spread of incomes, in a long-term context. The long term is important as the rise in inequality, in some countries, since the 1970s stands in marked contrast to its fall in the period from 1900 to 1970 among now-rich countries. High inequality is now a much more common characteristic of poor than of rich countries when measured, as far as we can, by a common yardstick. That yardstick is consumption per capita and such a measure hides the respective roles of markets and governments in outcomes for inequality. The importance of that distinction has been shown by our comparison of the US and the UK since the 1970s. The extent of the success of New Labour in the UK in raising both market incomes, and incomes with transfers, for the poorest section of the society is largely unknown. Indeed, as we noted in Chapter 7, the assertion that New Labour was an extension of the Thatcher premiership has been a widely propagated myth within Jeremy Corbyn's Labour Party. A myth within right-wing circles is that the UK economy has been held back by its membership of the EU and, freed from its restraints, will be able to perform like the regulation-lite US. In fact, the UK economy, by virtually every measure, outperformed that of the US from the 1980s until the financial crash. This is particularly true of its ability to increase the absolute, and relative, incomes of the poorest sections of society. It was the collapse in productivity under the Coalition and Conservative governments that led to the general fall in earnings after 2010.

Absolute poverty, which the World Bank measures at some US$2 per day using purchasing power parity dollars, is almost exclusively confined to poor countries. Measuring the poor in this absolute sense has been a contentious exercise. The reasons for the contention are not hard to discern. There are the apparently technical problems of measuring incomes in countries where the poorest do not earn wages and much of their 'incomes' is produced within the household. Probably more important for the disputes is that much hangs on the numbers for the purposes of political arguments. The World Bank is in the business of reducing poverty, what the numbers show can be interpreted as indicative of the extent of its success. It cannot be assumed, of course, that any fall that has occurred has anything to do with the World Bank. More generally the dire poverty of some people in some of the poorest countries inevitably suggests that poverty of an extreme kind remains a major problem and claims that such poverty is falling, as the World Bank does, excite scepticism.

There is, of course, no contradiction between a claim that poverty is falling and that much dire poverty continues to exist. The two statements simply imply that there was even more such dire poverty in the past. In one sense the fierce arguments that have been conducted as to whether absolute poverty is falling rather misses the point. In some countries, of which by far the most important is China, the answer is clearly yes. In others, many in sub-Saharan Africa, the answer is clearly no. An average across countries which have been successful and those which have not hides what we need to know as to the causes of continuing absolute poverty. However, in a wider sense, it is certainly useful to know whether, on balance, the world economy has been reducing poverty. Not simply for the purposes of political rhetoric but to know if the enormous success in the overall growth of the world economy, which we documented in Chapter 4, has benefited an increasing number of people.

So, has the total number of poor people in the world been declining? We answered that question in Chapter 6 and the answer does depend on the income level you use for defining absolute poverty. Using the World Bank's poverty line of US$(PPP 2011 prices) 1.9 per day the answer is yes, at least comparing 1993 with 2008. Using a much higher poverty line, argued for by Jason Hickel (2017), of US$ (PPP 2011 prices) 7.0 per day, the answer is only since 2003. Now it is obviously not surprising that as you choose a higher poverty line you get, by definition, more poor people. But why does it matter for the change? The reason is the changing shape of the distribution of world income which we showed in Figure 6.3 and reproduce again here as Figure 11.1, except that now, rather than highlighting alternative poverty lines, we highlight the range over which incomes have increased. Many more people now have incomes in the range of US$1,000 to US$8,000, both in PPP 2011 prices, in 2008 than they did in 1988. By far the most important factor underlying this change is the rise of China. Above the US$8,000 level there has been only a very modest change in the distribution, its most noticeable feature has been the elongation of the curve. The result

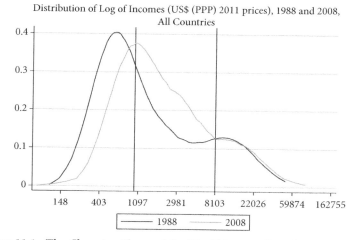

Figure 11.1. The Changing Shape of the World Income Distribution

Note: The distribution is of the log of per capita annual incomes. The logs have been converted to actual incomes on the horizontal axis.

Source: Lakner-Milanovic (2013) World Panel Income Distribution (LM-WPID) database.

of these changes is to further extend the range of incomes we see across the world.

If we confine our attention to data drawn from household consumption surveys, the basis of the data in the figure, then the poor have been getting richer faster than the rich, but at very different rates—see Chapter 6. Confining our attention to such data misses the richest of the rich. It is these super-rich people who have been the focus of attention in rich countries where the rise of the 1 per cent has been seen as self-evident evidence for the rise in inequality. We have investigated that issue in detail for both the US and the UK, two countries which have been singled out as examples of such rising inequality. The evidence here is much more complex than is widely appreciated.

It is true that in both countries the incomes of the super-rich, the top 1 per cent, have been increasing faster than that of everyone else. But, and it is an important qualification, most of the gain for the top 1 per cent has been within the top 10 per cent. This was shown in Chapter 7 and we reproduce that part of Table 7.2 where a direct comparison can be made between the UK and the US in Table 11.1 below. Comparing the period after 1990 with the period before we see that the rates of growth for the top 1 per cent increase five times for the UK and doubled for the US. However, the rates of

Table 11.1. Trend Rates of Growth of Tax Income (per cent per annum)

United Kingdom				
	Top 1 per cent	Top 10 per cent	Bottom 90 per cent	Average
Before 1990	0.6	1.5	1.7	1.6
After 1990	3.1	1.8	1.3	1.5
United States				
	Top 1 per cent	Top 10 per cent	Bottom 90 per cent	Average
Before 1990	1.2	1.7	2.4	2.1
After 1990	2.5	1.6	0.0	0.7

Source: See Table 7.2.

growth of income for the top 10 per cent changed relatively little. Indeed, for the US the growth rate fell marginally after 1990. Recall these are individual incomes for tax and so not directly comparable with the household survey data used in Figure 11.1 above.

The picture of poverty and inequality that emerges from this comparison of household data across the globe and tax data for two comparatively rich countries is one where rapid rises in incomes are being achieved among some poor countries and even more rapid increases in income for the richest in some rich countries. These comparisons enable us to see the paradoxes that underlie the increasing spread of incomes across the world. Yes, the gap between the richest and the poorest is growing apace. But, among the relatively global poor incomes are rising faster than the average of the top 20 per cent of the world's income. At the very bottom there is dire poverty with incomes lower than any for the last 1000 years; at the top are incomes in the millions; at the summit, incomes in the billions.

The factors driving the increases in poverty at the bottom are quite distinct from the factors driving the increasing spread of incomes at the very top. Understanding increases in poverty and inequality among people in poor countries requires an answer to the question as to why some of these countries have been so much more successful than others in enabling growth to occur. Sometimes that is a question as to why they have not grown at all, sometimes it is a question as to why they have not grown in a way that benefits the poor. At the other end of the scale we need to know why, among the very rich, the super-rich have emerged on the scale they have.

Incomes of the Absolutely Poor: Unskilled Wages and TFP

Incomes of the poor depend on the price of the assets they own (always unskilled labour and sometimes land) and their employment opportunities for their labour and the productivity of the land they own. Low prices for these assets—namely low wages for the unskilled and small rents from poor quality land—combined with low opportunities for employment are the factors which drive low market incomes for the poor. In now-rich countries how those market incomes translate into household disposable incomes is a function of government policies towards the poor. We have shown how important those policies are for both the UK and the US in Chapter 7 where we have provided a comparison of market income, what households earn from their market opportunities, with disposable income which is after the government's taxes and transfers.

In poor countries substantial transfers to the poor are usually not possible—a conspicuous exception is South Africa where such transfers are an important source of household income for the poorer members of society. Absent such transfers the incomes of the landless unskilled depend on the prices of that labour. That price may be an explicit wage or an implicit one resulting from tasks performed in informal or household enterprises. To understand absolute poverty in poor countries we need to understand why the price of unskilled labour is so low.

Now as with poverty within countries being unskilled is a relative term. In poor countries a generation ago being unskilled would have meant having no education; now, in most, it would mean having only primary or middle school. It is those at the bottom of the education ladder whose relative lack of skills makes them dependent on the price of their labour rather than the value of their education. Its price is so low because its productivity is so low and the possible causes of such low productivity are numerous. They include the absence of sufficient capital to employ the workers and the poor quality of public services that prevent what capital there is being used more productively. An example across much of sub-Saharan Africa is poor power supply handicapping the ability of firms to produce. However, the most important factor determining its low price is where the unskilled worker is born and seeks work. The poor are poor in poor countries because their countries are very bad at using the resources they have. For those countries whose poverty rates are increasing they are also very bad at increasing their resources.

In fact, we can measure just how bad some countries are as we have data on how TFP differs across countries which we present in Figure 11.2. The

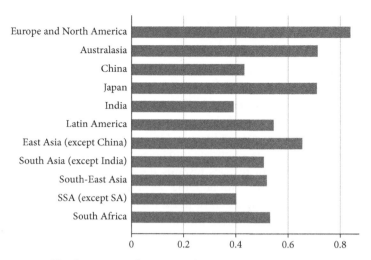

Figure 11.2. Total Factor Productivity Relative to the US across the World: 2014
Source: PENN World Tables 9.0.

figure shows TFP relative to the US. So, China and sub-Saharan Africa with a reading of 0.40 implies that all the factors in these countries would produce over twice its level of income if it had the same magic X factor as the US.

That might suggest we should all be very anxious to know what the magic X factor is and to some extent we should—spoiler, we don't actually know, although economists have made lots of plausible suggestions as to what it might be which we briefly reviewed at the end of Chapter 4. A more useful way to think about this magic X factor, which does not involve knowing what it is, is to recognize that if labour, and possibly capital as well, were to move to a country with a higher TFP its productivity would be greatly increased. The key to people remaining poor is being unable to move to places where they could be richer.

Incomes of the Relatively Poor: Wages, Employment, and Movement

That inability to move can be a key factor in relative poverty within now-rich countries, indeed currently it is possibly the most important. The reason an ability to move has become so important is the changes in technology and job types over the last twenty years.

Current problems stand in marked contrast to those in the past for countries such as the UK and the US. The Thatcher years were marked by sustained rises in wages for those relatively unskilled who obtained, or retained, their jobs. The dire outcomes for those in the bottom quintile (see Figure 7.4) was due to the lack of employment opportunities for the unskilled and limited governmental transfers. The extraordinary success of New Labour in the UK (shown in Figure 7.5) was the result of combining rises in the wages for the unskilled, in substantial part through the introduction of a minimum wage, and sustained rise in employment. The result was, for the bottom quintile, a far larger increase in their market incomes than in their disposable incomes. Even so the rises in the bottom quintile's disposable income was more than twice that of the top quintile. The contrast with the George W. Bush years in the US could scarcely be greater with a rise in disposable income for the bottom twenty per cent less than half that for the UK and far larger rises for the top than the bottom quintiles (also shown in Figure 7.5). Stagnant wages combined with limited employment opportunities ensured an outcome dramatically worse than that in the UK.

At the time of the 2016 EU Referendum the result of the vote to leave the EU was often interpreted as the revenge of the left-behinds against the 'metropolitan elite'. Again, the data directly contradicts this interpretation. As was shown in Figure 7.5 it was the bottom quintile that saw the largest increases in household incomes over the period from 2010 to 2016; the exact opposite is true for the US in terms of market incomes. The problem in the UK was not that household incomes at the bottom were falling (they were not), but how they were rising. Falling wages were combined with rising employment. The 1980s scourge of unemployment among the unskilled had been replaced by falling wages and rising employment.

For the decades after 1980 only in the New Labour years in the UK and in the Bush Senior and Clinton years in the US did it prove possible to combine rising wages for the relatively unskilled with rising employment. The replacement of these governments by ones of the right naturally fuels the suspicion that right-wing governments are the cause of the resulting problems. But it is possible the problems lie deeper, in the inherent difficulty in a modern service-dominated economy in enabling the relatively unskilled to benefit from rising incomes.

A common factor across both the UK and the US since the 1980s has been a rapid rise in the price of housing in cities where there are jobs. In *The New Geography of Jobs* Enrico Moretti (2013) graphically describes this process of shifting jobs and rising house prices in cities where those jobs are created in the US. The same is true of the UK with metropolitan areas generally, but pre-eminently London, creating jobs and such jobs being made increasingly inaccessible due to the rising costs of housing. The new jobs that come in these 'job-rich' areas are not simply skilled ones or, more accurately, the relatively unskilled can benefit too from working in areas where there are a lot of skilled jobs. Higher incomes generate higher incomes for all, not simply for the highly skilled.

New Jobs and Matching Skills to Jobs

The new technologies come with very different demands for labour than the technologies of the pre-1970s period. Skills carry a premium they had not before. Unskilled labour finds itself faced with increased dependence on a service, rather than a manufacturing, sector for employment. It is this failure to match the changing demands of technology with changes in the supply of skills which, it is frequently argued, is central to the problems faced by the unskilled. In their influential book *The Race Between Education and Technology*, Claudia Goldin and Lawrence Katz (2008) argue that the US relative success, and now relative failure, is due to the failure of education to keep pace with technology. At present it is technology that is winning the race and the implication is that as the supply of skilled labour fails to rise sufficiently its price will continue to rise. In this view the failure of education is the cause of the failure to turn the potential gains from trade into actual ones by appropriately skilling the workforce.

This process of skilling the workforce is inextricably linked to the increasing importance of matching workers to jobs. With the rise of the digital economy this process of matching has gone well beyond simply the ability of workers with various skills to move to where the jobs are, it now involves a complex process by which a very wide range of skills need to be matched to an equally wide range of jobs. It is within this process of matching that the fate of the relatively unskilled will be determined. If the unskilled can match to jobs in areas where the returns are high then inequality will be reduced. If, as appears in the UK at least to be the norm, the unskilled are geographically isolated in areas with poor jobs then inequality will be enhanced. It is important to note none of this is driven by markets; it is caused by markets not being able to operate to link workers with high-return employment opportunities. It is driven by policies which prevent movement and the ability of people to search for better jobs in more productive areas. The failure of the market in housing is making this as true within countries as it is true across countries. Increasing numbers of workers are simply in the wrong place and cannot move.[1] This is, of course most true across countries rather than within countries; however the inability to move is an important factor for relative poverty within countries.

Globalization, TFP, and Wages across the World

A point made by Joseph Stiglitz (2013) in *The Price of Inequality* is that globalization has been far more focused on liberalizing the market for capital than for labour. While capital can flow very freely across borders, labour cannot, and when it can, as in the case of freedom of movement in the EU, it sparks strong political opposition. One cause of this opposition is that the gap between the wages of unskilled labour across countries remains very large, just how large we showed at the end of Chapter 3. It is this failure to ensure that unskilled labour wages rise in poor countries that explains absolute poverty there and their failure to rise in rich countries relative poverty there.

It is how globalization is, or could be, changing the wages of the unskilled that is key to understanding how globalization links to changing poverty. Globalization could close this gap partly by trade as countries with a lot of low-priced unskilled labour export goods to countries with higher-priced unskilled labour. That indeed is what China has been doing with consequences we discussed in Chapter 9. Globalization could also close the gap by allowing both capital and labour to flow freely across countries. As demonstrated by the fierce political hostility to both trade and migration, these are the two aspects of globalization that its critics most dislike. The fear of the

---

[1] Housing costs are an important aspect of the creation of relative poverty. 'The growing crisis in the UK's housing market has created especially stark problems for low-income families with children. Housing costs have grown much faster for these families than for those who are better off. This has been driven by rising costs for renters and the rapid increase in the number of families renting privately due to a lack of social rented housing and the high costs of buying a home. The proportion of children in the bottom quintile living in the private rented sector rose from 17% in 2005/6 to 37% in 2016/17. At the same time, Housing Benefit has been weakened, leaving many families with less protection. Since the mid-1990s, the proportion of single-parent households who are claiming full Housing Benefit and who have to use other income to help pay their rent has more than doubled—from 17% to 43%. Over the same period, the number of couple family households with children receiving Housing Benefit and who have to use other income to top it up has also more than doubled—from 15% to 37%' (Joseph Rowntree Foundation, 2018, p. 4).

low-skilled in the host country—and it is a fear across decades and across almost every country, not even confined to rich ones—is that such migration will lower relative wages for the unskilled and quite possibly lower them in absolute terms as well. While the critics may not put the point so brutally what they mean is—we are rich, you are not, so stay poor so we can stay rich.

Indeed, it is possibly the only aspect of economics where popular intuition appears to coincide with basic economics. In this case if you increase the supply of a good its price will fall. Demand curves for labour slope downwards, which is the title of a well-known paper arguing that it is true unskilled migration reduces the wages of the unskilled. We cited this paper (Borjas, 2003) in Chapter 9 where it was noted that the issue in assessing the full impact of immigration is that, even if such falls occur (and that is disputed), it is not the end of the story. Falls in the price of labour will make investment more profitable and such investment can ameliorate, or fully eliminate, any fall in wages. We noted in Chapter 9 the balance of evidence for the UK with respect to recent waves of immigration indicating that the effect had been, on average, to raise wages.

While arguments that immigrants are the cause of lower wages can be, and are, exploited by demagogic politicians to stir fear of immigrants, it is not the case that reducing such gaps in wages needs to lead to lower wages in now-rich countries. The most important reason why that is so is the importance of TFP in driving income differences across countries. Labour is simply much more productive in some countries than others and allowing it to move will increase the income both of the country and the mover—that is what a higher level of TFP in the host country means.

The Four Steps to Get from the Poor to the Plutocrats

We are now in a position to summarize our answer to the question posed by the facts we have presented in this and preceding chapters and, indeed, posed at the very beginning of this book: what can explain the extraordinary diversity of incomes we observe in the world today? As we argued in Chapter 1 our problem is not to explain a remorseless rise of inequality as capitalism spread across the world, nor is it to explain a rising tide of poverty—neither is true. Our problem is to explain the (extraordinarily large) rise in some incomes and their fall among some of the poorest. Our answer to the question is in four steps.

Step 1: Get Lucky Where You Are Born

The first, and most important, step for seeing who ends up being absolutely poor is to note the spread in incomes across countries. This is partly caused by falling national incomes in some countries, but it is mainly due to countries failing to grow in a world in which most countries are growing. Such falls will be the principal means by which both some people become absolutely poorer and many more stay absolutely poor.

The primary source of absolute poverty is the existence of countries which are absolutely poor. It is not due to inequality. The reason is simple. In rich countries inequality is, on average, much lower than in poor countries and even in the most unequal of rich countries the inequality is insufficient to make the poorest in those countries absolutely poor if, that is, by absolutely poor we mean the standards of living judged poor by the World Bank poverty measures of US$2 (PPP) per day.

We have shown across the world for the last 300 years that growth of countries has been extraordinarily variable. In fact, these growth rates follow a distribution with which we are now very familiar, they look like a normal distribution. While variability is a common factor across the two waves of globalization—the first from 1700 to 1913, the second from 1950 to the present day—average growth rates were far higher in the second wave. In the second wave most growth rates clustered in the range of 1 to 3 per cent per annum but there were significant numbers outside that range. The implication will be that the spread of incomes has increased steadily over the last 300 years—at an increasing rate. It is this dispersion of growth rates which explains the peak in 1980 of the divergence of incomes across countries and this peak implied an enormous gap between the living standards of those in rich and poor countries. The reason that this increased spread is consistent with a decline in inequality at the global level since then is that over the last thirty years the countries which have grown fastest have the largest populations, by far the most important being China. The mirror image of the success of China is the existence of countries with substantial negative growth rate. Many of these have been in sub-Saharan Africa (SSA). In 2014 of the twenty poorest countries in the world only one, Haiti, was not in SSA. The key to reducing poverty is growth and poverty in SSA has been the creation of the policies their governments have pursued. Absolute poverty in the twenty-first century is a choice made by governments. Figure 11.3 provides a summary of this

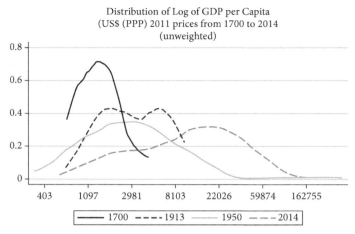

Figure 11.3. The Distribution of World GDP per Capita: 1700–2014
Note: On the horizontal axis the logs have been converted to actual incomes.
Source: Updated Maddison data and PENN World Tables 9.0.

history of global growth showing the distribution of those incomes in 1700, 1913, 1950, and 2014.

The spread in 1700 was comparatively narrow. By 1913 the world was 'twin peaked' with a mass of relatively rich countries and another mass point of relatively poor countries, all in the framework of a widening spread. Finally, in 2014 the density function looks much closer to normality with a vastly higher spread of incomes than in 1700. Such a pattern of global growth is entirely consistent with the 'random' process we first described in Chapter 2, where growth rates are unrelated to the level of income.

Step 2: Get Lucky When You Are Born (If Unskilled You Want the Early Twentieth Century, If Skilled After That)

Our second step in understanding the scale of the differences in income we observe across the world is to focus on the price of unskilled labour. This price is key as it is the most important asset which the poor own. Its price is critical for both their absolute, and relative, income. To understand changes in both, the changes in the price of unskilled labour need to be understood. We have traced this price in two countries, the UK and the US, for which we have long runs of data. As we have shown it is the rise in the price of this labour in both these countries from the early part of the twentieth century until the 1970s that saw not only the rapid rises in the incomes of such labour but a rapid decline in inequality. For the space of more than half a century the relatively poor saw higher increases in their income than the relatively rich. In this period the US outperformed the UK, and indeed the rest of the world, in the level to which it managed to raise the price of such labour. In the US this wage basically stopped rising in the 1970s. Just how successful the US economy had been up to this point was shown in Figure 3.10 which compared unskilled manufacturing wages some 35 years after the 1970s when the US was still second, behind Germany. The relatively unskilled in the US remain very rich indeed by world standards. While it would not be politic to say so in the US, today this wage is by historical, and comparative, standards extraordinarily high.

This process of rapid rises in the price of relatively unskilled labour has been documented in detail for the UK and the US for the period from 1900 to 1970. Something very similar seems to have occurred in a large number of countries which found a path to higher incomes and low, or lower, inequality. However, where most poor people lived in the 1970s, overwhelmingly in Asia and SSA, their growth since then has not been a replication of that earlier process. In China, which has seen rapid rises in national income and in wages, inequality has been rising. Even after thirty years of spectacularly high growth rates, wages in China remain far below those in rich countries. No country that was poor in the 1970s has managed to replicate the patterns of now-rich countries up to the 1970s.

Step 3: Get Lucky in Being Able to Move (If Born in the Wrong Place)

Movement is the single most important factor in being able to become less poor. It won't by itself make you rich but its impact on incomes can be dramatic. By far the most important recent example of this is the movement from rural areas in China. The creation of hundreds of millions of jobs that underlie its economic transformation involved massive movement of people. It is the barriers to such movements across countries that is the single most important factor enabling the extreme poverty we observe in those countries to continue. It is the barriers to movements within countries, of which the most important is the failure of housing policy, that limit economically their opportunities.

Movement of course only works if there is something to move to. That is where the dispersion of growth rates across countries comes into play. Some countries have proved much more successful than others in creating those opportunities. By far the most successful country over the last centuries which we have sought to cover has been the US. This became a colossus not because it grew particularly rapidly but because its population grew rapidly, fuelled in substantial part by migration.

It is politicians, and their electorates, that propagate poverty not only within poor countries, but ironically, among those who elect them.

Step 4: Get Ultra-Lucky with a Great Idea, or Own an Oil Company, or Have Rich Parents, or Eliminate the Competition

Our fourth step is from the wealthy to the super-wealthy, the plutocrats, the billionaires and those whose incomes are in the tens, or hundreds, of millions. As the heading for the step indicates, there is a variety of routes to becoming super-rich, several of which are entirely a matter of luck. Those who are born to rich parents, or own land on which oil is found, have done nothing to earn their wealth. Rather oddly it is not those plutocrats who seem to excite the most opprobrium. That is reserved for the bankers, financiers and (possibly) the owners of retail or IT mega-firms.

The reason for this distinction is possibly that while luck is seen as an inevitable aspect of life the earnings of bankers and others among the super-rich are seem as the result of market manipulation that renders their wealth at the expense of the rest. As we showed in Chapter 10 there is a widely argued case that such wealth does result from the failure of markets to be allowed to compete away the very high profits of such firms.

The Future: Utopia or Dystopia

We are suffering just now from a bad attack of economic pessimism. It is common to hear people say that the epoch of enormous economic progress which characterized the nineteenth century is over; that the rapid improvement in the standard of life is now going to slow down—at any rate in Great Britain; that a decline in prosperity is more likely than an improvement in the decade which lies ahead of us.   (Keynes, 1963, p. 358)

The essay from which that quotation is taken, 'Economic Possibilities for Our Grandchildren', was written in 1930 at the height of the Great Depression when national incomes in the US had fallen by nearly 25 per cent. Keynes went on to argue that such pessimism was unjustified and that the future would be far better than the present. The early years of the 1930s were to prove the prelude to political events that destroyed millions of lives in wars which cumulated in the catastrophe of the Second World War. But the essay was concerned with the grandchildren of Keynes' generation and, with them in mind, he was if anything too pessimistic himself. If we substitute the twentieth for the nineteenth century in the above quote, it is clearly as true today as it was in the early 1930s that we are suffering from a bad attack of economic pessimism. Indeed, President Trump won the US Presidency with a truly dystopian picture of what has already happened to the US in recent decades.

The basis for Keynes' faith in the well-being of future generations was the power of compound interest. As his essay illustrates, with striking examples, compound interest can transform lives in a few generations. We have seen over the decades since the 1950s that with the rates of growth achieved first in the Asian tigers—Singapore, South Korea, Hong Kong, and Taiwan—and later in China that the time for that transformation can be reduced to one generation. We have also seen that the problems in the US are not that the growth rates have fallen—true they are far below those of the rapidly growing countries of Asia but, by historical standards, they are very average. The source of the dystopian vision for the future in the US in recent decades is the failure of that country to adjust to an economy dominated much more than in the past by the service sector.

Compound interest works well only for the average. Economists have devoted a very large amount of effort to seeking to document that education is a valuable investment to ensure that those with more of it perform better than the average. Indeed, one of the liveliest political issues in both the US and the UK is the increasing cost of acquiring high levels of that education. The truth is that education can be a very valuable investment, but that is far from guaranteed. Changes in education and changes in the technology that uses that education are, we have argued, the driving forces behind the changes we have observed in the distribution of incomes within now-rich countries. In particular the factors that have changed the relative wages of those with relatively little education are the factors driving a vision of Trumpian dystopia. In contrast stand the countries which have seized the opportunities offered by technology, and the knowledge that underlies that technology, to transform the lives of their citizens. For them Keynes' optimism was more than justified.

The irony underlying the dystopian vision would not have escaped Keynes. Having solved what Keynes rightly saw as the problems of poverty and mass unemployment, raised their incomes to levels even he would have been surprised by, the politics of using those high incomes has proved so intractable. It is the divide across education that defines the battle lines of the Trump presidency and Brexit and the additional irony, given the rhetoric of elites and the people, is that the newly educated young are among those most disadvantaged by the policies that Republicans have pursued in the US and the Conservative-led governments in the UK.

This divide is well-illustrated by the voting patterns in the UK's EU referendum shown in Table 11.2. In that referendum those aged 18–34 and those aged more than 65 had mirror-image voting patterns. The same was true for the educated. The consequence is that the young, productive members of society are being outvoted by the old and unproductive. With the populist policies of hostility to trade and immigration diverting attention

Table 11.2. The UK EU Referendum: The Roles of Age and Education

| | | | Whether voted Leave or Remain | |
			Remain	Leave
Age	18–34	(%)	**60**	**40**
	35–44	(%)	50	50
	45–54	(%)	48	52
	55–64	(%)	49	51
	65+	(%)	**39**	**61**
	Total	(%)	49	51

		Remain	Leave
Degree	(%)	**74**	**26**
Higher education below degree/A level	(%)	50	50
O level or equivalent/CSE	(%)	39	61
No qualification	(%)	**22**	**78**
Total	(%)	49	51

Source: How Britain voted at the EU referendum. In International Politics and Current Affairs, 27 June, 2016, 1:58 PM. The YouGov web site: https://yougov.co.uk/topics/politics/articles-reports/2016/06/27/how-britain-voted.

from the problems of productivity and skills a dystopian future may well be the outcome.

While now-rich countries look back in anger, now-richer-than-they-were countries see, if not a utopian future, at least one where the opportunities to emulate the now-rich seem very possible. The problem here, we have argued, is that the mechanisms that worked so well for the now-rich are no longer in place. Wages for the unskilled remain far below those in rich countries. Possibly Keynes was right by accident. Yes, compound interest can work its wonders when technology and unskilled labour work together. In a world where they don't optimism for this generation's future will prove unjustified.

References

Acemoglu, D. and J. Robinson (2012) *Why Nations Fail—The Origins of Power, Prosperity and Poverty*. London: Profile Books.

Alvaredo, F., Chancel, L., Piketty, T., Saez, E., and G. Zucman (Eds.) (2018) *World Inequality Report*. Cambridge, MA: Harvard University Press.

Atkinson, A.B. (2015) *Inequality: What Can Be Done?* Cambridge, MA: Harvard University Press.

Atkinson, A.B., Hasell, J., Morelli, S., and M. Roser (2017) 'The Chartbook of Economic Inequality'. Hosted at the Institute for New Economic Thinking, The Oxford Martin School, University of Oxford.

Atkinson, A.B. and T. Piketty (Eds.) (2007) *Top Incomes Over the Twentieth Century: A Contrast Between European and English-speaking Countries*. Oxford: Oxford University Press.

Autor, D., Dorn, D., and G. Hanson (2013) 'The China Syndrome: Local Labor Market Effects of Import Competition in the United States', *American Economic Review*, 103(6): 2121–68.

Bloom, N., Draca, M. and J. Van Reenen (2016) 'Trade Induced Technical Change? The Impact of Chinese Imports on Innovation, IT and Productivity', *The Review of Economic Studies*, 83(1): 87–117.

Bolt, J. and J.L. Van Zanden (2014) 'The Maddison Project: Collaborative Research on Historical National Accounts', *Economic History Review*, 67(3): 627–51. https://www.rug.nl/ggdc/historicaldevelopment/maddison/releases/maddison-project-database-2013 (accessed 11 August 2020).

Borjas, G.J. (2003) 'The Labor Demand Curve Is Downward Sloping: Re-examining the Impact of Immigration on the Labor Market', *Quarterly Journal of Economics*, 118(4): 1335–74.

Broadberry, S., Campbell, B., Klein, A., Overton, M., and B. van Leeuwen (2014) *British Economic Growth, 1270–1870*. Cambridge: Cambridge University Press.

Broadberry, S., Guan, H., and David Daokui Li (2017) 'China, Europe and the Great Divergence: A Study in Historical National Accounting, 980–1850', Discussion Papers in Economic and Social History Number 155, April 2017, University of Oxford.

CBO (Congressional Budget Office) (2019) *The Distribution of Household Incomes*, July 2016. Washington DC.

Chiang, A. (1984) *Fundamental Methods of Mathematical Economics*. New York: McGraw-Hill, Third edition.

Clark, G. (2007) *A Farewell to Alms—A Brief Economic History of the World*. Princeton, NJ: Princeton University Press.

Clark, G. (2016) 'What Were the British Earnings and Prices Then? (New Series)', MeasuringWorth, 2016, http://www.measuringworth.com (accessed 11 August 2020).

Deaton, A. (2013) *The Great Escape: Health, Wealth, and the Origins of Inequality*. Princeton, NJ: Princeton University Press.

Dustmann, C., Frattini, T., and I.P. Preston, (2013) 'The Effect of Immigration Along the Distribution of Wages', *Review of Economic Studies*, 80(1): 145–73.

Dustmann, C., Schönberg, U., and J. Stuhler (2016) 'The Impact of Immigration: Why Do Studies Reach Such Different Results?', *Journal of Economic Perspectives*, 30(4): 31–56.

Easterly, W. (2002) *The Elusive Quest for Growth: Economists' Adventures and Misadventures in the Tropics*. Cambridge, MA: MIT Press.

Eatwell, R. and M. Goodwin (2018) *National Populism: The Revolt Against Liberal Democracy*. London: Pelican Books.

Ebenstein, A., Harrison, A., McMillan, M., and S. Phillips (2014) 'Estimating the Impact of Trade and Offshoring on American Workers Using the Current Population Surveys', *The Review of Economics and Statistics*, 96(4): 581–95.

Feenstra, R. C, Inklaar, R., and M.P. Timmer (2015) 'The Next Generation of the Penn World Table.' *American Economic Review*, 105(10): 3150–82. http://www.ggdc.net/pwt/ (accessed 11 August 2020).

Freeman, R. and R. Oostendorp (2013) Occupational Wages around the World (OWW) Database: http://www.nber.org/oww/ (accessed 7 August 2020). A paper explaining this data can be found at R. Oostendorp *The Occupational Wages around the World (OWW) Database: Update for 1983–2008*, Background Paper for the World Development Report.

Freund, C. (2016) *Rich People, Poor Countries: The Rise of Emerging-Market Tycoons and Their Mega Firms*. Washington DC: Peterson Institute for International Economics.

Freund, C. and S. Oliver (2016) *The Billionaire Characteristics Database*: https://www.piie.com/publications/working-papers/origins-superrich-billionaire-characteristics-database

Fukuyama, F. (2014) *Political Order and Political Decay*. London: Profile Books.

Gabaix, X. and A. Landier (2008) 'Why Has CEO Pay Increased So Much?' *The Quarterly Journal of Economics*, 123(1): 49–100.

Goldin, C. and L.F. Katz (2008) *The Race Between Education and Technology*. Cambridge, MA: Harvard University Press.

Gordon, R.J. (2016) *The Rise and Fall of American Growth*. Princeton, NJ: Princeton University Press.

Hall, R.E. and C.I. Jones (1999) 'Why Do Some Countries Produce So Much More Output Per Worker Than Others?' *Quarterly Journal of Economics*, 114(1): 83–116.

Harris, R. and J. Moffat (2017) 'The UK Productivity Puzzle, 2008–2012: Evidence Using Plant-Level Estimates of Total Factor Productivity', *Oxford Economic Papers*, 69(3): 529–54.

Hickel, J. (2017) *The Divide: A Brief Gide to Global Inequality and its Solutions*. London: Windmill Books.

HMRC (2017) *Survey of Personal Incomes for 2014–15,* Knowledge, Analysis and Intelligence Data, Policy & Co-ordination, HM Revenue and Customs, London.

Jones, C.I. and J. Kim (2018) 'A Schumpeterian Model of Top Income Inequality', *Journal of Political Economy,* 126(5): 1785–826.

Joseph Rowntree Foundation (2018) *UK Poverty 2018,* https://www.jrf.org.uk/report/uk-poverty-2018 (accessed 11 August 2020).

Kay, J. (2016) *Other People's Money: Masters of the Universe or Servants of the People?* London: Profile Books.

Keynes, J.M. (1963) *Essays in Persuasion.* New York: W.W. Norton & Co., pp. 358–73

Kuznets, S. (1966) *Modern Economic Growth—Rate, Structure and Spread.* New Haven, CT: Yale University Press.

Lakner, C. and B. Milanovic (2013) 'Global Income Distribution: From the Fall of the Berlin Wall to the Great Recession.' World Bank Policy Research Working Paper No. 6719.

Lakner, C. and B. Milanovic (2016) 'Global Income Distribution: From the Fall of the Berlin Wall to the Great Recession.' *World Bank Economic Review* 30(2).

Lindsey, B. and S.M. Teles (2017) *The Captured Economy: How the Powerful Enrich Themselves, Slow Down Growth, and Increase Inequality.* Oxford: Oxford University Press.

Lucas Jr., R.E. (2002) *Lectures on Economic Growth.* Cambridge, MA: Harvard University Press.

Maddison, A. (2006) *The World Economy Volume 1: A Millennial Perspective and Volume 2: Historical Statistics.* Paris: OECD, Development Studies Centre.

Mian, A. and A. Sufi (2014) *House of Debt: How They (and You) Caused the Great Recession, and How We Can Prevent It from Happening Again.* Chicago, IL: University of Chicago Press.

Moretti, E. (2013) *The New Geography of Jobs.* Boston, MA: Mariner Books.

Morris, I. (2011) *Why the West Rules—For Now.* London: Profile Books.

Myrdal, G. (1968) *An Asian Drama: An Enquiry into the Poverty of Nations.* Twentieth Century Fox Fund.

Nolan, B., Roser, M., and S. Thewissen (2016) 'GDP per Capita Versus Median Household Income: What Gives Rise to Divergence Over Time?' INET Oxford Working Paper No. 2016–03. https://stefanthewissen.files.wordpress.com/2015/08/nolan-et-al-2016-gdp-per-capita-versus-median-household-income-inet-wp.pdf (accessed 11 August 2020).

Officer, L.H. and S.H. Williamson (2020) Annual Wages in the United States, 1774-Present, http://www.measuringworth.com

Piketty, T. (2014) *Capital in the Twenty-First Century.* Cambridge, MA: Harvard University Press.

Rosen, S. (1981) 'The Economics of Superstars', *The American Economic Review,* 71 (5): 845–58.

Rostow, W.W. (1969) *The Stages of Economic Growth: A Non-Communist Manifesto.* Cambridge: Cambridge University Press.

Rubinstein, W.D. (1983) 'The End of "Old Corruption" in Britain 1780–1860', *Past and Present,* 1001: 55–86.

Rubinstein, W.D. (2006) *Men of Property: The Very Wealthy in Britain Since the Industrial Revolution.* Second Edition. The Social Affairs Unit.

Stiglitz, J.E. (2013) *The Price of Inequality.* London: Penguin Books.

Stiglitz, J.E. (2015) *The Great Divide.* Random House, UK: Penguin Books.

Thewissen, S., Nolan, B., and Roser, M. (2016). Incomes Across the Distribution Database. https://ourworldindata.org/incomes-across-the-distribution (accessed 11 August 2020).

Williamson, S.H. (2020) 'What Was the UK GDP Then?', MeasuringWorth, http://www.measuringworth.com (accessed 11 August 2020).

Index

Note: Figures and tables are indicated by an italic "*f* ", "*t*" and notes are indicated by "*n*" following the page numbers.